DISCARD

Images in a Crystal Ball

Images in a Crystal Ball

World Futures in Novels for Young People

Lillian Biermann Wehmeyer

LIBRARIES UNLIMITED, INC.
Littleton, Colorado
1981

LIBRARIES UNLIMITED, INC.
P.O. Box 263
Littleton, Colorado 80160

Library of Congress Cataloging in Publication Data

Wehmeyer, Lillian Biermann, 1933-
    Images in a crystal ball.

    Includes index.
    1. Science fiction—Indexes. 2. Children's
stories—Indexes. I. Title.
Z5917.S36W43 [PN3433.6] 016.823'008'0355 80-26892
ISBN 0-87287-219-X

Libraries Unlimited books are bound with Type II nonwoven material that meets and exceeds National Association of State Textbook Administrators' Type II nonwoven material specifications Class A through E.

FOREWORD

This resource book is designed to assist teachers and librarians who are considering novels as a vehicle to explore with young people the future of the human species in this universe. The first pages provide a brief background to such study. However, the primary focus is on the body of futuristic fiction itself—the variety of ideas and inventions, the range of attitudes, the genuinely literary features—which are embodied in these novels.

The approach is practical, rather than theoretical. The book is directed toward classroom teachers who may wish to develop a unit on futuristic literature itself, teachers who may use futuristic novels to enrich topics of study in science or social science, or teachers or librarians who wish to group and describe futuristic novels so as to stimulate students' interest in and speculation about the future. To meet such needs, this book proceeds as follows.

Part I outlines background information for the study of futuristic literature. Also discussed in Part I are classroom and library approaches to futuristic fiction.

Part II describes the range of ideas and inventions encompassed within these novels. This section provides a broadbrush overview of some of the topics which are indexed in greater detail in Part IV. Part II also discusses attitudes toward the future—ranging from extreme optimism to extreme pessimism—which are evident in futuristic novels for young people. It is this writer's conviction that teachers and librarians must insure a balance between optimism and pessimism in future-oriented units of study and in library collections of futuristic fiction.

Part III, the heart of this manual, describes some 150 individual novels, arranged alphabetically by author. These books are: 1) set in future time; 2) full-length novels (not story collections); 3) published in or since 1964 and still in print during 1975-1979; 4) intended for readers in grade 8 or below, although many titles will also appeal to high school students.

For each title in Part III, theme and plot are outlined in a "Summary." Then, "Notes" suggest aspects of each novel significant in relation to futuristics and/or to literature. All books which meet the above criteria have been included, but about 50 of the titles are starred to indicate that they are recommended as an initial selection for a classroom or media center. These titles have been selected to include a variety of authors, topics, and attitudes; nearly all of them are of high literary quality, although a few have been chosen for the situations or topics which they uniquely present. Part III, therefore, assists teachers and librarians to choose, share, and discuss futuristic novels.

If Part III is the heart, then Part IV is the nerve center of this book. Here are indexed the various futuristic topics and themes occurring in the novels described. As one example of the relationship of the "Index of Themes and Motifs" (Part IV) to the earlier general categorical descriptions (Part II), note that whereas Part II considers improved human capacities in general, Part IV shows, in alphabetical arrangement, which novels deal with each particular psychic power—clairvoyance, telepathy, etc. Librarians will use the "Index of Themes and Motifs" to group novels for book talks and to guide readers to stories which touch on appealing topics. Classroom teachers and students will consult the index to locate books which may readily be compared and contrasted, or related to a particular topic of classroom study. The symbol † marks those titles which include sufficient detail to permit discussion of the topic after reading just that book alone; two or three of the other titles might be combined to explore the topic under which they are listed.

Thus, approach is provided both by general and specific topic and (in the general index) by title, publisher, illustrator, author and co-author. Multiple access permits flexible application of futuristic fiction to various educational needs.

TABLE OF CONTENTS

PART I

WORKING WITH FUTURISTIC FICTION:
Why and How

The purpose here is to explore world-future images as they are depicted in literature for young people. Are they optimistic or pessimistic? Do they encourage hope or counsel despair? Are they earthbound, or flung across the reaches of space? How do they describe personal freedom, social conditions, government, environment, technology, and other aspects of future society? From a literary standpoint, are these novels worthy of classroom study and discussion? Are they sufficiently thought-provoking and varied to help prepare students for the future? Finally, equipped with answers to such questions, how may teachers and librarians use futuristic fiction to heighten young people's awareness of alternative futures?

WHY TEACH ABOUT THE FUTURE?

Commonsense Arguments

Futuristics has already become a topic for classroom work, and has occasionally even been the basis for re-orienting an entire curriculum. Some 11,000 teachers have reported that they are teaching units on futuristics, motivated by a rationale such as the following:

> *The students in school today will spend most of their lives in the next century.* It is doubtful that they are even being prepared very well by society for what is left of this one. Education which takes that time lag into account is essential for the well-being of our students, for the survival of society, and for the continuing good health and self-respect of the education profession.[1]

Alvin Toffler, the "future shock" man, believes that students need help in relating world-future alternatives to their own lives. High school students, he found, could readily list numerous changes that would occur in the future, but when asked to list seven events in their personal futures,

> their response indicated an unchanged way of life. There was an absolute gulf between their perception of rapid change in the environment and their lack of understanding that the changes would have an effect on their personal lives.

As means of preparing students for the future, Toffler proposes attention to inter-personal relationships, exposure to various organizational patterns (not always one teacher with thirty students), instruction in valuing and choice making, community involvement (perhaps by finding useful community tasks for pupils), and curricular units on alternative futures.[2] Toffler argues that "in most situations we can help individuals adapt better if we simply provide them with advance information about what lies ahead."[3] At least one science fiction critic agrees, noting that the primary value of literature set in the future is that it "teaches adaptability and elasticity of mind in the face of change."[4] These statements are typical among educators, sociologists, and others who believe futuristic fiction can help broaden young readers' familiarity with alternative world-future images.

Persuasive though such arguments may be, we must be cautious about proposing future studies as the new panacea, the latest road to salvation, in education. Too often, educators have claimed too much too soon, only to be forced to retrench when promised improvements in pupil performance were not demonstrable. Nevertheless, although we can make only modest claims for the value of future studies, the rationale for introducing future-oriented materials into the curriculum, as outlined above, develops by sound logic from good commonsense evidence.

Research-Based Arguments

Beyond the commonsense rationale, moreover, some strands of research offer at least partial support for a futuristic orientation in school curricula. For instance, Fred L. Polak examined the future images held by various cultures in Western civilization, from ancient times to the present. Upon completing that analysis, he wrote, "The rise and fall of images of the future precedes or accompanies the rise and fall of cultures." That is to say, when an image of the future begins to decay, the culture associated with that image decays as well. At the present time, he continued, Western civilization has lost its future images. It has gone further, to attack all images of the future. "In the absence of a diligent application of counterforces, the defunct condition of current images predisposes Western culture to breakdown."[5]

Polak originally wrote that statement in 1955. In 1976, he continued to be "moderately optimistic" that such counterforces would be mustered.[6] Others, however, disagree with him. Some critics go so far as to call Polak's ideas "dangerous." They agree that a new image is needed, but not on any earlier Western model. Rather, these analysts argue, Westerners must accept their own obsolescence, support the Third World in finding its own future image, and ultimately accept that new image for themselves.[7]

We do not presume to know what future image will revitalize or replace that which has guided Western civilization in recent centuries, nor whether that image will strengthen or drastically redirect the course of our society. However, if we accept Polak's basic thesis that decline of a culture is associated with corresponding decay in that society's image of its own future, then surely images of the future are of crucial significance for young people. This is true regardless of whether erosion of future images is in cause-and-effect relationship with cultural decline, or which is the cause and which the effect. Polak sees the breakdown of the image as the cause and cultural decline as the effect. On the other hand, it may be eminently reasonable to distrust the future if one is surrounded by incontrovertible signs of social breakdown. Seemingly thinking along these lines, John Christopher, one of the more prolific writers of futuristic juvenile novels, recently responded to the question "Are you pessimistic about the future?" by indicating that, yes, he has some worries about the future. "I believe that we are in a 'decline and fall' situation," he added.[8]

But we need not resolve the question as to whether a viable future image can be deliberately revitalized or created anew or, further, whether such an image can avert or at least stave off cultural decay. Surely we are dealing with a case of self-fulfilling prophecy: if everyone becomes convinced that no action can avoid nuclear war, environmental pollution, or some other man-made disaster, then no one will seek such preventive actions. Thus, at the worst, to study the future, pursuing positive alternatives at least as diligently as negative alternatives, can scarcely do harm. At best, such studies may spark one or more individuals who have the capacity to solve a problem or actualize a brighter future.

WHY LITERATURE?

Toward "Possibilism"

Whether we choose the grandiose goal of counterbalancing a decline of Western civilization, or a more modest effort to equip our students to cope with the future regardless of the fate of a particular culture—can literature contribute to such efforts? Are young readers' views of the world future, their concepts or attitudes, likely to be influenced by the futuristic literature they read?

The foregoing pages argue that young people need ideas about alternative future possibilities so as to prepare for and cope with them; further, that they need a sense of control over their own destinies, a recognition that choices today affect personal and social realities tomorrow. Next, let us turn to the proposition that futuristic novels are one vehicle for such ideas and awareness, and the notion that many such novels written for young people also provide opportunities to teach literary appreciation and analysis, including characteristics of science fiction and of utopian literature.

Taken as a whole, futuristic novels for young people explore a wide range of circumstances and issues, and reflect a full spectrum of attitudes from pessimism to optimism. If students begin to read futuristic novels, it is essential that they read widely enough to encounter a range of views, and in particular, both optimism and pessimism. As the editor of *Future Survey* writes, after reviewing futurists' forecasts and ideas published in 1979,

> The conscious combining of areas of anticipated positive development and areas of potential disaster—the good news and the bad news about the future—cannot be overstressed. Far too much thinking about the future has dwelled solely on one side or the other. The probable future, though, is not described well by either Pollyanna or Cassandra. Rather, it is a mixture of good and bad, and we should strive to incorporate both in our worldviews.[9]

Indeed, perhaps the best answer is to move beyond either pessimism or optimism to "possibilism." Max Lerner declares:

> Our destiny as a people rests not in our stars but in ourselves. I am neither optimist nor pessimist. I am a possibilist.
> To believe either that everything is bound to work out or that nothing will ever work out is equally an exercise in mindlessness. There are no blank-check guarantees that we will survive and prosper, and no inevitability that we won't. I believe in the possible. More options are open for us than we dare admit. Everything depends on our collective intelligence in making choices, and our will to carry them out.[10]

If we guide young people to an appropriate range and balance of future images in literature, perhaps we can help them, too, to become "possibilists."

Young People's Literature as Literature

The foregoing assertion that futuristic novels for young people presently available actually include a range of varied situations and attitudes will be demonstrated in Part II of this book. However, the case for studying futuristic literature in the classroom is enhanced if other objectives will be accomplished at the same time. To put it more strongly, this literature, like any other, has no place in the educational program if it fails to contribute to the objectives of literature study *per se*, whether or not reference is made to the field of futuristics.

Fortunately, literature for young people has the same features—plot, characterization, style, tone, symbolism and the like—as adult literature, and can be discussed in those terms.[11] Furthermore, it has been demonstrated that junior novels can be used successfully to teach literary concepts.[12] These findings about young people's literature in general are applicable to many of the 150 novels summarized in Part III. Approximately 50 of these titles are asterisked there for "first purchase." Nearly all of these recommended titles have been chosen on the basis of high literary quality, although a very few, though certainly acceptable from a literary standpoint, have been selected more with regard to their unique treatment of a particular topic.

One function of literature study is to expand the reader's experience. Therefore, it is relevant to note a study which finds that children's novels, like adult literature, are capable of conveying a socially significant message. Specifically, themes of individualism, technology, social organization, war, and destruction are extensively treated in science fiction for children. Therefore,

> this literature can be used to help create in children an awareness of social problems and a more perceptive understanding of the decisions one must make in the world.[13]

This statement applies to the novels we are considering, although there is some limitation in that one out of three futuristic novels for young people fails to include descriptions of economic, political, or social circumstances.

In Part III, the "Notes" for each novel remark on important qualities of style, characterization, plot, and the like. In addition, socially significant topics are mentioned in the "Notes" in Part III and indexed in Part IV. Thus, this manual serves as a resource to teachers and librarians in achieving through futuristic fiction an expanded literary appreciation and awareness on the part of students.

Not only general literary characteristics, but also the genres of adult literature find counterparts in the juvenile field. To cite one example, all but the most devastating subtypes of adult literary tragedy have been found also in literature for children.[14] Similarly, science fiction and utopian literature, both of which have been extensively analyzed as adult genres, deserve attention in a study of futuristic fiction for young people.

Science Fiction

Junior science fiction novels fall into four categories which have been described in adult works: space opera, literature, extrapolation, and humanoid relations.[15] Unfortunately, science fiction has been for many years regarded as a weak sister in the world of literature. August Derleth has been quoted as follows:

Fundamentally, seven out of every ten science fiction stories are only orthodox adventure tales with the trappings of interplanetary travel.[16]

Or, as J.B. Priestley puts it, much science fiction

takes to distant planets men who should not be taken to the nearest big town—aggressive and unbalanced 12-year-olds in possession of "atomic blast guns."[17]

Children's science fiction stories also suffer at times from vague purpose; flat, static—even stereotyped—characterization; detailed explanations that interrupt the flow of narrative; dominance of setting over characters; simplistic plot; and overemphasis on fancy rather than an appropriate balance between fantasy and reality.[18]

However, science fiction has gradually won recognition as a serious and valuable genre. Priestley recognizes that "science fiction can be an admirable medium for oblique satire and protest."[19] The range of children's science fiction also includes books which evince cohesive purpose, dynamic characterization, and other qualities of fine literature.[20] Science fiction critics have analyzed the literary devices, the strengths and weaknesses, the settings and themes of this literary form. Since such analyses are readily available, we will not take the many pages that would be required to repeat their findings here. However, teachers' reference books on science fiction are listed in the bibliography at the end of Part I.

Before turning from this topic, it is necessary to point out that *science* fiction and *futuristic* fiction are not wholly synonymous. On the one hand, some science fiction (such as the Danny Dunn books by Jay Williams or the Matthew Looney series by Jerome Beatty, Jr.) is not really set in future time. Rather, a single futuristic element intrudes into what is otherwise a present-day setting—or a futuristic notion becomes the basis for wholly imaginative fantasy. On the other hand, some futuristic novels (for example, *The Mountain of Truth* by Dale Carlson and *The Empty World* by John Christopher) are not usually regarded as science fiction since they do not involve progress based on scientific knowledge. Science fiction—like utopian literature, to be discussed next—largely overlaps, but is not identical with, futuristic fiction.

Utopian Literature

In utopian literature, as in science fiction, we find literary forms for adults mirrored in futuristic novels for young readers. What are the relevant characteristics of utopian literature?

In the more recent examples of utopian writing "getting to the utopia has tended increasingly to be a journey in time rather than space." Only future-time utopian literature, of course, concerns us here. However, any utopian writer purposes to expose the weaknesses of his own time and place, either by extrapolating its virtues to a nearly-perfect contrast with present reality, or by projecting its vices to an anti-utopia. Few writers create both.[21] In adult literature anti-utopias now appear far more frequently than do utopias.[22] Generally, the customs of a utopian society are given rational explanations. A frequent device in adult utopias has been to have someone "enter the utopia and be shown around it by a sort of Intourist guide."[23]

Looking first at the positive form, we may define "utopia" as a portrayal of a perfect society, built upon selected strands extrapolated from present reality—those strands which the author views as most harmonious with his convictions about the best of all possible worlds. In the nineteenth century, utopias, previously portrayed as isolated communities, were more frequently described as global societies. These societies were static—carefully planned and controlled. A small elite group analogous to a priesthood—often transformed to scientists in more recent science fiction—usually controlled a utopian society, which frequently resembled a monastic community. Although the individual was subordinate to the state—his leisure, privacy, and freedom of movement limited; his goods part of the communal property—he gained inner freedom through a liberal education. Perhaps the most recent widely known utopia in adult literature, Edward Bellamy's *Looking Backward*, was published nearly a century ago. According to Fred L. Polak, there have been no genuine utopias written since World War II.[24]

Conversely, anti-utopian novels reflect a distrust of such extensive government planning. They are extrapolated from those present-day trends which the author regards as most antithetical to an ideal society. As noted earlier, they may take one of two forms. The utopian satire, or dystopia, portrays the horrors of an over-planned, over-controlled society. Recent popularity of this form in adult fiction is attributed in part to disenchantment with communism as realized in Soviet Russia, although the form also stems from the anti-utopian novel as first explored before World War I, most notably by H. G. Wells.[25] The classic example in adult literature, of course, is George Orwell's *1984*.

Another anti-utopian form, the pastoral utopia, portrays the "simple life," often by return to a lifestyle borrowed from history and revived in a setting created by cataclysmic disaster. The pastoral utopia rejects "the assumption that to increase man's control over his environment is also to increase his control over his destiny."[26] Thus, although a pastoral utopia appears peaceful and idyllic in contrast to the harsh circumstances depicted in a dystopia, the pastoral form is no less a protest against complexity and inhumanity in this technological age. Walter M. Miller's *Canticle for Leibowitz* exemplifies the pastoral utopia in adult fiction.

In a representative sample of futuristic novels for young people, about half the books resemble adult utopian forms, and of these, about two-thirds are dystopias. Only one in seven utopian types in juvenile futuristic fiction is the positive variety. Thus, children's novels reflect the trend toward anti-utopian forms already noted in literature for adults.

Like writers for mature readers, our authors for young people extrapolate trends to create future situations. Their dystopias project the consequences of failure to prevent environmental pollution, overpopulation, or war. Although legal and political structures are seldom explicated and the Intourist device is employed rarely, these novels succeed in portraying social attitudes and customs, rationalizing them on the basis of necessity and the imagined history of the future situation. Although the nineteenth century communal or monastic model rarely appears in juvenile fiction (exceptions: *The Mountain of Truth* by Dale Carlson and *Conversations* by Barry Malzberg), other factors, perhaps mental telepathy for example, may closely bind a community. Juvenile novels which exemplify each of the three utopian forms are listed in Part IV, the "Index of Themes and Motifs."

Novels for young people bear recognizable resemblance to utopias, pastoral utopias, and dystopias in adult literature. Therefore, these novels may serve to introduce students to these three forms and to several of their typical characteristics. Although dystopias and pastoral novels outnumber idealized utopias in world-future novels for young people, the overall balance between optimistic and pessimistic images, as we shall see, is about even. Thus, while drawing comparisons with the genres of adult utopian literature, it is still possible to maintain an appropriate balance in attitudes toward the future.

Effect of Literature on Readers

We have indicated that students can gain in literary insights from the study of futuristic novels. Can we also look for changes in their attitudes toward their future as a consequence of such reading?

Until now, research in response to literature has yielded ambiguous results.[27] For every study that claims to demonstrate positive impact of literature on young people's cognitive or affective response, there seems to be another which contradicts those findings. One study, in fact, appeared to demonstrate that exposure to stories about honesty increased *dis*honesty.[28] On the whole, however, the body of research into literature's effects on young readers combines to suggest that while reading *alone* may not change—perhaps, in fact, often intensifies—readers' attitudes toward such matters as ethnic groups or sex roles, nevertheless, reading *combined with overt response* may have a positive effect. Overt responses might take the form of discussion, role play, or other opportunities to rehearse desirable attitudes. It follows that teachers or librarians who hope to affect their students' attitudes toward the future, to move them toward "possibilism," must provide each pupil with opportunities to discuss, act out, or otherwise respond to what has been read. Several suggestions for such response are listed toward the end of this chapter.

Of course, the ambiguity of much previous research on the effects of literature is disappointing to teachers and librarians, whose professions are built on the assumption that literature broadens experience, develops insights, and deepens understanding. Let us take a moment to examine three factors which have contributed to these sometimes contradictory results. First, so many other influences impinge upon a child's concepts of ethnic groups, sex roles, or whatever content has been studied, that it is nearly impossible to isolate the effects of literature. Second, although there have been content analyses of children's literature on the one hand and studies of response on the other, children's reactions to previously analyzed material have not been investigated. Finally, although reader characteristics have occasionally been considered and related to the genres of books youngsters prefer to read, differential characteristics of readers have not been placed in interaction with differential qualities of reading matter which has been subjected to content analysis.

Perhaps a study of the interaction of optimism/pessimism in futuristic literature with characteristics of individual readers will one day provide more definitive information about the effects of literature on readers. Such a study can be designed to overcome all three problems just noted. For one thing, study of children's response to futuristic literature at least eliminates firsthand experience with the topic as a variable (although it must take into account the influences of motion pictures and television). Secondly, as will be noted in Part II, futuristic novels can be rated for degree of optimism/pessimism, a quality which can in turn be expected to produce differing responses on the part of young readers. Finally, considering those readers, perhaps anxiety level of a child and optimism/pessimism of a futuristic novel interact. That is to say, perhaps high-anxious and low-anxious youngsters will be found correspondingly more or less willing to choose, to believe, or to recall a particular depiction of world future according to the degree of optimism or pessimism that novel evinces.

As teachers and librarians share futuristic novels with students, they may observe these or other differences in response. (The writer would appreciate receiving word of such observations.) Until more definitive research is available, however, we have a fair basis in limited studies and in commonsense experience to assert that students who read and respond to novels set in future time will expand their awareness of world-future images. The question still remains: how might we approach these novels in a classroom or library?

TEACHING WITH FUTURISTIC NOVELS

In the Library

For a librarian, the usual modes of presentation via book talk, display, or bibliography are obvious possibilities. For these purposes the topical index in Part IV of this book should prove useful. A librarian might do a series of presentations—one on robots, another on aliens, and still others directing attention to themes of environmental pollution, psychic powers, space exploration, technological advances in any of several specific areas, and so on.

The "Index of Themes and Motifs" (Part IV) will also assist librarians to locate "another book like the last one" as they guide the reading of individual students. And, of course, the index will enable librarians to locate books for classroom teachers who wish to use futuristic fiction in their teaching.

To this end some 50 titles are starred in Part III; these novels may be regarded as first purchase suggestions to provide as wide a range as possible of authors, themes, and topics while maintaining a good to excellent standard of literary quality. If, on the other hand, books are needed to supplement a narrowly defined unit—say, on maintaining balance among organisms in their natural environments—the topical index in Part IV will prove more useful as a selection guide.

Finally, librarians may want to use futuristic fiction in a reading discussion group under their own direction. In this instance many of the classroom-oriented suggestions which follow will prove useful.

In the Classroom

Focus on Literature

The primary focus of a unit of study may be futuristic fiction itself. Here, probably as part of the English program, attention will center on theme, plot, characterization, style—all the usual aspects of literature study. These novels are especially amenable, as well, to approach through the avenue of each reader's personal response, including emotional reactions and interpretations. In addition, features typical of the genres of science fiction and utopian literature may be drawn to students' attention. With literature the primary consideration, futuristics as a social science may well serve a secondary, enriching function.

We will not review here techniques for teaching students about literature. Suffice it to say that the same techniques one might use to develop students' literary insights into any novel—its plot, style, characterization, etc.—may be applied also to futuristic fiction. To assist teachers, the "Notes" for each title described in Part III draw attention to structural or stylistic features which merit classroom study. Since the purpose of a literature unit on futuristic fiction is likely to be to acquaint students with a wide range of authors, styles, themes and the like, the titles which have been starred in Part III will merit first examination.

Future Studies Focus

Although futuristic fiction will be approached first from a literary standpoint in an English class, teachers of social science or science may prefer to focus on future studies, using fiction as but one secondary resource. In these subject fields futuristic novels may spark interest in or enrich a study of such topics as environmental pollution, mutation, adaptation, computers, sports, energy sources, mental telepathy, political control, or race relations. For additional possibilities, teachers might read through the topic headings in Part IV, the "Index of Themes and Motifs." Suggestions for follow-up activities in the classroom are offered on the following pages.

Units in future studies are not included in this book. However, teacher resource books for this purpose are listed at the end of Part I. In addition, Part II of this book draws together thoughts of scientific futurists and creations of novelists on each of several broad topics. Moreover, the "Notes" for the 150 novels described in Part III point out dominant aspects of each novel which are worthy of study from a futurist point of view. Thus, whether the teacher must begin from a broad topic, from a specific set of available books, or from specific futuristic notions, one of the remaining parts of this book provides a means to select and discuss novels appropriate to the instructional purpose.

Follow-up Activities

Before turning to a description of the body of futuristic novels for young people, however, a brief description is now offered of some learning activities which might follow upon reading these books. These suggestions do not exhaust all the possibilities, certainly, but may bring to mind activities appropriate to a particular class or pupil. They include writing scenarios, compiling a futures catalog, comparing and contrasting novels, synthesizing a composite prediction or history, checking accuracy or probability, dramatizing, and responding subjectively.

Writing scenarios. A scenario is simply a description, a word picture, of a future world. (We use the word "scenario" as futurists do, not in the sense of a dramatic scenario or plot outline.) Students can readily paraphrase a scenario from nearly any novel set in future time. As a model for this follow-up activity, junior or senior high school students may read Paul Ehrlich's scenario, "Eco-Catastrophe!"[29] Younger pupils or less capable readers may turn to *2010: Living in the Future* by Geoffrey Hoyle,[30] a scenario with cartoon-style drawings depicting some ways in which life may be quite different a few decades from now. For an example of a scenario paraphrased from a novel, turn to the description of environmental destruction drawn from H. M. Hoover's *Children of Morrow* and *Treasures of Morrow* (Part II, page 29).

Compiling a Futures Catalog. Among topics suitable for such a compilation are land or space vehicles, robots, recreations, and alien beings. A model for the latter is available in *Barlowe's Guide to Extra-Terrestrials*, which illustrates and describes a number of aliens from science fiction.[31] Although most of the creatures are taken from adult novels, two are drawn from books in this bibliography. Aliens in juvenile fiction range from almost human in appearance to very different species. The Imbur look much like us, although they lack a nose and have six fingers on each hand (the Ziax II books by John Morressy). Toward the other extreme, Argans are four foot tall furry spiders—and geniuses in their own musical system (*Sweetwater* by Laurence Yep). Somewhere in the middle are the Lasbutsilians, a space-faring species closely resembling humans in form, but so small that they are seen sitting on strawberries in a basket (Bulychev's *Alice*). One of the most varied collections of alien beings described in a single novel—albeit some of them very briefly—occurs in *The Goblin Reservation* by Clifford Simak.

Another model for a futures catalog, although not drawn from descriptions in novels, is Stewart Cowley's *Spacecraft 2000 to 2100 A.D.*[32] A richly illustrated catalog of twenty-first century spaceships, this book is validated as a publication of the year 2100 by everything but the copyright date. The jacket even says of the author that he is a "Terran Defence Authority Commander," also noting that his current project is building a full-size SSF21D Cutlass spacecraft out of—yes—macaroni. Each craft in the catalog is illustrated in full color, facing a one-page description and chart of specifications. Spaceships, aliens, or other topics for a futures catalog may be pursued with the help of the "Index of Themes and Motifs" (Part IV).

Comparing and Contrasting Novels. The "Index of Themes and Motifs" demonstrates the recurrence of many futuristic elements from novel to novel. Part II reinforces this notion and demonstrates that authors' attitudes range from extreme pessimism to extreme optimism.

For example, technology is handled with sharp satire in *The Endless Pavement* by Jackson and Perlmutter, but with lighthearted humor in *My Robot Buddy* by Alfred Slote. Nuclear bombing eventually leads to cooperation in Ruth Hooker's *Kennaquhair*, but to suspicion and separation in *Z for Zachariah* by Robert C. O'Brien. Plague is followed by Lisa's success in creating a miniature libertarian society in *The Girl Who Owned a City* by O. T. Nelson, but Neil's encounters with insanity, suicide, and attempted murder follow the plague in John Christopher's *The Empty World*. In discussion, essays, charts, or drawings, students may identify and compare common elements, as well as contrast the different treatments accorded those same elements, in various novels.

Synthesizing a Composite Prediction or Composite History. Another follow-up project might be integration of information from several novels to develop a composite prediction for any technology, nation, or planet. Books selected for this project must indicate an approximate time setting (*see* the century headings in Part IV). If the books propose opposite situations—if one depicts total environmental deterioration in the same century that another shows an environmental paradise—they would need to be incorporated into alternative predictions.

A sample composite prediction is included in the section on space exploration in Part II (page 33). While this prediction is written in the future tense, such a chronological account might also be written as history—in the past tense because the narrator is looking backward from a point in future time. Chapters in Jean Karl's *The Turning Place; Stories of a Future Past* offer a model of such "future history."

Checking Accuracy or Probability. In the composite prediction about space travel just referred to, errors are already apparent. Man first landed on the moon in 1969, not 1972. At the close of 1978, no space station wheels were yet in orbit. These bits of the prediction were taken from Ted White's *Secret of the Marauder Satellite*, published in 1965, which was therefore out of date four years later.

Writers not only misjudge; sometimes they describe technologies (such as instantaneous transmission of matter) or events (like the one-man rendezvous with a space station in *Secret of the Marauder Satellite*) which stretch the reader's credulity. Students may be fascinated with checking the accuracy or likelihood of such predictions. Fiction titles for this purpose may be located with the aid of the "Index of Themes and Motifs" (Part IV). Among the nonfiction resources students may consult in this quest are *The New Challenge of the Stars: A Science Fact Look at Science Fiction* by Partick Moore and David Hardy,[33] and Arthur C. Clarke's *Profiles of the Future: An Inquiry into the Limits of the Possible*.[34] To reverse the process, students might also gather a number of appealing future possibilities from nonfiction sources, infer consequences of these, and weave original stories around those notions.

Dramatizing. From *Star Trek* to *Star Wars* and *Battlestar Galactica*, motion pictures and television have provided young people with models for dramatized science fiction. Moreover, masks, costumes, and toys are readily available to encourage young thespians to emulate those exciting scenes. As we have seen, overt response helps to establish or change attitudes as a consequence of involvement with literature. Surely this must be equally or more applicable to movies and television. Thus, if our goal is to expand the range of alternative future images available to young people, then dramatization of short stories and novels, especially those whose world futures differ from the movie and television variety, is an activity to be encouraged.

Responding Subjectively. All the follow-up suggestions proposed require that students go beyond merely reading futuristic novels. An approach to literature which capitalizes on personal response and therefore may be particularly appropriate for working with futuristic literature is described in *Readings and Feelings; An Introduction to Subjective Criticism* by David Bleich.[35] This guide provides a framework for encouraging and evaluating students' response to literature. In most classrooms this approach will be balanced by more objective analysis after subjective responses have been fully explored.

Other Activities. These proposed activities are but a few follow-up suggestions for reading futuristic novels. Certainly short stories may be handed in similar fashion. Students may become interested in the historical development of science fiction or utopian literature. They may decide to pursue a study of futuristics as a social science, or turn to a scientific approach to space technology, astronomy, environmental design, or any number of future-oriented topics. If they have a bent for creative work, pupils may develop original scenarios, art work, predictions, poetry, or stories. They may enjoy formulating space age rewrites of traditional material like those in Frederick Winsor's *Space Child's Mother Goose*.[36] Teachers will develop many other activities (and I would be most interested if you would share those that work out well).

RESOURCES FOR TEACHERS

Literature

Ash, Brian, ed. *Visual Encyclopedia of Science Fiction.* New York: Harmony Books, 1977.

Thematic discussions of science fiction for adults. Useful in suggesting what to look for in juvenile science fiction.

Barron, Neil. *Anatomy of Wonder: Science Fiction.* New York: Bowker, 1976.

An historical bibliography and discussion of science fiction. Includes a chapter on science fiction for young people. Revised edition in press.

Calkin, Elizabeth and Barry McGhan. *Teaching Tomorrow: A Handbook of Science Fiction for Teachers.* Dayton, OH: Pflaum/Standard, 1972.

LaConte, Ronald T. *Teaching Tomorrow Today.* New York: Bantam, 1975.

Manuel, Frank E., ed. *Utopias and Utopian Thought.* Boston: Houghton Mifflin, 1966.

A series of historical and critical articles essential to a study of utopianism; originally an issue of *Daedalus* magazine.

Scholes, Robert and Eric S. Rabkin. *Science Fiction: History, Science, Vision.* New York: Oxford University Press, 1977.

Useful discussion of themes and motifs.

Futuristics

Allain, Violet Anselmini. *Futuristics and Education*. Bloomington, IN: Phi Delta Kappa, 1979.

Berry, Adrian. *The Next Ten Thousand Years; A Vision of Man's Future in the Universe*. New York: Saturday Review Press/Dutton, 1974.

Cornish, Edward, et al. *The Study of the Future; An Introduction to the Art and Science of Understanding and Shaping Tomorrow's World*. Washington, DC: World Future Society, 1977.

Students' study guide available.

Dickson, Paul. *The Future File; A Guide for People with One Foot in the 21st Century*. New York: Rawson Associates, 1977.

Includes lists of organizations, books and magazines, as well as descriptions of future-oriented activities in several communities and states.

The Futurist. Monthly journal of the World Future Society, Washington, DC.

Kahn, Herman, et al. *The Next 200 Years; A Scenario for America and the World*. New York: Morrow, 1976.

A product of the Hudson Institute, an East coast "think tank."

Kauffman, Draper L., Jr. *Futurism and Future Studies*. Washington, DC: National Education Association, 1976.

Kauffman, Draper L., Jr. *Teaching the Future: A Guide to Future-Oriented Education*. Palm Springs, CA: ETC Publications, 1976.

A wealth of teaching ideas, especially related to social studies.

Laszlo, Ervin, et al. *Goals for Mankind; A Report to the Club of Rome on the New Horizons of Global Community*. New York: E. P. Dutton, 1977.

A more optimistic view than that enunciated in earlier documents from the Club of Rome.

NOTES

[1] Draper L. Kauffman, Jr., *Futurism and Future Studies* (Washington, DC: National Education Association, 1976), pp. 8-9, 51.

[2] James J. Morisseau, "Alternative Futures: A Conversation with Alvin Toffler," In *Curriculum: Quest for Relevance*, 2nd ed. William Van Til, ed. (Boston: Houghton Mifflin, 1974), pp. 353-58.

[3] Alvin Toffler, *Future Shock* (New York: Bantam, 1971), p. 418.

[4] David Ketterer, *New Worlds for Old; The Apocalyptic Imagination, Science Fiction, and American Literature* (Garden City, NJ: Anchor Press/Doubleday, 1974), p. 25.

[5] Fred L. Polak, *The Image of the Future*, trans. and abridged by Elise Boulding (New York: Elsevier, 1973), pp. 19, 222-23.

[6] Fred L. Polak, "Responsibility for the Future," In *Images of the Future: The Twenty-First Century and Beyond*, Robert Bundy, ed. (Buffalo: Prometheus Books, 1976), p. 15.

[7] Bundy, ed., *Images of the Future*, pp. 16-53, 234-36.

[8] In conversation following an address to librarians at the Berkeley Public Library, Berkeley, CA, Oct. 24, 1978.

[9] Michael Marien, "The Good News and the Bad News; Optimism vs. Pessimism in Recent Writing about the Future," *The Futurist* 14 (June, 1980), p. 4.

[10] Max Lerner, "On Being a Possibilist," *Newsweek* 94 (Oct. 8, 1979), p. 21.

[11] William Anderson and Patrick Groff, *A New Look at Children's Literature* (Belmont, CA: Wadsworth, 1972).

[12] Nathan S. Blount, "The Effect of Selected Junior Novels and Selected Adult Novels on Student Attitudes toward the 'Ideal' Novel" (Dissertation, Florida State University, 1963).

[13] M. Jean Greenlaw, "Science Fiction: Impossible! Improbable! or Prophetic?" *Elementary English* 48 (April, 1971), pp. 196-202.

[14] Carolyn Tietje Kingston, "Exemplifications of the Tragic Mode in Selected Realistic Fiction for 8 to 12 Year Old Children" (Dissertation, Teachers' College, Columbia University, 1968).

[15] Virginia F. Bereit, "The Genre of Science Fiction," *Elementary English* 66 (November, 1969), pp. 895-96.

[16] Ibid., p. 895.

[17] J. B. Priestley, *Man and Time* (London: Aldus Books, 1964), pp. 128-29.

[18] Bereit, op. cit., pp. 897-900.

[19] Priestley, loc. cit.

[20] Bereit, loc. cit.

[21] Northrop Frye, "Varieties of Literary Utopias," In *Utopias and Utopian Thought*, Frank E. Manuel, ed. The Daedalus Library (Boston: Houghton Mifflin, 1966), pp. 27-29.

[22] Mark R. Hillegas, *The Future as Nightmare; H. G. Wells and the Anti-Utopians* (New York: Oxford University Press, 1967), p. 3.

[23] Frye, op. cit., pp. 26-28.

[24] Polak, *The Image of the Future*, pp. 189, 191.

[25] Charles I. Glicksberg, "Anti-Utopianism in Modern Literature," *Southwest Review* 37 (Summer, 1952), pp. 221-28; Hillegas, op. cit., p. 4.

[26] Frye, op. cit., pp. 43-44.

[27] For a more extended summary of this research, see chapter 11 in *The School Librarian as Educator*, Lillian Biermann Wehmeyer (Littleton, CO: Libraries Unlimited, 1976), pp. 197-213.

[28] H. W. Hartley, "Developing Personality through Books," *English Journal* 40 (April, 1951), pp. 198-204.

[29] In *The Futurists*, Alvin Toffler, ed. (New York: Random House, 1972), pp. 13-26.

[30] Illus. Alasdair Anderson (New York: Parents Magazine Press, 1973).

[31] By Wayne Douglas Barlowe and Ian Summers (New York: Workman, 1979).

[32] (Seacucus, NJ: Chartwell Books, 1978).

[33] (New York: Rand McNally, 1977).

[34] (New York: Popular Library, 1973).

[35] (Urbana, IL: National Council of Teachers of English, 1975).

[36] Illus. Marian Parry (New York: Simon and Schuster, 1958).

PART II

FUTURISTICS AND FUTURISTIC NOVELS

Mankind's desire to foreknow the future is recorded in the earliest written records and oral traditions. We have examined the entrails of birds, tea leaves, and lines on the palms of our hands; plotted the courses of the stars; and consulted prophets, seers, and psychics in our quest to penetrate the curtain which shields tomorrow from our vision. Only rarely has success rewarded our efforts. Witness Croesus, who was told by the oracle at Delphi, "When you cross over the river Halys, you will destroy a great empire." Imagine his anguish when he realized, too late, that the "great empire" was his own!

FUTURISTICS

Within the last 15 years or so a new approach to the future has emerged. "Futuristics," "futurism," "futurology" or "future studies"—the field is too new even to have settled firmly on a name—is a new branch of the social sciences which attempts to predict the future using rational, rather than mystical, processes. Futuristics draws upon sociology, economics, and political science, as well as biological and physical sciences and technology. Its methods include trend analysis and extrapolation, cross-impact matrix, Delphi survey technique, decision tree, scenario, and simulation.[1] The intent of future study is not to foretell the future, but to generate a set of alternative futures, each related to particular preconditions. As this new science becomes more refined, decision makers will be able to examine the set of alternatives, select the description or descriptions that appear most desirable, and then guide governments and institutions into conditions which favor those futures and mitigate against their less acceptable counterparts.

The year 1964 may be accepted as an initial date for futuristics as a serious academic field since in that year the Commission for the Year 2000 was organized under the aegis of the American Academy of Arts and Sciences. (For this reason 1964 has been chosen as the boundary for this bibliography; we analyze and index novels published from that year forward.) However, not all futurists limit themselves to so short a time span as the remainder of the twentieth century. Although a major work resulting from the commission's studies is entitled *The Year 2000*,[2] other futurists have extended their time horizons to *The Next 200 Years*, *The Next 500 Years*, and even *The Next Ten Thousand Years*.[3]

OPTIMISM, PESSIMISM, AND POSSIBILISM

Moreover, futurists' writings include a broad range of attitudes toward the future, a range which is reflected in futuristic novels for young people. When we began to consider images of the future offered in children's novels, we included in that study a concern for their degree of optimism or pessimism. We happened upon a chart of futurist views developed by Herman Kahn and the Hudson Institute.[4] The chart describes four attitudes, ranging from convinced pessimist to convinced optimist.

Kahn describes the view of the convinced pessimist, or "convinced neo-Malthusian," as

> a modern version of the analysis of the 19th-century English economist Thomas Malthus, who argued that population would eventually grow faster than food supply, thus implying that starvation would soon become mankind's perennial lot, at least for the poor.

At the other extreme is the view of the convinced optimist, whom Kahn dubs a "technology-and-growth enthusiast." This image, Kahn writes,

> stems from the premise that in the next 100 years material needs can be met so easily in the currently developed world that the more advanced nations will develop super-industrial and then post-industrial economies, and that the rest of the world will soon follow.

Between these extreme views are more moderate positions. According to Kahn,

> both of the moderate positions argue that we can expect serious problems in energy shortfalls, resource scarcities and food distribution. Both also raise the real possibility of cataclysmic or irreversible environmental damage.

The guarded pessimist or "moderate neo-Malthusian"

> hold[s] open the possibility . . . barely . . . that with technological progress, wise policies, competent management and good luck, mankind can deal with these problems and survive into a future where, at least, opportunity is not foreclosed and disaster is not foreordained.

A bit more hopeful, the guarded optimist or "moderate advocate of technology and economic growth" offers that possibility "relatively clearly" rather than just "barely" and, moreover,

> goes even further, holding that we may still avert ultimate disaster even if policies are not so wise, management not so competent and luck not so good, but the worse the policies, management and luck, the greater the potential for tragedy along the way and even for final cataclysm.

Which of these views predominates among futurists? Writing in 1976, Kahn felt that the movement toward neo-Malthusian attitudes had already gone too far. "Spurred now by well-publicized studies, it has acquired a momentum of its own which, if continued, will only deepen the malaise it depicts and make longer and more difficult the recovery that is required."

John Maddox, in *The Doomsday Syndrome*, has also criticized the prophets of calamity. "Their most common error," he charges

is to suppose that the worst will always happen [and to] ignore the
ways in which social institutions and human aspirations can conspire
to solve the most daunting problems. . . . Throughout history, hope
for the future has been a powerful incentive for constructive change.
What will happen if it is now needlessly blighted?

He asks whether "anxiety about the environment" may be a "convenient lightning
rod for diverting anxiety" from the pressing social problems of our own times. At
the same time, however, Maddox admits that environmentalists in America "have
helped to dramatize a set of problems that might otherwise have been neglected,"
while Europeans, lacking this dramatic outcry, may be ignoring those problems to
their detriment.[5] More recently, as we shall note in our discussion of the environment
theme in futuristic novels for young people, American environmentalists have begun
to strike a slightly more encouraging note. The 1977 report of the Club of Rome,[6]
previously associated with gloomy prognostications for the future, also offers a more
optimistic, if still somber, appraisal.

Nevertheless, it is likely that we need both the optimists and the pessimists to
help us avoid paralyzing fear on the one hand and careless apathy on the other. If so,
it is important that both positive and negative future-world images are available to
young people so that they will develop an awareness of the problems and dangers
they must eventually face, along with confidence in their ability to overcome those
problems. Therefore, it is reassuring to find that novelists strike an appropriate
balance between optimism and pessimism. In a representative sample, the attitudes
reflected just about a 50-50 split:

Convinced pessimist	16%
Guarded pessimist	30%
Guarded optimist	33%
Convinced optimist	21%

This balance is retained across age levels; readers as young as age eight are presented
with both extremes. (The very few titles for six- and seven-year-olds, however, are
decidedly optimistic.)[7] Furthermore, an analysis of the novels' conclusions indicates
that these books are far more likely to end in an improved or improving situation than
in one which is deteriorating.

This latter finding supports expectations of literary critics. Benjamin Appel,
who anthologized science fiction from the second century forward, writes:

Scientists and writers of science fiction share a common belief, or if not
belief, a hope that the many unanswered questions of the universe are
capable of solution. If not by this generation, by the next.[8]

Jean Karl, editor of children's books for Atheneum, comments in the same vein:

A children's book looks at life with hope, even when it is painting the
most disastrous of circumstances. . . . This is when children's books
depart most radically from adult books. . . . They retain the belief in
the future that is the heritage of the young. . . . When hope is gone,
childhood is gone.[9]

Although nearly all futuristic novels for young people retain that "belief in the future," sometimes hope is expressed through the characters' ability to survive and cope with disaster. A very few of these books, indeed, reflect that loss of faith in the future which Fred L. Polak sees in Western society today.[10] This inclusion of less encouraging along with more optimistic world-future images in fiction for young people, of course, reflects a shift in the range of children's literature generally, a shift which dates from the mid-sixties and has been dubbed "new realism." If children's writers and editors, in the role which communications theorists know as "gatekeeper," once sifted reality so that children would read only about "nice" things, they now seem to present a much larger portion of that reality.[11]

Consequently, just as futuristic novels for young people offer a wide range in time, from the immediate future to the fortieth century, and in space, from Earth to 220 light years distant, so they provide a wide range of attitudes, situations, and ideas. From the 150 novels described and analyzed in Parts III and IV of this manual it is possible to select a balance between optimism and pessimism. By this means we can avoid inadvertently leading students to conclude either that "everything is bound to work out" or that "nothing will ever work out." Exposed to a broad range of alternative world-future images, students are more likely to adopt Max Lerner's "possibilism"—to assert that "Everything depends on our collective intelligence in making choices, and our will to carry them out."[12] Thus they will develop "competence and potency" to deal with the future.[13]

Beyond reflecting the range of optimism and pessimism which Kahn describes for scientific futurists, however, children's futuristic novels also reflect many of the ideas and concerns which form the serious focus of social-scientific future studies. The remainder of this chapter will be devoted to examining world-future novels for young people as they relate to several topics in futuristics, science and technology, social studies, and humanities. This discussion is based on a detailed, carefully structured content analysis which was applied to one novel by each of 43 authors.[14] Other futuristic novels are included as appropriate for each topic. In most cases a topic is approached by summarizing the views of futurists as background to the novels.

SYSTEM BREAKS

Futurists usually make "surprise-free" predictions, assuming no major, unexpected events. Yet they recognize that such events are "likely to occur and may be unpredictable," so they have coined the term "system break" to describe such events. System breaks are sudden occurrences which bring about a sharp change in the direction of society, whether for better or worse. Sources of possible system breaks include world war or famine, as well as technological, biological, and international developments.[15] Even catastrophes need not mean total destruction. One futurist estimates, for example, that nuclear war would have to destroy 80% of the world's population to stop social progress.[16] However, a system break can provide impetus for, or climax to, the plot of a novel, no matter what its probabilities in actuality.

In a representative sample of futuristic novels for young people, nearly half include or follow upon a system break. Of these, not a single one is positive in nature. A few are events beyond human control: a mysterious madness causing people to hate machines, rays projected from alien spaceships to destroy nearly all life on Earth, a plague killing everyone over 12 years of age, a sun exploding in its nova phase. Typically, however, the system break could have been prevented by mankind; examples include nuclear or magnetic war on earth, galactic war, famine, crises in environmental pollution, and overpopulation. Of the types of system breaks outlined by the futurist quoted in the preceding paragraph, world war, famine, and technological and biological developments all occur in juvenile novels. In most cases the system break occurs as or before the novel "opens," and the story follows the characters' efforts to cope with these difficult situations. (To locate novels which include the various forms of system break, consult "System Break" and related headings in Part IV. Similar events which do not result in system breaks are also indexed in Part IV.)

Occasionally a novel speaks of more gradual deterioration which does not lead to a redirection of society; for instance, a situation in which oxygen and nitrogen are expected to disappear in just over five years (novels in which environmental disaster arrives gradually, rather than suddenly), and those in which an authoritarian state gradually evolves.

Sometimes developments that hold promise of a positive system break do not materialize. For example, in *The Mountain of Truth* (Carlson), vaguely reminiscent of *Lost Horizon*, a group of young people, guided initially by ancient Tibetan monks, hopes to develop psychic power to combat "insoluble" problems due to misuse of technology, and thereby save the world. However, at the close of the narrative, Carlson leaves the reader uncertain as to whether the group still functions. Similarly, in Bova's *Exiled from Earth*, scientists are well on the way to a breakthrough in genetic engineering permitting them to produce children with improved minds and bodies. Although this might be regarded as a positive system break of millennial proportions, the leaders of the world government decide they must exile the scientists and destroy their laboratories for fear that some power-hungry group might use these same techniques to turn other humans into mindless zombies.

In fact, less than one title in four fails at least to mention environmental or social problems similar to those which operate as system breaks in other novels. While writers who build their stories on system breaks or other difficulties typically describe how those situations are dealt with, the more optimistic writers, on the other hand, often skip ahead to future time without explaining how environmental pollution, shortage of resources, political conflict, or other present-day difficulties have been overcome. An important exception are the several novels which suggest cultural evolution (*see* index, Part IV) as a process by which humankind can work through or avoid disaster. Like writers of science fiction for adults, who employ the notion of evolution in forms of government,[17] several novelists for young people adopt an evolutionist view, assuming that all societies must experience developmental stages resembling the major historical periods of the history of Earth—or, more accurately, of Western civilization.

In summary, unlike futurists, who avoid predicting system breaks (presumably because they are among those unique, chance occurrences which lie outside the realm of statistics and which André Norton refers to as "the X factor"), novelists capitalize on the dramatic and imaginative capacity of such events. To balance this apparent pessimism, however, we must note that the novelists usually follow up on disaster with some degree of recovery, or at least anticipated recovery. Only two novels in all 150 assume human extinction (*see* index, Part IV), and one of those is more a fable than a realistic story. Two people survive nuclear war in *Z for Zachariah* (O'Brien), only to part company out of fear. However, in *Kennaquhair* (Hooker) six children and an adult escape nuclear destruction, and the children go on to learn the necessity of self-discipline and cooperation. Plague leads to loneliness and to encounters with insanity, suicide and attempted murder for Neil in *The Empty World* (Christopher), yet he finally locates and establishes a promising relationship with another survivor. Even more optimistically, plague in *The Girl Who Owned a City* (Nelson) provides an opportunity for Lisa to establish a miniature libertarian society— a little utopia. Thus, system breaks in novels often create a situation which, though not desirable in itself, calls forth resourcefulness and courage in the characters who survive.

NATURAL RESOURCES

Food, energy sources, and other essentials for life and production are topics of great concern to futurists. Their predictions range from the gloomy statement that "a massive famine within the decade seems probable," to assurance that "there are many means for providing ample food for the world during the next 200 years";[18] from a prediction that 19 mineral resources will be exhausted within periods ranging from 6 to 154 years, to the argument that better resource exploitation, ocean mining and extraction from seawater and ordinary rock will take care of 99.9% of the demand for mineral resources for the next 200 years[19] —not to mention the possibility of mining on the moon.[20] Shall we experience depletion, or abundance, of natural resources?

Food

About one novel in four can be expected to mention food shortages, often accompanied by rationing and/or malnutrition (*see* "Food Shortages" and "Famine" in Part IV). An extreme case is *Survival Planet*, in which Tofte depicts mass starvation on Earth. The only escape is for those few who have an opportunity—obtained by wealth or political power in most cases—to flee to another planet.

More often, whether the food supply is ample or not, it is totally or partially artificial (*see* "Food, Artificial" in Part IV). Opinion is unanimous that all artificial food is less tasty than natural food, and often less nourishing as well.

Methods of cultivation vary from food gathering and hand agriculture to hydroponics. Ingenious examples are provided by Bonham and Biemiller. Brian in *The Missing Persons League* (Bonham) has a farm under his house. He has excavated soil and secreted the excess within the walls of his home. Fluorescent light and recycled garbage help him grow vegetables and raise hens and rabbits to offset the diet of algae-based foods like AlmosTomato available at State stores. A much larger operation is sea farming as practiced by the hydronauts (Biemiller trilogy). Since nothing can grow in the nuclear-wasted soil, most foodstuffs are derived from sharks, whales, algae, and seaweed.

Children's novelists describe food supply situations which match the futurists' range from famine to abundance. The majority of fiction writers, however, predict adequate—if not epicurean—food resources.

Fuel and Energy Resources

Similarly, most children's authors anticipate a solution to shortages of fuel and energy. Less than one in three is likely to mention such shortages, or to describe situations limited to comparatively primitive energy sources—societies where the consequences of a system break have forced reversion to sources ranging from sheer muscle to waterwheels or windmills. In some cases, development to regain more advanced levels remains theoretically possible; in others, depleted fuel supplies or taboos limit use of advanced energy sources. An example of the latter is Lightner's *Day of the Drones*, in which solar energy use is taboo, permitted only with express approval of the Wasan (chief) and Council of Medics. Theoretically, of course, new or alternative fuel sources are still possibilities in such a situation. None of the novels projects a world in which all fuels have been consumed and no other sources can be developed.

Advanced energy sources suggested by our writers include luminescent organisms, earth-core forces, nuclear energy, lasers, and solar energy. As predicted by the futurist Adrian Berry, mining on the moon or the asteroids occurs in *The Jupiter Project* (Benford) and in *Prisoners in Space* (Del Rey). (For other novels that deal with the energy motif, *see* Part IV under "Fuel Shortages," "Energy, Solar" and similar topics.)

Children's novels avoid the direst of the futurists' predictions: depletion of all energy sources. However, many writers have borrowed from scientists in creating their energy sources of the future. Although the novelists offer a range of predictions, from shortage to abundance, most of them anticipate adequate fuel and energy supplies.

ENVIRONMENT

"The end of the ocean came late in the summer of 1979, and it came even more rapidly than the biologists had expected." Thus commences a scenario written by Paul Ehrlich in 1969.[21] Rachel Carson, Barry Commoner and other environmental alarmists have aroused public awareness in the movement John Maddox has dubbed "the doomsday syndrome."[22] On New Year's Day, 1979, however, Ehrlich and two other doomsayers indicated that they had become a bit less worried than a decade or so earlier because progress had been made and continued to be made in controlling and reducing environmental pollution. They warned that this effort must not slacken.

Kahn et al. take a more sanguine view, predicting that by the year 2000 "we will breathe clean air, drink directly from rivers and enjoy pleasing landscapes," although they agree that concern and prudence are certainly warranted if we are to assure our longer-term survival.[23] Must we face suffering and ultimate extinction on a polluted planet, or have we the means and the will to rehabilitate our biosphere?

Here is one novelist's view:

> It had begun when the oceans turned gray, then brown with scum. Smog covered the cities; plants and trees died; riots, starvation, disease and suicides followed. In the decade known as the Death of the Seas, 93% of all living creatures died of simple suffocation. The ozone layer was destroyed so that humans were forced to avoid exposure to direct sunlight thereafter. Later, in the 24th century, earthquakes raised the Chilean Andes and dropped San Francisco Bay as much as twelve feet. The Morrowans had survived for six generations in LIFESPAN, a subterranean complex, before they emerged to begin life anew on the earth's surface.

This is the background Hoover provides for her Morrow novels, set in California in the twenty-fifth century. Her gloomy prediction matches the pessimism of Ehrlich's scenario, although Hoover sets these events farther into the future.

Consider another image of the future, early in the twenty-first century, paraphrased from Adrien Stoutenburg (*Out There*).

> How beautiful the world had been before the disasters of misapplied technology—before pesticides, oil spills, nuclear wastes, erosion and war had done their work. The Trans-Alaska Pipeline spilled oil into the

ocean; sonic booms knocked trees over. Experiments in chemical warfare sprang out of control and defoliated the land. People crowded into
a few widely scattered population centers and became afraid of venturing
out into the wilderness. The Bushman, Pygmy and Aborigine were no
more. Carp, sunfish, trout and salmon died out, along with the king-
fisher and eagle. Robins and wrens dashed themselves to death against
the dome over New York City, although the non-native sparrows and
starlings survived. Open land was devoid of animal life except for wild
dogs who stayed near cities and military bases and lived on garbage.
When no mountain lion had been seen for 50 years, the Wildlife Service
was phased out.

Stoutenburg goes on to relate the story of Aunt Zeb and her carload of young
animal lovers who set out across the wasted land with the hope that some animals
have survived. Although they succeed in spotting deer, squirrels, turkey vultures,
trout, and several other species, they also have several mishaps and must ultimately
be rescued by helicopter. The pilot is so taken with the little mountain oasis of life
the group has located that, as the story closes, he is thinking of turning the area into
a tourist attraction—a step which would mean, of course, its destruction.

These are certainly pessimistic views of the future of the environment. This
pessimism is reflected generally in futuristic novels—a majority of which either
describe, or occur subsequently to, environmental damage due to pollution, overcrowding, or nuclear war. (To locate examples, *see* Part IV under headings for pollution, population, and war.)

How, one wonders, can the human species survive? In some cases, of course,
the solutions—if there are any—lie in a future beyond the time frame of the story.
However, novelists suggest a number of possibilities: underground cities or cryogenic
sleep until the earth renews itself; natural protection of valleys or caves; rebuilding
cities in new locations; domed cities or totally enclosed megastructures; population
control; smog towers to suck in and clean polluted air; a growth inhibitor in food;
colonization of other planets; and time travel. (*See* such headings as "Time Travel,"
"Cities, Enclosed," etc., in Part IV.)

These "solutions" are sometimes limited. They may stave off disaster only for
a time. In Bova's *Flight of Exiles*, domed cities are located in Siberia, while most
inner cities in the U.S. and Western Europe, though not domed, nevertheless are
closed off and occupied by uneducated, vicious, uncontrollable gangs who permit
no outsider to survive the night. Where multi-level cities have been built to house
the great numbers of people, the lower levels are slums. Underground cities, cryogenic sleep, and safe valleys are high risk solutions to environmental problems, and
time travel is hardly a realistic proposal.

Nevertheless, it is precisely freedom to explore *un*likely solutions which makes
literature a valuable resource in the minds of some serious futurist scholars. Therefore,
we may contemplate a society which gives moral sanction only to operations that
coincide with natural forces—using sun, wind, water, and temperature changes—without destroying or interfering with natural processes (Parker). We need not spurn even
the sparkling towers and silver-paved roadways of Elana's Federation (Engdahl). However unlikely in themselves, such ideas may inspire more realistic solutions as we
ponder them.

Moreover, although a preponderance of futuristic novels for young people
reflects serious concern for the fragility of environmental quality, some depict situations which gradually improve, rather than deteriorate. Much of the earth's surface
is still uninhabitable in the Morrow books, it is true, as well as in *Day of the Drones*

and Biemiller's hydronaut trilogy. But the circumstances in these novels already represent improvement over preceding devastation. Consider another example: for generations the forebears of Luke 15P9 (Martel) have lived underground, forbidden to visit the fatal surface. Fortunately, Luke has both curiosity and courage, and discovers that the earth has already renewed itself.

The folly of interfering with the balance of nature is a special aspect of environmental concern which is demonstrated in several novels (*see* "Balance of Nature" in Part IV). Such folly costs us a space age equivalent of the fountain of youth in *The Thursday Toads* (Lightner), wherein humans systematically exterminate a giant, poisonous species of toad on a distant planet. Eventually they discover from the planet's native inhabitants that a bite from that toad during adolescence confers long life, on the order of 200 years or more! But of course, not a single toad can be found. In *Space Gypsies* (also by Lightner), settlers have been killing native wiskits to protect their crops. Unknown to them, wiskits are the natural enemies of giant-sized worms which now multiply, causing earthquake-like disturbances. And again, John Morressy deals with humans who, out of fear, destroy sorks on Ziax II. The species is nearly extinct when the pioneers realize that it had kept in check an orange grass which, because of its insatiable capacity to absorb water, threatens their very survival.

Environmental balance, disaster, and survival all figure in world-future novels for young readers. The environment is probably treated in more novels and in greater depth than any other social or economic issue, at least in books published in the 15-year period covered by this bibliography. Since environmentalists themselves remark that they are somewhat less alarmed than previously, it will be of interest to note whether these concerns also abate somewhat in juvenile novels in the next several years.

TECHNOLOGY

One futurist view of technology argues that

the technology of our industrial civilization has reached a peak in putting a man on the moon, but, as the ancients knew, the peak is also the moment of descent.

Thus William Thompson begins his thesis that machine technology and a new consciousness are coming together to bring mankind to a cataclysm—which may result in either rebirth or death.[24] Technology has been blamed for consuming our resources, polluting our environment, and creating social problems.

Nevertheless, technology is also the means to correct the pollution it has itself created, and perhaps to alleviate shortages and some of our societal difficulties as well. The movement to slow technological growth by halting economic development is called "misguided" by the Hudson Institute.[25] Victor Papanek, the designer, although recognizing the damaging by-products of technology, calls upon committed industrial designers to repair the errors of poor technology by working in design teams. "The ultimate job of design is to transform man's environment and tools and, by extension, man himself," he asserts.[26] Can we expect technology to transform us for the better, or is this promise merely an illusion bringing us only more quickly to Thompson's "moment of despair"?

A majority of novelists strike a positive note in their attitude toward technology. Generally they are moderate rather than extreme in their position, whether it be positive or negative. Nevertheless, the strongest novel in this area is a highly pessimistic

picture painted by Jackson and Perlmutter in *The Endless Pavement*. Two lanes of
vehicles circle continually in opposite directions. The Home-a-rollas are in one lane;
the School-a-rolla, Assembla-rolla (factory) and other service units are in a second
lane. An empty lane lies between them so that repair vehicles can move as needed
in either direction. The entire arrangement is enclosed by a chain link fence beyond
which the Great Autos race without respite on the endless pavement.

In this story, technology rules the world. Humans are kept alive only to repair
the Great Autos and their master, the Great Computer-Mobile. Each person is strapped
into his personal rollabout shortly after birth and is not permitted to leave it. School
begins each day with the recitation:

> I pledge allegiance
> To the great autos
> And to the concrete on which they roll;
> One pavement under Ford, indivisible,
> With mobility and power steering
> For all (p. 8).

A red fruit grows to maturity despite the interminable concrete; Josette manages
to reach the fruit and ultimately uses it to disable the Great Computer-Mobile. The
book closes with the pitiable sight of human beings, their legs atrophied, crawling
as best they can to pull themselves up and over the fence—only to face the endless
pavement.

Other authors, too, are concerned with the threat of technology going out of
control:

> Machines are hellish (Dickinson).

> The human race has screwed itself with technology (Carlson).

> What good is technology if we breed cave men in the cities! (Bova)

For the most part, however, writers speak of controlling and guiding technology, rather
than eliminating it. Even in *Day of the Drones*, where machines are taboo, there is a
recognition that this may not always be so. *The Mountain of Truth* proposes that
technology must be combined with psychic powers, much as predicted by futurist
William Thompson. Perhaps technology can be controlled by avoiding operations that
destroy or interfere with nature, as in *A Time to Choose*, or by withholding technological information from peoples who are judged not yet ready for it, as in *Star Prince
Charlie*. A novel which debates the question is *The Pale Invaders* by Kestavan. In a
world once destroyed by misused technology, the villagers believe it is better to stay
away from machines entirely, while the "invaders" try to recover the lost knowledge,
confident that they will be able to avoid repeating those earlier blunders.

Taken collectively, novelists are as uncertain as futurists about the threats and
promises of developing technology. (*See* "Technology—Negative Attitudes" and
headings for the various forms of technology in Part IV to locate additional novels
on this motif.) Let us examine a number of specific technologies to gain a clearer
picture of the futures drawn by novelists.

Space Exploration

The British astronomer Adrian Berry sees expansion into space as the answer to numerous problems. As a first step he predicts that by the year 2050 shells on the moon will house engineers and miners who will retrieve its natural resources, astronomers who will want a clearer view of the heavens, and victims of burns, muscle diseases, arthritis and rheumatism, who will benefit from its weaker gravity.[27] A contrary view is held by Kenneth Boulding, who argues that we must view our earth as a closed system, "spaceship earth," because a "spacemen economy" is too far into the future—"at least beyond the lifetime of any now living"—to help us.[28]

Will we continue the exploration of space? If so, will this endeavor merely accelerate the depletion of our natural resources, or will it instead help us to break out of several approaching dilemmas?

Most of us probably think of space exploration as virtually synonymous with "the future." Nevertheless, just as some futurists do not share that view, so only about half the young people's futuristic novels mention space travel. Where space travel does occur, and where dates are clearly indicated, we note that space frontiers expand and means of reaching them become more sophisticated as novels are set farther into the future. The following prediction is synthesized from several novels.[29]

The first men will have landed on the moon in 1972. By 1978, the primary wheel of our first space station will be in orbit.[30] Later, comfortable passenger capsules will shuttle people between a consumer-oriented launch facility on Earth and the orbiting station. By the end of the twentieth century, we will see a base and/or an experimental smelting station on the moon, as well as supplies dropped on Mars to prepare for the first manned space flight to that planet.

In the twenty-first century, colonies will exist on the moon. After an abortive attempt early in the century, man will succeed in establishing a base or city on Mars. This century will also bring a manned space laboratory orbiting Jupiter, mining of the asteroids, and unmanned space flight to Alpha Centauri. Scientists will make progress toward a ship capable of manned flight beyond the solar system to other stars. They will begin experiments in transmission of matter.

Space travel may drop off and the moon station be abandoned as people become bored, but a breakthrough to permit travel at 80 times the speed of light—perhaps fuel derived from a new high-density material discovered on an asteroid—will bring about its revival in the twenty-third century. At this time man will be able to travel ten light years from Earth.

In the twenty-sixth or twenty-seventh century, interplanetary transmitters will permit individuals to travel instantly from one planet to another, although space ships will still be used to expand the frontiers of the known universe. These frontiers will have extended at least as far as Virgo (220 light years away) by the thirty-first century.

What a contrast—from novels that omit space travel, and even suppose no knowledge of or interest in space exploration, to journeys measured in hundreds of light years! (*See* headings under "Space" in Part IV to locate novels of both types.) Such expansion is not without its dangers, however. Occasional novels involve individuals or groups stranded on alien planets; another tells us that one out of every three star voyagers does not return. *The Earth Is Near*, by Ludek Pesek, details a manned exploration of Mars, clearly delineating both physical and psychological dangers of such an undertaking. Mark's *Ennead*, a novel surrealistic in tone, portrays for older readers the dehumanization that may occur in the harsh environment of a colonial planet. Besides the dangers of space travel, writers raise other objections: that it is too costly in relation to its benefits; that people should not be used as guinea pigs; or that the money would be better used to deal with problems on Earth. The latter argument is unconvincing, however, in Christopher's *The Guardians*, where the real motivation for abandoning space travel is probably the need of the elite tyrants in the County to maintain the *status quo* and thereby safeguard their covert authoritarian control.

Countering such objections to space exploration, on the other hand, is the thesis that expanding to other planets is "both natural and right." Sylvia Engdahl expands this thought in *The Far Side of Evil*. Characters in this novel discuss the "Critical Stage" in each planet's evolution—called "critical" because

> if they have the technology to cross space, they also have the technology for a war of annihilation; and every case that's ever been recorded shows that a people will do one or the other, but not both . . . The natural outlet of the effort [to prepare for war] is the conquest of space, which all peoples must achieve in order to become mature.[31]

This idea—that aggressive instincts can be channeled into space exploration—has been found also in science fiction for adults.[32]

The topic "space exploration" divides fiction writers sharply and evenly, much as it divides futurists. Expansion into space is a topic, apparently, on which one cannot easily take a middle-of-the-road position.

Transportation

Despite their worries about technology, our authors envision a wide range of ingenious innovations in transportation. (*See* "Transportation Technology" and cross-references in the index, Part IV.) For example, the gasoline engine may be replaced by electric-, solar-, or laser-powered vehicles; by police cruisers, buses, scooters, or cars that ride just above the ground on a cushion of air; or by anti-gravity buses or submarines. Other inventions for transportation described in novels for young people include automatically guided cars, helicopters, and jet fliers, and moving roadways and sidewalks. Perhaps the most astonishing vehicle of all is the "yachina," a box mounted inside a wheel-like contraption that moves forward as six kangaroo-like creatures ("yachi") hop from one platform on the wheel to the next (*Star Prince Charlie* by Anderson and Dickson).

Communication and Information Systems

If gasoline engines are headed toward obsolescence, books may join them. For example, in Kestavan's village only one boy was chosen every ten years to learn "the Reading and Writing" (*The Pale Invaders*). Books may shrink through microphotography; Bonham speaks of an encyclopedia reduced to the size of six Fig Newtons. Tape cassettes, picture tapes, or computer archives are among the information storage devices foreseen by novelists. Parker mentions tape cassettes which project arrangements of dots, rather than letters, onto a reading panel. Ultimately, layers of atoms may be stacked on top of one another to store information (Simak, *Goblin Reservation*). (*See* "Information Storage—Nonbook" in Part IV for other examples.)

Of course, information storage devices are not foolproof. They may be altered as in *Follow the Whales*, where historical records have been censored and much "good" removed to justify the "bad" which had to be imposed to save humanity from extinction. Alternately, records are sometimes misinterpreted. For example, Grandfather Peter mistakes a photo of a soccer game in an old newspaper fragment for a battle with a bomb (Kestavan). Shakespeare's plays are attributed to his "contemporary BernShaw" in Lightner's *Afria*. And we, from our "prehistoric" twentieth century vantage point, are taken aback to read that "Ghengin Kaan's name . . . derived from a great conqueror of prehistory who was said to have invented and used the first nuclear weapon in the Battle of Waterloo" or to encounter the "Ancient Temple of Kennedy XXVII, hereditary president of the First Terran Empire" (*Lord of the Stars*). (For more titles, *see* "Information Storage—Errors" in the index, Part IV.)

Although books may disappear or change form, newspapers and magazines appear more likely to survive, according to our novelists. The staff of the space lab JABOL (*The Jupiter Project*) receive their magazines photostatically reproduced on plastic sheets which can be erased and used again. Television, often three-dimensional, is mentioned frequently, and may even be carried in one's pocket. Telephones, too, come in pocket size, or more frequently with a picture; the latter are known variously as viewphones, videophones, visiphones, and vistaphones. Users of Parker's wireless thoughtfone place calls by mental contact with a human operator. To avoid the problem of different languages, instant translation devices, usually worn at the neck, facilitate face-to-face communication with beings on other worlds. Alternately, a world or intergalactic language may be invented. (*See* "Communications Technology" and cross-references in Part IV.)

Computers (*see* index, Part IV) figure in other inventions for communications. Computers take messages when one is away from home and may understand and speak English. A pocket computer gives legal advice (*Lord of the Stars*). Later, in our discussion of physical and mental powers, psychic communication will be added to the technological methods already described.

Recreation Technology

Some of the communications technology just discussed provides recreation to listeners and viewers, of course. Apart from this, futuristic books often do not mention recreation at all, or give only passing acknowledgement to sports, games, or hobbies. (Indeed, this is generally a very somber group of books; note the few titles under "Humor" in the index, Part IV.)

Futuristic novels mention such familiar recreations as piano playing, singing and storytelling, chess and cribbage. Children's games, parties, and dancing also occur, not to mention dining and drinking. There are circuses, amusement parks, fairs, and festivals. We also find well-known sports: ball games such as volleyball, soccer, tennis, baseball; swimming, sailing and surfing; judo and boxing; fox hunting, flower shows, horse racing, archery, biking, and track meets—even galactic Olympic Games.

More germane to our purpose here, however, are technological innovations in recreation (included in books listed under "Recreation Technology" in Part IV). Among these is a cylindrical squash court in zero gravity with appropriate rules (Benford). In an adaptation of old Roman games, electro-cars race on a high-banked course, occasionally airborne briefly by a jetburst, and gladiators fence on high wires using fiberglass swords (Christopher's *Guardians*). When an entire people lives underground, speleology becomes a national sport (Martel). On a distant planet youngsters sit in jet jumpers to play a new version of polo (Earnshaw). Perhaps we can also look forward to vacation trips to the moon.

Despite these examples, most of our writers seem to expect recreational activities to continue, for the most part, much as we know them today. We may need to be more creative if we are to avoid the sense of purposelessness which leads people to sheer boredom, as foreseen in Benford's novel.

Educational Technology

Many futurists are interested in education. At one extreme, Esfandiary believes that schools are already obsolete. Rather than to maintain schools, he asserts, we should make use of electronic media and world travel, thereby learning more and learning it faster.[33] Alvin Toffler expects more education to take place in the home, aided by computer-assisted instruction, with schools providing course modules, athletics, and social activities.[34]

Conversely, Beckwith expects children of the future to begin school at earlier ages and spend *more* time there, probably in boarding school situations, as parents pursue their careers. He predicts homogeneous grouping of students on the basis of ability, although asserting that these groups will no longer correspond to socio-economic strata. A universal language and, ultimately, world government will make education even more uniform around the globe.[35]

Margaret Mead argues for a "prefigurative culture"—a virtual reversal of the process of education as we know it—whereby the young, "free to act on their own initiative, can lead their elders in the direction of the unknown."[36] Clearly, futurists have envisioned several disparate possibilities for education.

In futuristic novels for young people, schools range from dismal to exciting. On the dismal side, Rob in *The Guardians* is harrassed by his teachers and hazed by his fellow students in the state school in the Conurb. In the County, however, conditions are better; there is a sense that everyone is being trained for authority. Equally forbidding, Brian's school in *The Missing Persons League* meets in condemned tarpaper bungalows with oxygen canisters mounted on the cracked walls. The students are too sedated to concentrate, so perhaps it is of little consequence that English will be made an elective course. We have already described *The Endless Pavement*, in which Josette spends each day in the School-a-rolla learning to tighten lug-nuts and bolt plenum tubes from her Teach-UR-Self Kit, and is chided by the Great Computer-Mobile on the screen should she drop her screwdriver too often. The most distressing feature of the futuristic school in Grohskopf's *Notes on the Hauter Experiment* is the lack of human contact. No adults appear—lessons are returned through a chute and meals are already on the tables when the cafeteria doors unlock—and social interaction among the students themselves is carefully controlled. (*See* "Schools" in Part IV for additional examples.) Perhaps the most depressing image of education in the future is the conditioning experiment which provides the entire plot for Sleator's *House of Stairs* (*see* "Interpersonal Relations," Part II).

By contrast, the reader's imagination may be stimulated by such opportunities as Rover or Anthropological Service training, Moon Mechanics, Space School, or the College of Supernatural Phenomena. Then there is the fascinating possibility of consciously training and directing one's psychic powers (*see* "Mental and Physical Powers," Part II).

Educational technology may prove to have flaws. Benford fears that it may be so expensive that the 30-pupil classroom is reinstated; Tofte fears that students may fail to apply themselves if free instruction is broadcast into homes without follow-up.

Nevertheless, what fun it would be to record homework assignments or lab demonstrations on a dictavision (Martel), learn from tapes while you sleep (Earnshaw) or from electronic signals while still in the womb (Jakes), or to interact with a computer that persists until it finds a way to teach that fits one's individual mental processes (Benford). (*See* "Educational Technology" in the index, Part IV, for additional examples). Again in education, we find that futurists and novelists offer a range of predictions about the future.

Medicine

Perhaps young readers are not interested in advances in medicine. At any rate, many novels do not touch on the subject at all. Those novels that do treat the future of medicine provide only sketchy information. In a few novels, genetic engineering prevents health problems before they can arise.

However, in a few instances, diagnosis is assisted by "life form scanners," and treatment by "therapy beds" or "iron wombs." Martel's upsilon rays kill viruses. Synthetic organs, synthoflesh to cover burns, and a regrown thumb or arm are other examples of medical advances.

West's *Dark Wing*, the only novel in this bibliography which uses medicine as its dominant theme, describes a society in which the practice of medicine has become illegal (as also happens under certain circumstances in Nourse's adult novel, *The Bladerunner*, which some older students may enjoy). West's hero, Gordon Travis, happens upon an old paramedic kit, complete with computerized instructions for diagnosis and treatment of illnesses and injuries. While Gordon's self-education in medicine is fascinating, his equipment is necessarily makeshift, and it is difficult to believe that he performs all his surgeries with success. Readers should perhaps be cautioned to regard that aspect of the novel with scepticism. (*See* "Medical Technology" in Part IV for novels that touch on that topic.)

The terms "psychomedician" (*Lord of the Stars*) and "sike" healer (*A Time to Choose*) suggest combinations of psychiatry and physical medicine. However, psychiatric advances are also shown to be used in harmful ways—witness the brain operation used to control rebels in Christopher's *The Guardians*. Medical progress may not be an unmixed blessing—as in Bonham's *Forever Formula*, where people live long lives, but eventually fall victim to sheer boredom. In most novels which mention advances in medical technology, however, such advances are depicted as beneficial.

Weapons and Defense

The power and variety of weapons are more impressive in these novels, unfortunately, than is progress in medical technology. Personal weapons range from a relatively innocuous tear gas pencil for personal defense to ray and laser guns that stun, paralyze, kill, or even totally disintegrate an enemy. Other variations are micro-miniaturized whistle guns, poison needle guns and molecule displacers, cobalt rifles and lignite fuses that destroy all oxygen in the atmosphere, and an algin container that could disintegrate an iceberg. Alien Kroons (*Lord of the Stars*) can unleash the Wind of Death, a swarm of virulent microorganisms that leaves a planet uninhabitable for generations.

Forms of defense include a personal transceiver capable of contacting emergency headquarters from anywhere in the world, a plastic suit and tent to permit travel through areas poisoned by radiation, a personal invisibility shield, and protective shields surrounding an entire planet. Technology appears to have been far more successful at devising formidable weapons than at perfecting means of defense. (Consult headings under "Weapons" and "Defense" to locate books that mention these topics.)

Artificial Beings

Science fiction fans are well acquainted with the idea that technology may devise machines resembling living beings. Nevertheless, few novels for young readers are deeply concerned with artificial beings (*see* that heading and cross-references in Part IV).

We have already discussed the malevolent machine creatures in *The Endless Pavement*. Fairman's "Barney" and Slote's "Danny," by contrast, are intelligent, loyal companions—able to cook, care for babies, climb trees, and converse. Barney can carry out general directives and solve unexpected problems on his own, while Danny can be extended and re-programmed to grow taller and smarter right along with Jack, his owner. Danny resembles a real boy so closely, in fact, that a would-be robot-napper is not sure which to abduct, Jack or Danny.

An abrasive artificial creature is "Sidney Six," a persistent robot journalist who rather resembles a box with stalks (*The Time Gate*). Simak's Sylvester, on the other hand, looks like his real life model—a sabertoothed tiger. The Suttons have created three types of artificial beings in *Lord of the Stars*—tracker birds, sky hounds and androids—all servants of the evil, octopoid Kroon. Finally, Norton's *Android at Arms* spins a tale of mystery and intrigue around a half dozen androids created by the "Psychocrats" to redirect world politics after they are substituted for the six world leaders of whom they are copies.

These fictional robots far exceed the bounds of present technology. Some are dismissed by futurists as impractical. Nevertheless, writers' fantasies in this area may provide a wealth of ideas to be sifted by inventors.

Other Inventions

What else may the future hold in store? Novelists suggest several fascinating inventions, among them a sound-wave shower, automated all-night shopping centers, machines that extract oxygen or water from rocks, doors made of a curtain of light or ozone, time travel, autopods for milking whales, silco-membrane diving suits with pore-penetrating hair follicles that permit a human being to absorb oxygen and discharge carbon dioxide under water, and finally, a self-heating can of corned beef. Although our authors certainly project serious reservations about the role of technology in our world, for the most part they do not hesitate to conjecture about new and surprising products of that same technology.

GROWTH

In a book entitled *The Death of Progress*, Bernard James argues for a steady-state ideology. He writes,

A basic and profoundly powerful dynamism is in trouble, and the heart of that dynamism is the belief in endless material progress. So we may anticipate a bewildered and panic-ridden immediate future and a series of frantic and largely ineffectual responses to our problems.[37]

In the same vein, Paul Ehrlich tells us that the imbalance of birth rate over death rate must inevitably be redressed, certainly by 1980, either by thermonuclear war, worldwide plague, or famine.[38]

Conversely, the Hudson Institute views economic growth and population growth from the stance of a guarded optimist. Both, they believe, will level off as a result of built-in braking factors before disaster strikes.[39]

Beckwith presents another alternative: population size will stabilize, but through imposition of birth control on peoples in poorer nations by governments of advanced countries. Thus, the growth problem is optimistically viewed, but with a compensating restriction on personal freedom.[40] Only Berry foresees no difficulty should population and economic growth continue apace since, as noted earlier, he envisions people and enterprises spread throughout the galaxy.[41]

Information on economic and population growth, although a prime focus of futurists' investigations, is sparse in novels for young readers. Children's authors probably surmise—and rightly so—that their readers will not be interested in large doses of economic background. In several novels, curbs are placed on population growth in response to environmental pollution, overcrowding, or political purposes. (*See* headings under "Pollution" and "Population" and cross-references in the index, Part IV.)

In societies rebuilding after environmental or nuclear disaster, on the other hand, growth is sought just as rapidly as the environment can support it. And where space travel has become commonplace, space traders (*see* Part IV) soon make their appearance.

Just one novel, *Noah's Castle* by Townsend, demonstrates the breakdown of distribution of food and other goods through runaway inflation. Barry Mortimer's father foresees the problem and gathers several months' supply of food for his family, only to have it stolen when food supplies become scarce.

Although growth is scantily treated in children's futuristic fiction, examples that do exist (excluding system break or space exploration, discussed above) view uncontrolled growth with a jaundiced eye.

POLITICS

Futurists' predictions dealing with politics are even more sharply contradictory than those that deal with growth. James sees governmental breakdown followed by a move toward totalitarianism; while others anticipate that democracy will spread, evolving ultimately into world government guided by global public opinion polls or referenda made possible by pocket computers or similar technology.[42]

As with the subject of growth, the topics of government and politics are rarely well developed in novels for young readers. Four models typically found in adult science fiction (Roman Empire, feudal Western Europe, federal United States, and Stalinist Russia),[43] are borrowed only rarely. Infrequent, too, are references to communism, democracy, or other present-day forms of government. However, the broader conflict of freedom versus authority is not uncommon. In many instances this latter conflict centers on individuals or groups, rather than on the governmental level, as will be seen later in this chapter.

Some novels, on the other hand, are exceptions to the general rule and do focus on political themes. In *The Guardians* (Christopher), a self-appointed minority living in the County controls English society, including that majority of the populace crowded into several Conurbs. Rob escapes from a Conurb to the apparent peace and tranquility of the County, where landed gentry hunt foxes, race sailboats, embroider, and raise miniature trees. Beneath this leisurely facade, as Rob eventually discovers, an organizational structure ruthlessly and efficiently snuffs out any hint of rebellion. As the novel closes, Rob is returning to the Conurb to join a rebel group whose efforts may or may not succeed in overthrowing repression.

Rebellion prevails in Malzberg's *Conversations*. The Youthers oust the Elders, although living conditions show only minor improvements thereafter.

In *The Incredible Tide* (Key), two groups of people have survived a war employing magnetic weapons. The city of Industria resembles a communist society, while the village at High Harbor is nearly anarchic. Before the two groups can come to blows, an earthquake and tidal wave destroy Industria. The charismatic "Teacher" manages to reach High Harbor to warn its people about the approaching tidal wave. We are left with the hope that he will not only save the lives of the people of High Harbor, but will teach them to adopt a spirit of cooperation and justice.

Evolution, rather than confrontation, is the political process described in *Star Prince Charlie*. In this novel, a young Earthman unwittingly fulfills certain prophecies and is hailed as a long-awaited prince. Two feudal lords attempt to use him to extend their respective powers. Charlie manages to balance them off one against the other, and then to establish a House of Lords and a House of Commons. He thereafter departs, leaving his new government in power until his promised return. Since he has no intention of keeping that promise, however, Charlie has served as the catalyst in New Lemuria's transition from feudalism to democracy.

Political philosophy wholly dominates *The Girl Who Owned a City* (Nelson). Writing in the classic utopian tradition, Nelson's purpose is clearly didactic: to describe an ideal society in a manner comprehensible to children. After a mysterious illness kills everyone over the age of 12, young Lisa and her followers establish a miniature libertarian state based on her father's precepts and the ideas she reads in an unnamed book. Lisa is always able to "figure something out." Her guiding principle is:

Having things is something, but not everything.
Earning the values for your life is not just
something; it is everything (p. 93).

She writes a contract for those who enter her "city" (actually a large city high school building), whereby they promise to earn their place and never to use force offensively. Lisa owns her city—this is her right, she asserts, because she has created the city and assumed the worries and responsibility connected with it. For others to vote away what she has earned through her own effort would be an injustice. But she maintains that everyone, even the little tots, can contribute services and earn their own rewards—and indeed, must do so if they are to achieve happiness.

Thus, in several novels, political themes successfully provide momentum. (*See* "Conformity vs. Individuality" and "Government" headings and cross-references in Part IV to locate other novels which deal with this topic.)

WAR AND PEACE

War is one of the "system breaks" which would radically alter the course of history. Although we have noted Beckwith's confidence that progress would continue as it has after previous calamities, the Hudson Institute is far less confident that historical experience is reliable in the face of thermonuclear war.[44] Moreover, the likelihood of such war escalates as more and more nations acquire nuclear capability.

Futurists, however, continue to make surprise-free predictions; that is, they virtually ignore the possible effects of system breaks and can only reiterate the importance of such steps as arms limitation to avoid them. As to the results of war, the scientists leave it to the fiction writers to paint scenes of a world after nuclear conflagration.

And indeed, about three-quarters of juvenile world-future novels mention war. We have already discussed the various weapons available and noted that war precipitated a system break in several novels. Typically, however, war is mentioned only in passing. Christopher, in *The Guardians*, refers to a war with China which no one wants to end because it is useful as a place to send "hooligans." (*See* "War" headings in Part IV for further examples.)

On the other hand, *The Galactic Rejects* is a genuine "war novel." In this story, three psychic spies bail out of a damaged space ship and land on the peaceful planet Bor, only to find themselves some months later once again facing the enemy Azuli.

To close on a more encouraging note, war has been avoided or eliminated in some novels, most often by establishing a world government at some cost to individual freedom. In a larger arena, interplanetary peace has sometimes been achieved through federation or a common legal system. Thus, some novelists, like *most* futurists, envision a future without war.

GROUP DYNAMICS

We have thus far discussed topics related to economics. Most work in futuristics is directed toward that field. Although many futurists are social scientists by background, they do not give extended attention to the social dynamics of projected scenarios.

Intergroup Relations

One important question deals with relations among groups identifiable by ethnicity, nationality, social or economic class, sex, and so on. A majority of these novels anticipate competition, suspicion, or hostility among social groups. This apparent pessimism may be a function of the nature of novel writing—that the conflict which the plot spins out is, often, a conflict between groups of people.

In some settings personal differentiations, by contrast, have been eradicated, although other groups in the same novel may not share that enlightened state. For example, the Order of the Children of Truth (*Mountain of Truth*) accepts members without regard to their social group background, although the world outside their Tibetan hideaway is not many years beyond our own and is divided by the same national, economic, and social strife with which we are so familiar. Again, in the Anthropological Service of the Federation (*Enchantress from the Stars*), people of all races work together as one family, but less mature societies in the same novel engage in warfare nonetheless. Maxwell, hero of *The Goblin Reservation*, announces that intolerance does not exist because the universe offers no basis for it, but literature students nevertheless fight with Time College students, and trolls quarrel with goblins, fairies, and banshees. Maxwell himself finds that he has an instinctive aversion to touching the alien Wheeler species.

Readers of futuristic novels for young people will encounter gangs, vandals, robbers, and rough neighborhoods. The People of the Ax channel their aggressive instincts into mock raids between villages, thereby avoiding violent outbreaks. A similar rationale operates in Christopher's Conurbs (*The Guardians*), where social conflict is deliberately fostered by encouraging people to identify with the Blacks, Whites,

Greens, or Reds in the daily Games. These factions are permitted to engage in riots, occasionally even to the point of causing deaths.

Group tensions are ameliorated in the course of several novels. Processes by which group lines are broken down include personal contact between individuals, a shared emergency, and monastic discipline. The three *Galactic Rejects*, in another example, hope to end the 19-year-old Azuli-Earth war by offering the Azuli a vaccine they desperately need.

More unusual than these approaches is the quality passed on to young "ax people" in their early teens through a laying-on of hands. Thereafter, as "Finished People" with souls, they sense one another's feelings at times of stress or passion and therefore cannot commit violent acts against one another. The less-than-human *crom*, however, must be killed if the world is to survive—until Arne demonstrates that the *crom*, too, have souls which can be awakened (*People of the Ax*).

Thus, the novels in this bibliography describe intergroup relations and resolve intergroup conflicts in a variety of ways. (*See* "Intergroup Dynamics" in Part IV for the subject headings related to this topic.) With this overview of intergroup relations in mind, we now turn to several specific aspects of social structure. These include social classes and mobility; relations based on race, culture, and sex; and contact with nonhuman intelligent beings.

Social Classes and Mobility

Kahn et al. point out that even if one day we have an open, classless society, one consequence may be a lack of "sense of place," and a ceaseless struggle for any tangible or intangible evidence of privilege.[45] Beckwith does not anticipate a classless society. Contrariwise, he predicts government by a meritocracy, an elite class not democratically selected. "It has been argued that government by social scientists would create a slave world," he writes, but scientists "are and always will be servants of mankind, not its masters."[46] Can we believe that scientists will be immune to the temptations of power where others have not? This very uncertainty may be the reason few futurists address the question of social structure.

Details regarding social class structure are frequently lacking in children's novels as well. Social mobility is carefully controlled in some instances, perhaps to retain power, or to increase the likelihood of survival in a post-disaster environment. Occasionally such rigid control is overthrown by force.

Conformity to dictates of government is one basis for class stratification. For example, in Surréal (Martel) one is assessed penalty points for such breaches as failing to shower when entering the family home, too frequent consumption of a double order of dessert, noisy behavior on the express train, or careless schoolwork. Failure to achieve or to maintain first class citizenship precludes advanced education; too many penalty points leads to being branded as a traitor and, apparently, banishment.

Apprentice citizens of Industria (*The Incredible Tide*) must not only conform to government regulations, but also find it necessary to inform on those who do not if they hope to accumulate the 1,000 points required to move up to "citizen third." Slaves in that society are branded on the forehead with a large red cross.

Perhaps the greatest number of class levels occurs in *The Missing Persons League*, where Bonham tells us there are "at least eight levels." Apparently, government employees are among those who receive higher status and are entitled to a larger food ration and access to natural, rather than artificial, foods. (Refer to "Social Classes" in Part IV to locate additional examples.)

In addition to obedience, other bases for social status include intelligence or ability, achievement, family membership, personality type, age, race, sex, and fertility. As an example of elitism (*see* "Elitism" in the index, Part IV), Biemiller's hydronauts are those people who could not be conditioned to live in the crowded hive cities; those who work in the sea regard themselves as members of an elite class who will govern the world when the environment permits a greater degree of individual freedom. In another case, Lightner describes a society in post-disaster Africa where light skin excludes even the most intelligent from advanced education and positions of leadership based on the argument that it was white men who had destroyed most of the planet. A Committee on Race Purity regulates these decisions and also decides which babies are so light-skinned that they should not be permitted to live. Among the surviving Anglics in Britain, however, women who are fertile have the highest status because many women cannot bear healthy children. Lacking mammals as models, the Anglics base their social structure on that of bees. Despite these examples, class structures, like political forms, frequently receive scanty treatment in these novels for young people.

Racial and Cultural Accommodation

Racial and cultural relations, like other noneconomic topics, are discussed by futurists less frequently than more readily measurable items such as population and gross national product. Beckwith ventures a prediction, however, that racial conflicts will disappear because racial lines will blur through miscegenation.[47] Berry shifts the question to the interplanetary level but, far from describing relations between intelligent species, he foresees that such beings will avoid one another due to the fear of hurting a less advanced culture on the one hand, or being conquered by a more advanced group on the other.[48]

As in adult science fiction, race relations are infrequent as a focus in children's futuristic novels. Racial attitudes in the latter range from stereotyping ("Oriental inscrutability" in Benford, "Neanderthal stupidity" in Simak) through disparagement to actual violence. Racial attitudes are not always explicit. For instance, Biemiller's team of four hydronauts tease one another about their race and sex, displaying humor that would seemingly fail if not for the survival of our familiar stereotypes. Similarly, the need to observe that Paul did not hold another team member's Harlem background against him suggests racial prejudice somewhere in that society (*Secret of the Marauder Satellite*).

In several cases it is not the fact of demonstrated racial prejudice that is remarkable, but that only one race or nationality is shown where more are expected. The illustrations may show only Caucasians, or surnames may all be European.

On the other hand, some authors seem to have made a point of showing that racial and ethnic tensions have been overcome. Several novels mingle races and nationalities. In *Conversations*, people of different types and backgrounds "no longer" live together. In *The City Under Ground* differences have been removed genetically so that all children of the same age look virtually alike except for eye color. Shared calamity seems to have erased all racial awareness from the minds of the children who reach the valley *Kennaquhair*—at least judging from the illustrations which show children of different races together. However, since the text never refers to this fact, we cannot be sure whether the racial mix was intended by the writer or was conceived by the artist.

The one novel which deals more than incidentally with race is Lightner's *Day of the Drones*. As previously indicated, the direction of prejudice is opposite to a pattern common in the United States; in Lightner's imagined world, light skin is a handicap.

At the story's close, however, distrust of light-skinned people is replaced by mutual respect and common purpose, at least among those few of the Africans who reconnoiter England and bring a fair-skinned Anglic back with them.

In view of the significance of racial intolerance in our society today, and since there is some evidence that reading, if combined with discussion, may positively affect children's attitudes toward minority races, we are disappointed to find that, like adult science fiction, some children's books reinforce stereotypes and others avoid the racial issue altogether. (*See* "Racial" headings in Part IV to locate novels which illustrate conflict, cooperation, or stereotyping.)

Sex Stereotypes

Like stereotypes related to race, those associated with the sexes are perpetuated in some novels, erased in some, and simply bypassed in still others. An image of women as weak, irrational, and subservient is projected about as frequently in stories as is the image of girls and women who clearly take equal risks, make equal contributions, and hold equal rank with males. (*See* headings under "Sex" in the index, Part IV.)

Aliens

We have noted already that astronomer Adrian Berry shifts interracial concerns to the realm of inter-species contacts. Typically, writers of science fiction for adults also replace the minority groups with which we are familiar with nonhuman robots (discussed earlier) and aliens. Human-machine and human-alien relations are then used to explore themes of racial conflict and cooperation, as well as other elements of the human situation.

However, less than one-third of young readers' world-future novels involve direct contact with aliens. Several other books involve human-alien contact set in present time, rather than in the future. A very few of these present-time stories, selected for their quality and usefulness in connection with a futures unit, are included in Part III and indexed in Part IV (*see* "Alien" headings) of this bibliography.

Aliens may be friendly, like the telepathic little Minims (Earnshaw), or hostile, like the warlike Bantons (Del Rey). They may resemble humans, as do the Boreans (Offutt); or octopi, as do Kroons (*Lord of the Stars*); or spiders, like Argans (Yep). They may be small enough to stand in the palm of your hand (Bulychev's Lasbutsilians), or twice the size of a human being (Benford). Perhaps they look like bushes or waves (Karl).

Undoubtedly the most astonishing array of intelligent species in a single novel is described in Simak's *Goblin Reservation*. First, there are all the Little Folk we thought did not really exist: fairies, goblins, trolls, and banshees. The latter have telepathic links with the ghostlike people of the "crystal planet," who had managed to survive the contraction of the universe before our own planet was reborn from a cosmic egg. Other intelligent life forms in this novel include hoppers, creepers, crawlers, wrigglers, and rollers—even a visiting professor from a liquid planet who must travel inside a tank. Survivors from Jurassic times, the treacherous Wheelers have roly-poly bodies suspended between two wheels, the lower half transparent and filled with a hive of writhing, worm-like insects.

Earthlings' attitudes toward aliens range from open warfare through exploitation and distrust to noninterference or benevolent protection. On the one hand, racial reaction to the unknown brings a "dog snarl" to the lips (White); on the other, determined efforts are made to train young people in new modes of communication so that they can establish mutual understanding with other-minded species, however different (Karl). The range of expectations we noted for interracial relations is matched by the range of novelists' predictions for inter-species contact.

INTERPERSONAL DYNAMICS

Interpersonal Relations

Esfandiary proclaims:

The private possession of people is even more reprehensible than the possession of objects. . . . Love must be inclusive not exclusive.

At one time the individual who could not commit himself to a one-to-one relationship was considered neurotic. In our fluid times it is precisely the individual committed to an exclusive relationship who is immature. . . .

Do not look for some one to love. Look for some *ones* to love. . . .

To be deeply involved with one person is to thwart your potential for growth.[49]

Thus one futurist sees an entirely new basis for human relationships. The psychologist Carl Rogers, although he also believes in personal growth and self-realization, simply declines to predict the nature of interpersonal relations in the future. Such a prediction cannot be made at this time, he says, because man is studying the future and endeavoring to make choices on the basis of this study for the first time in history; this fact will alter interpersonal relations in unpredictable ways.[50]

Beckwith, in contrast to Esfandiary, predicts *more* long-term friendships resulting from grouping students according to similar ability, and intervention of governmental agencies established to bring congenial people together.[51] Whatever the nature of interpersonal relations, however, all seem to agree that they should offer greater satisfaction and self-fulfillment to the individual.

In their interpersonal relations—apart from interactions based on group membership, already discussed—the characters in children's futuristic novels cover a wide range. We find teasing, bickering, and hostility as well as concern, warmth, and love—often intermingled in the same story. Interpersonal relations, after all, are the very stuff of fiction.

Two models of interpersonal relations come into sharp contrast in *The Treasures of Morrow*. Tia and Rabbit, when they first reach Morrow, are unaccustomed to hugs and do not understand that a gift may be made as a gesture of caring, without expectation of something in return. At Base, where the children had been reared, kindness is despised as weakness. Morrowans, on the other hand, can be ruthless, but are above deliberate cruelty. A similar contrast occurs in *Survival Planet*, where the mutual concern of the Evenson family puts into sharp relief the selfishness and irresponsibility of Chairman Taggart and Zurik, each of whom schemes to reach a safe planet with no regard for the other's group, the millions left starving on Earth, or the alien beings they encounter when they land.

Most of the novels portray trust and self-fulfillment. The relationship between orphaned Karen Orlov and Dr. Theodora Leslie in *The Rains of Eridan* is drawn particularly well; an adolescent girl and young woman scientist grow from fear of involvement to mutual commitment.

Those novels which show the highest quality of interpersonal relations frequently involve conscious use of psychic powers. In *A Time to Choose*, for example, those one-in-a-thousand persons who have natural psi-factor potential are trained for five years so that they can straighten out "bent minds." In the commune, we are told, there had been only one case of a "hang-up" in ten years, and he drowned himself before the sike arrived.

At the other extreme, three novels depict incredibly destructive situations. In William Sleator's *House of Stairs* five orphaned sixteen-year-olds are locked into an enormous space filled with stairs and landings, but no visible walls, floor, or ceiling. To obtain food from a flashing light machine, they must eventually do hurtful things to one another. Two of the five young people spoil the researcher's experiment by resisting, but the reader knows that starvation had driven them to surrender just when the psychologist decided to stop the conditioning process.

We have referred previously to *The Endless Pavement*, in which, thanks to the never-ending televised auto races and the unchanging routine, scarcely anyone talks in a Home-a-rolla, or needs to do so. Undoubtedly one of the most pessimistic of portrayals, however, is *Z for Zachariah*. John, who is very likely the last man alive in the world, manages—more by luck than by wit—to find Ann, who is probably the last woman. Suspicion drives them apart and Ann ultimately leaves her valley, having stolen John's radiation-proof gear, hoping against hope to find a haven elsewhere.

Futurists agree that interpersonal relations are likely to offer greater satisfaction and fulfillment in the future than at present. Even though optimism has a slight edge among the novels, children's writers are less sanguine.

Family Life

Toffler predicts several radical alterations in family life, all born of the accelerated rate of change: widespread acceptance of trial and serial marriages, purchase of embryos by retired persons as well as young people, professional parents paid to carry out the task of rearing society's children, communes formed in response to shared interests, marriage of homosexuals, and polygamy.[52] Esfandiary believes that presently the mother-child relationship becomes transformed into a need for husband or wife, and into patriotism, chauvinism, ethnocentrism, and racism. Therefore, he regards the family as "a destructive system" which should be replaced by shifting communes called "mobilia." A rule of thumb would be never to remain with one group more than six months.[53] This, of course, would be the end of the family as we know it.

Fiction writers are far more conservative than are futurists in predicting family structures. Whereas futurists speak of serial marriages and communes, the nuclear family survives in two-thirds of futuristic novels for young readers. (For the exceptions, *see* "Communal Living" in Part IV.)

Communes for all ages, or for infants or young adults only, occasionally appear. Malzberg's "Group" is the least traditional living arrangement. Three boys and three girls of the same age live together, apparently from early childhood. Within the Group each boy-girl pair has a particularly close relationship, continuing for life. The purpose of the Group is that its members shelter and protect one another. This socialization is so strong that even when Dal becomes estranged from his Group, all of his training and background "shriek at him" to comfort his Group mate.

Sociological aspects of future life—economics, politics, and human relations—have received less attention than have scientific topics among our novels. Probably sensing their readers' interests quite accurately, children's writers have been more inventive and more exhaustive in describing technological change than they have in describing social change.

PERSONAL DEVELOPMENT

Personal Freedom

Mankind has developed many mechanisms to control human behavior. Surveillance, backed by the possibility of physical force, takes many forms. Beckwith argues that some regimentation—for instance, driving on the right side of the road—expands freedom (in this case, the freedom to drive safely). More often, regimentation limits personal freedom. Beckwith regards the following practice as freedom-*expanding* regimentation because it will permit scientists to study diseases, crime, and associated factors. He predicts:

> At birth each person will be assigned a number to be used throughout his life for identification. . . . By 2100 this number will be indelibly tattooed on the body of each infant shortly after birth.[54]

Other means of control are already becoming more numerous and more efficient. Quarton lists modifications of the genetic code, selective mating, controlled nutrition, hormones, drugs, neurosurgery, and environmental manipulations as such efficient means of control already in practice.[55]

How different is the picture painted by Esfandiary—although this scenario may not strike some readers as particularly more desirable. He writes:

> Why go through a lifetime trapped within the same body the same mind the same personality? What a bore. Future-people will look back and wonder how an individual could have gone through an entire lifetime with its one and only self. . . . [The individual] wants to maximize his fluidity not simply by merging and demerging with different people but different colors and designs different admixtures of personalities and brains the option to plug into human-machine systems and be such systems. . . . We are in the age of the cyborg. . . . The day will come when the death of one single human—any human—will be so rare and tragic that the news flashed across the planet will stun humanity.[56]

What about personal development—especially treatment of personal freedom, mental and physical powers, religion and philosophy in futuristic novels for young people? Personal freedom is likely to be noticeably restricted; this is true in about half the stories. Again, escape from such restrictions is always a likely theme for a novel. Restrictions on personal freedom result from harsh environmental conditions, voluntary acceptance of group regulations, governmental repression, and fear. As an example of the latter, we cite the dome that Earthlings build on Ziax II (Morressy) even though the atmosphere is entirely safe.

In some instances, these restrictions are recognized as temporary—to be eased when the crisis situation will have passed. Indeed, movement toward greater freedom as environmental conditions improve is already evident in Lightner's African settlement and in Martel's underground Surréal.

Among the means used to control personal freedom are: genetic engineering or eugenic sterilization, psychological conditioning, drugs or regimented diet, information control, police or machine surveillance, physical restraint, conscription into military service, dictated selection for marriage and/or vocation, group pressure, no opportunity to be alone or to meet apart from the larger group, and the fostering of informers. (Refer to many of the foregoing and to "Conformity vs. Individuality" in the index, Part IV.) In addition, penalties for nonconformity, such as brain operations, loss of food or other privileges, slave labor, exile, or death are implemented to restrict freedom.

Extremely severe restriction on personal freedom occurs in Christopher's Tripod Trilogy, in which the alien Tripods cap all humans as they enter adolescence. The mesh cap, which is not removable, makes impossible any action other than that intended by these alien rulers. Unbeknownst to the Tripods, however, a growing cluster of young men escape capping and plot to overthrow this totalitarian control.

Children's novels demonstrate many forms of regimentation, including all but one of the means of control listed by Quarton. On the other hand, while none of the novelists draws so radical a picture of freedom as does Esfandiary, several of the writers do predict emergence in humankind of new capacities.

Mental and Physical Powers

People of the future may be taller, able to hear vibrations above the normal range, able to "bind" oxygen through their skin, or have wider eyes or hairless skulls in adaptation to their environments. Novelists also suggest that a predominance of our successors may be geniuses—IQ 310 and above—due to chemical stimulation of embryos (Jakes). Biemiller describes a new form of man, developed by geneticists to hatch when Earth again becomes livable. Resembling sea otters but triple their size, these "Kirl" survive to populate the earth alongside humans as we know them. (See "Genetic Engineering" and "Mutations" in Part IV to locate novels on these topics.)

The most frequently mentioned and most intriguing development, however, is the conscious direction of telepathic powers. (See "Psychic Powers" for cross-references in Part IV.) Novelists may be stretching reality in this instance. From a scientist's viewpoint, Colin Blakemore writes:

> If any species had had genuine second sight, not only would it necessarily have spread like a flood through the gene pool, but also that species could rule the world. For this reason alone the biologist must regard with extreme suspicion the claim that some individuals have extra-sensory perception or true clairvoyance.[57]

Nevertheless, several novels unabashedly credit humans with psychic capabilities. The increase in the number of telepathic adepts is sometimes attributed to nuclear radiation—a positive by-product of disaster.

In *Treasures of Morrow* a child accidentally causes the death of a man who threatens his sister; in *Lord of the Stars* telepaths must register because they are regarded as a threat to the state. For the most part, however, the assumption prevails that telepathic skill brings about such deep understanding that violence becomes impossible, as already described in *People of the Ax*.

Novelists assume that where telepathic power exists, it will be trained and consciously directed. Privacy of others is in some cases protected by a moral commitment not to enter another's mind without consent or by the ability to raise a protective screen against telepathic incursion; nevertheless, the dreadful possibility of reading peoples' minds against their wills occurs in a few novels. With training, one may learn to transport himself to another planet or to enter the mind of an animal as a witch is said to enter his "familiar." The responsibilities attendant upon having such power at full strength had been so great a burden to some thus gifted among the People of the Ax that they destroyed themselves. Nevertheless, psychic power most often offers new means of expanding personal freedom.

Religion and Philosophy

Predictions of the future of religion and philosophy are relatively uncommon in futurists' writings, although Toffler gives extensive attention to changes in life-styles and mores already in progress.[58] Beckwith believes that religion is already giving way to philosophic thinking—which in 200 years will have been replaced in its turn by scientific rationality.[59] "God was a crude concept—vengeful wrathful destructive. We want humans to evolve beyond God," says Esfandiary, uttering the ultimate heresy in the eyes of anyone who is today still committed to a traditional religious faith.[60] Will we thus abandon the wisdom of our past? Such a change may be more powerful, if more gradual, than war or famine in altering man's day to day existence.

One contrasting view is the recent argument of Christian theologians, most notably Jürgen Moltmann, which posits the future as the mode of God's being—the time in which the anticipatory event of Christ's resurrection becomes eschatological reality. This "theology of hope" is not a prediction of the future of religion, of course, as much as it is a religious view of the future, akin to the eschatological spirit of first century Christianity.[61]

For our novelists, psychic power is sometimes conjoined with religion. For instance, psychic power is an integral part of the new faith of the Order of the Children of the Mountain of Truth (Carlson). Given its first impetus by ancient Tibetan monks, the new order worships light as the source and symbol of life, but with no deity, no structured religion, no creed. Despite this disclaimer, the order teaches that the meaning of life is the continuance of life itself for all eternity, that to know one's necessity and follow it is to find one's own Truth, and that it is necessary to surrender one's ego to escape shame and guilt. The power of the mind can heal bodily diseases, read another's conscious thought and enter his subconscious memory banks, materialize and dematerialize objects and oneself, and perhaps contact minds on other worlds. Psychic power is viewed in this novel as the salvation of mankind.

Carlson predicts in this novel that Tibet will be the last stronghold of deep religious conviction in the world. Perhaps sharing that expectation, Simak places his College of Comparative Religions on the Himalayan Campus of the galactic university which occupies all of the planet Earth. Integration of psychic powers with religion is also suggested by Parker, in whose novel "sike" candidates live in cloisters and the principal of Sike College is also dean of the cathedral.

More familiar religious beliefs also survive, at least in novels set in the immediate future. Their faith had served to hold Sikh young people together against intolerance and had grown stronger when they immigrated to the British Isles (Dickinson). The Sikhs are not affected by the madness which turns all Englishmen against machines. Whereas the British suddenly revive neglected Christian observances, the Sikhs simply continue in their well-established customs, reading from their holy book and praying each morning and evening.

Ann Burden tries prayer in church, reads the Bible, and plays her favorite Christian hymns when nuclear war leaves her entirely alone in an isolated valley (O'Brien). But she had not been very religious previously, and finds little help now.

In addition to instances of Hinduism and Christianity, brief references to surviving vestiges of unspecified religious beliefs occur among our novels. They include prayer; churches or services; Bible or other scriptures; and references to the soul, guardian angels, or paradise. The Bible itself is a classified document in *Follow the*

Whales (Biemiller), but the hydronauts are given a copy by their superior officer. They conclude that it is a fairy tale history that makes every individual count as an individual. In another novel with religious elements, Adam Warrington finds himself so hemmed in by moral strictures on the planet Jasper in the Reformation Group that he must leave in order to obtain university education (Kurland).

Novelists in some cases mention or describe God as a being so generalized that we cannot associate him with any specific faith of our own time. "God was one of man's better ideas," according to a computer named David (Benford). Teacher (Key) describes God as the well of all knowledge and declares that anyone can hear God in his inner ear unless he has permitted that ear to go deaf. The Voice declares, "There is reason and meaning in everything," according to Teacher. Dr. Manski, in the same novel, cannot believe that an intelligent person could possibly believe in God.

The conception of God is generalized in the above examples, but has atrophied in several novels. God has been reduced to an unexploded missile at Hoover's "Base," and to the "Prime Mover"—a machine that generates electric power from forces in the earth's core—in Martel's Surréal. Lightner's Council of Medics (*Day of the Drones*) has a religious system and ritual centered largely on the destruction of the world by white men, while the Anglics in the same novel focus their observances on giant bees, sacred to their Gods, which execute infertile or rebellious men. One of their chants is the familiar line, "Where the bee sucks, there suck I"! Finally, to take a satirical turn, "There used to be a Great Person whose name was Detroit and he made the first autos," according to Josette's mother—although the pledge of allegiance reads "one pavement, under Ford" (Jackson-Perlmutter).

Limited concepts of God in these societies result from the loss of earlier, more sophisticated, beliefs. In other novels, however, a society is still at an earlier point in evolution. The religious rites on New Lemuria (Anderson-Dickson) closely resemble those of ancient Greece; among the People of the Ax (Williams), those of tribal Europe; and on Andrecia (*Enchantress from the Stars*), medieval England. More advanced cultures do not disturb these convictions, perhaps sharing a view enunciated by the Morrowans that, regardless of the inadequacy of a religious belief, it would be unethical to destroy that faith unless one had something to put in its place (Hoover).

Religion emerges or is imposed as necessary to survival under hostile conditions in Engdahl's *This Star Shall Abide* and its sequel, in Christopher's *Prince* trilogy, in the trilogies of Snyder and Bova, and in *Time of the Kraken* by Williams. The first three of these authors create priesthoods which hold sway over their respective worlds, privy to technological knowledge others do not share. These priests are actually scientists; as already noted, scientists serve in modern science fiction as analogues to the priests of earlier utopian works.[62] Williams describes a religion which is a curious mixture of Icelandic mythology and misconceptions about their trip across space, which these refugees from Earth no longer have the technological background to understand. These five novelists, unlike most others considered here, have woven their plots around religious conflict (*see* "Religion" in the index, Part IV).

According to Elana's textbook in *Enchantress from the Stars*,

> Each [people] must pass through three stages: first childhood, when man admits that much is unknown to him, calling it "supernatural," yet believing. Then adolescence, when man discards superstition and reveres science. . . . And at last maturity, when the discovery is made that what was termed "supernatural" has been perfectly natural all along, and is in reality a part of the very science that sought to reject it (p. 16).

Our own stage, we infer, is adolescence, which Elana calls the most difficult because people have faith only in what they can see. The ultimate faith Engdahl predicts, however, is never clearly defined.

Therefore, we find little evidence that our children's authors foresee evolution beyond God to scientific rationality, as expected by Beckwith and Esfandiary. Neither do any of these books propose a Christian—or any other—millennium. Religion is one subject on which futurists and novelists are not in accord.

As to philosophy, we have already encountered philosophical positions in this discussion. In considering system breaks, space exploration, political dynamics, and religion, we noted evolutionist views of societal development. In discussing environment, we observed a moral commitment to restricting technology so that it coincides with natural forces. There were arguments that expansion into space is natural and right, and several counter-arguments. In our examination of political dynamics we found a model, albeit juvenile, libertarian society. Our discussion of group dynamics included several examples of elitism. All these instances reflect an underlying philosophy.

However, we would hardly expect a novel, especially a novel for young readers, to explicate a comprehensive philosophic system. Nevertheless, several novels thematically juxtapose contrasting ideas in situations where both extremes are justified, at least to some extent. These conflicts motivate explanatory conversations or thoughts in the novels, thus leading readers to reflect on these issues. Such dialogues involve individuality vs. conformity, communism vs. anarchy, tyranny vs. freedom, information vs. protection, and technology vs. the simple life.

Furthermore, although these novels are not treatises in systematic philosophy (nor should they be), they offer bits of advice and aphorisms. Here is a sampling:

On imagination . . .

Benford: Men need dreams to live.

Engdahl: If nobody believed anything except what they understood, how limited we would be!

Jones: You have to believe in the possibility of things.

Karl: Learn everything and jump to the unexpected.

Norton: Seeing's believing, no, no, no!
Believing's seeing, you can go!

On history . . .

Malzberg: We need to know our past to know what we have become.

White: Life is growth and change; we must remember where we have been to know where we are.

On difficulties . . .

Benford: Ultimately there is nothing worth fearing.

Engdahl: Human suffering is necessary because people advance only through solving problems. Sometimes one must be willing to do what is wrong and face the consequences.

Karl: Sometimes things get better, sometimes worse—but problems remain.

Key: Every man owes his brother a helping hand when he is in
trouble.

Norton: For every evil under the sun
 There is a remedy, or there is none.
 If there be one, seek till you find it.
 If there be none, never mind it.

On the purpose of life . . .

Key: The purpose of life is to help others and to learn.

Malzberg: One must accept some responsibility for one's life, for choice.

White: Life is too precious to throw away half-used; we need to learn
to care about other people.

And finally . . .

Morressy: Is it better to go fast, or to see the things around you?

Futuristic novels for young readers depict many future images—some of them
grim and forbidding. They include characters motivated by greed, lust for power, fear,
and resentment. However, the foregoing quotations indicate that many novels provide
food for thought and encourage a "possibilist" attitude.

TIME SETTINGS

We noted early in this chapter that although most futurist scholars limit their
focus to the next 20 or 30 years, a few have extended their vision as far as 200, 500,
or even 10,000 years hence. We find that many children's novelists, too, prefer the
near future. Sometimes a writer explicitly indicates a date; in other cases we may be
told that some number of years has elapsed since, for example, Shakespeare's birth
or lifetime, or some other reasonably exact date, so that at least a century setting
may be inferred. In those novels in which dates can be pinpointed, the late twentieth
and twenty-first centuries predominate. The most remote date ascertainable is 3987
A.D., just over 2,000 years into the future. None of our novelists approach the time
settings used in some adult fiction; Polak mentions the date 17,864,151 A.D.[63] (To
locate novels by time setting, consult headings in Part IV, e.g., "Twenty-first Century,"
"Fortieth Century.")

Just over half the novels in a representative sample provide no hints as to the
year, or even the century, in which the story is set. Occasionally authors provide
contradictory information, as in *The Missing Persons League*, in which one set of
"facts" yields a time setting of the year 2290, while another set of facts points to
1684 as the time setting. Consistently, however, regardless of when the novel takes
place, if a crisis occurs within or prior to the action—and whether it is ecological
disaster, political revolt, or nuclear war—it typically happens, or has already happened,
in the twentieth or twenty-first century. Also, if space exploration has continued, it
extends farther into space as the time setting moves farther into the future (as already
demonstrated in the composite prediction in our discussion of space exploration).

Taking all the novels together, however, and viewing them in chronological
sequence, it becomes apparent that they do not fall into a single logical or historical
progression—nor even into a pair of developmental lines, one assuming and the other
avoiding a system break. Rather, each author has imagined a distinctive "history" for

his or her future-world society. Although some of these histories may share certain elements, e.g., nuclear war, artificial food, or mental telepathy, each combination is unique.

PLACE SETTINGS

Principal place settings extend from our own United States to distant reaches of outer space. Most writers are firmly rooted on the earth, usually in the United States (no doubt because we have analyzed only books available in the U.S.). At the other extreme, about one author in four takes us beyond the solar system to planets with such romantic names as New Lemuria, Iduna, Clord, Wenda, Harmony, and Ziax II. Some of these distant planets are in the process of recapitulating the earth's history with local variations.

(To locate books by their future settings, consult names of countries, planets, stars, and constellations in Part IV. Novels whose setting cannot be determined are listed under "Earth" or "Universe," as appropriate.)

SUMMARY

In conclusion, we have shown that futuristic novels for young people are equally balanced between optimism and pessimism, and are far more likely than not to end on a hopeful note. Half these novels may be expected to open with or to follow upon a system break—a sudden, cataclysmic event bringing about a sharp change in the direction of society.

Most authors in a representative sample of futuristic novels for young people describe situations in which food and energy resources have been successfully obtained, and they paint encouraging pictures of both technology and interpersonal relations. On the other hand, most children's novelists envision serious difficulties with the environment. Likewise, intergroup relations and personal freedom are unfavorably depicted in a majority of instances. The representative books are about evenly divided in their expectations of space exploration and government.

In relation to the field of futuristics, however, ideas are as important as attitudes. These children's novelists collectively propose many intriguing innovations to produce food; generate energy; survive environmental damage; improve transportation, communication, recreation, education, and medicine; defuse intergroup tensions; and develop psychic talent.

World-future novels for young people match the range of attitudes and ideas set forth by social-scientific futurists. And while novelists may avoid the economic and political detail of futurists' scholarly tomes, they more than compensate for that lack by their use of imaginative and often fascinating portraits of people and circumstances.

With so vast a range of ideas and attitudes, it is sometimes difficult to find the novel or novels most responsive to a particular interest or most appropriate to a particular learning activity. To assist teachers and librarians in locating books to use with young adolescent and pre-adolescent readers, the next section of this book, Part III, describes world-future novels for that age group, summarizing each, and commenting on its relevance to the study of literature and futuristics. Following this title-by-title review, Part IV presents the "Index of Themes and Motifs."

NOTES

[1] Ronald T. LaConte, *Teaching Tomorrow Today* (New York: Bantam, 1975), pp. 51-60. *See also* Theodore J. Gordon, "The Current Methods of Futures Research," in *The Futurists*, Alvin Toffler, ed. (New York: Random House, 1972), pp. 164-89.

[2] Herman Kahn and Anthony J. Wiener, *The Year 2000, A Framework for Speculation on the Next Thirty-Three Years* (New York: Macmillan, 1967).

[3] Herman Kahn, et al., *The Next 200 Years: A Scenario for America and the World* (New York: Morrow, 1976).
Burnham Putnam Beckwith, *The Next 500 Years; Scientific Predictions of Major Social Trends* (New York: Exposition Press, 1967).
Adrian Berry, *The Next Ten Thousand Years; A Vision of Man's Future in the Universe* (New York: Saturday Review Press/Dutton, 1974).

[4] Kahn, op. cit., pp. 9-20.

[5] John Maddox, *The Doomsday Syndrome* (New York: McGraw-Hill, 1972), pp. v-vi, 276-78.

[6] Ervin Laszlo, et al., *Goals for Mankind; A Report to the Club of Rome on the New Horizons of Global Community* (New York: Dutton, 1977).

[7] The ratings used in this analysis were called "Author's View." The coding instructions read as follows:

> Finally, rate the author's viewpoint. It is true, of course, that a particular novel may not represent an author's actual prediction of the future. He may be painting a dismal picture as a warning, or a marvelous picture as an inspiration. He may merely be playing with imaginative ideas and have no serious message at all. Nevertheless, if you had nothing but this book to guide you—the entire book, including the ending—and you were to meet this author and question him on his views, into which of Kahn's four groups would you expect him to fall?

For details and further analysis, see the author's dissertation, "World-Future Images in Children's Literature" (University of California, Berkeley, 1978; *Dissertation Abstracts International*, Vol. 39, 1979).

[8] Benjamin Appel, *The Fantastic Mirror: Science Fiction Across the Ages* (New York: Pantheon Books, 1969), p. ii.

[9] Jean Karl, *From Childhood to Childhood: Children's Books and their Creators* (New York: John Day, 1970), p. 7.

[10] Fred L. Polak, *The Image of the Future*, trans. and abridged by Elise Boulding (New York: Elsevier, 1973). *See* Part I, p. 10, above.

[11] Lillian Wehmeyer, "Futuristic Children's Novels as a Mode of Communication," *Research in the Teaching of English* 13 (May, 1979), pp. 137-52.

[12] Max Lerner, "On Being a Possibilist," *Newsweek* 94 (Oct. 8, 1979), p. 21. *See* more extended quotation in Part I, p. 11, above.

[13] Thomas F. Green, "Stories and Images of the Future," in *Images of the Future: The Twenty-First Century and Beyond*, Robert Bundy, ed. (Buffalo: Prometheus Books, 1976), p. 39.

[14] *See* the dissertation cited in note 7 and the article cited in note 11, above.

[15] William Van Til, "Prologue: The Year 2000," in *Curriculum: Quest for Relevance*, 2nd ed. Van Til, ed. (Boston: Houghton Mifflin, 1974), pp. 323-27.

[16] Beckwith, op. cit., p. 19. Beckwith does not explain his basis for this statement.

[17] Dennis Livingston, "Science Fiction Models of Future World Order Systems," *International Organization* 25 (Spring, 1971), pp. 265-66.

[18] Draper L. Kauffman, Jr., *Futurism and Future Studies* (Washington, DC: National Education Association, 1976), p. 30; Kahn, op. cit., p. 138.

[19] Kahn, op. cit., pp. 88-89; quoting Dennis L. Meadows. Ibid., pp. 101-105.

[20] Berry, op. cit.

[21] Paul Ehrlich, "Eco-Catastrophe!" in *The Futurists*, Alvin Toffler, ed., pp. 13-26.

[22] Maddox, op. cit.

[23] Kahn, op. cit., pp. 162, 180.

[24] William Irwin Thompson, *At the Edge of History* (New York: Harper and Row, 1971), p. ix.

[25] Kahn, op. cit., pp. 150-51.

[26] Victor Papanek, *Design for the Real World; Human Ecology and Social Change* (New York: Bantam, 1973), p. 42.

[27] Berry, op. cit.

[28] Kenneth E. Boulding, "The Economics of the Coming Spaceship Earth," in *The Futurists*, Alvin Toffler, ed., pp. 235-43.

[29] Benford: *Jupiter*; Bonham: *Missing*; Bova: *Flight*; Bulychev: *Alice*; Jakes: *Time*; Stoutenburg: *Out*; White: *Secret*.

[30] Note that (as mentioned in Part I) White, published in 1965, missed the 1969 moon landing by three years and that 1978 has passed with no space station under way, as predicted. Students may find it challenging to check the predictions and scientific accuracy of both novelists and futurists.

[31] Sylvia Engdahl, *The Far Side of Evil* (New York: Atheneum, 1971), p. 23.

[32] Livingston, op. cit., p. 265.

[33] F. M. Esfandiary, *Up-Wingers* (New York: John Day, 1973), pp. 48-56.

[34] Alvin Toffler, *Future Shock* (New York: Bantam, 1971), pp. 398-427.

[35] Beckwith, op. cit., pp. 216-34.

[36] Margaret Mead, "The Future Prefigurative Cultures and Unknown Children," in *The Futurists*, Alvin Toffler, ed., pp. 27-50.

[37] (New York: Knopf, 1973), p. 143.

[38] Ehrlich, op. cit., p. 26.

[39] Kahn, op. cit., pp. 32-34, 49-54.

[40] Beckwith, op. cit., p. 67.

[41] Berry, op. cit.

[42] Bernard James, *The Death of Progress* (New York: Knopf, 1973), p. 143. Beckwith, op. cit., pp. 42, 56-63. Esfandiary, op. cit., pp. 77-78, 93. Kahn, op. cit., pp. 206-207.

[43] Livingston, op. cit., p. 267.

[44] Kahn, op. cit., pp. 219-21.

[45] Ibid., p. 202.

[46] Beckwith, op. cit., pp. 58-62.

[47] Ibid., pp. 73-75.

[48] Berry, op. cit.

[49] Esfandiary, op. cit., pp. 39-40.

[50] Carl R. Rogers, "Interpersonal Relationships: U.S.A. 2000," in *Curriculum: Quest for Relevance*, Van Til, ed., pp. 374-82.

[51] Beckwith, op. cit., p. 261.

[52] Toffler, *Future Shock*, pp. 238-59.

[53] Esfandiary, op. cit., pp. 26-38.

[54] Beckwith, op. cit., pp. 34, 80.

[55] Gardner C. Quarton, "Deliberate Efforts to Control Human Behavior and Modify Personality," *Daedalus* 96 (Summer 1967), pp. 837-53.

[56] Esfandiary, op. cit., pp. 116-17, 134, 142.

[57] Colin Blakemore, *Mechanics of the Mind* (Cambridge: Cambridge University Press, 1977), p. 115.

[58] Toffler, *Future Shock*, especially pp. 303-322.

[59] Beckwith, op. cit., pp. 291-92.

[60] Esfandiary, op. cit., p. 143.

[61] Jürgen Moltmann, et al., *The Future of Hope: Theology as Eschatology* (New York: Herder and Herder, 1970).

[62] Northrop Frye, "Varieties of Literary Utopias," in *Utopias and Utopian Thought*, Frank E. Manuel, ed., The Daedalus Library (Boston: Houghton Mifflin, 1966), p. 35.

[63] Polak, op. cit., p. 143.

PART III
FUTURISTIC NOVELS ANNOTATED

Following are listed and described more than 150 futuristic novels for students in elementary and junior high school grades. They are arranged in alphabetical order by author and then by title, except that pairs and trilogies are grouped together and listed in the order in which they should be read.

A summary is provided for each novel. If a theme or controlling idea has been identified, that statement opens the summary. Sometimes, of course, a futuristic novel is more of an adventure or mystery story with science fiction trappings than an explication of a theme. Following the thematic statement, the plot is summarized. These summaries are intended to assist librarians and teachers not only to select, but also to discuss the novels with students. If a unit is set up so that students are permitted to choose among some fifty or so books, it may not be possible for the teacher to read them all the first year or two the unit is taught. Consequently, the summaries are somewhat longer and more detailed than in bibliographies intended as selection guides only.

Following each summary are notes suggesting aspects of each novel significant in relation to either literature or futuristics. They may indicate parallels to utopian literature or science fiction for adults; strengths or problems in plot structure, characterization, style, symbolism, or the like; or scientific or social-scientific inventions or ideas of interest. Certainly not exhaustive, the notes suggest initial approaches to analysis and literary criticism with students. All the novels described in Part III are subsequently indexed in Part IV, the "Index of Themes and Motifs."

This bibliography covers books which are: 1) set in future time; 2) full-length novels (not story collections); 3) published 1964-1979 and in print 1975-1979; 4) intended for readers in grade 8 or below (although perhaps also including older students). An attempt has been made to include every novel which falls within this scope, regardless of literary quality, marking with an asterisk those 49 titles recommended for first consideration.

There are three reasons for this decision to discuss all available novels. The first is that even a story mediocre from a literary standpoint oftentimes is unique in treating a particular theme or motif, and may therefore be the most effective point of contact at which to capture the interest of a particular student. The second is that, in other instances, students may use the index, Part IV, to find and compare two different treatments of a similar notion, and thus to distinguish more readily those characteristics which contribute to differences in literary quality. A third, but less important, reason is a curiosity—perhaps shared by others—to see the full range of world-future images available to young people.

The criterion "set in future time" deserves further comment. As noted in Part I, not all science fiction books are set in future time; rather, they may introduce a technological novelty or an alien being into an otherwise present time setting. Furthermore, some novels fall on a border line between future and fantasy. For the most part, such books have not been included in this bibliography. However, a few of these titles are particularly well written and at the same time treat themes or ideas which are also handled in futuristic novels. Therefore, a very few such books (e.g., the novels of Zilpha Snyder and a few by André Norton which do not fully meet the criterion "set in future time") are described in the following pages so that students may compare them with futuristic novels.

An asterisk marks those 49 titles recommended for "first purchase," that is, as an initial collection for classroom or library. These novels have been selected to include a variety of authors, topics, and attitudes. They are nearly all of excellent literary quality. However, a very few "medium" rather than "excellent" titles are included because they treat an important topic in a unique way. It must be added that some unstarred titles are also of good quality, as the notes often indicate, but would add little breadth to the basic recommended selection.

Bibliographic information for each title includes the number of pages for hardbound editions and availability of paperbacks as of spring, 1980. Recommended grade levels are occasionally set higher than in publishers' blurbs or librarians' selection tools; the recommendations here indicate grade levels at which students can understand and evaluate world-future aspects of the novel, rather than simply follow and enjoy the story.

Abels, Harriette S. **Galaxy I Series**. Mankato, MN: Crestwood House, 1979. Grades 3-8.

This series was not available for examination but is listed for the information of teachers needing easy-to-read material for classroom use. Frye readability ranges from grade 3 to grade 5. All titles published both hardbound and paperbound. Titles are:

Mystery on Mars, 47p.

Meteor from the Moon, 46p.

Planet of Ice, 47p.

Strangers on NMA-6, 47p.

Unwanted Visitors, 47p.

Medical Emergency, 47p.

Green Invasion, 47p.

Silent Invaders, 47p.

Forgotten World, 46p.

See also easy reading series by Eve Bunting.

Anderson, Poul, and Gordon R. Dickson. **Star Prince Charlie**. New York: Putnam, 1975. 190p. Berkley paperback, 1976. Grade 7 up.

SUMMARY

All intelligent beings follow similar paths in their social evolution. Occasionally, however, a random factor may change, or at least speed up, the pattern. In this account, purportedly submitted toward "a master's degree in sociotechnics at the

University of Bagdadburgh" (prologue), a random factor is present in the person of Charles Stuart.

Charles Stuart is traveling with his tutor on the feudal planet New Lemuria, where humans have been assigned by the Interbeing League to be available to guide the New Lemurians in their social development. A human embassy has been established, but is forbidden to intervene directly in local politics.

Quite unintentionally Charlie finds himself mistaken for the long-prophesied red-haired prince who is to perform five feats, overcome the wicked king, and rule forever after. Baron Dzenko, who would like very much to oust King Olaghi, arranges to have Charlie brought to him and makes it clear that both Charlie and his tutor will not survive unless Charlie carries forward the prophecy as Dzenko's representative.

Dzenko contrives for Charlie to succeed in the first three trials, but at that point Olaghi kidnaps Charlie and his tutor. The latter is a Hoka, an alien who enjoys assuming roles from history. At the moment he has styled himself "Hector MacGregor," a Scotsman loyal to the original Charles Stuart, whom he sees reincarnated in his pupil. Just when Charlie thinks he will be returned safely to the human embassy, Hector MacGregor "rescues" him and carries him back to Dzenko, who Charlie gradually realizes is hungry for power and wants to replace Olaghi only to collect taxes and play the despot himself.

Charlie now takes the initiative. He manages to escape from Dzenko long enough to carry out the fourth feat—to confront the priests of Klash and guess their three riddles. Finally, he accomplishes the fifth task by remaining in the Grotto of Kroshch while it is inundated by the incoming tide. Dzenko and Olaghi are exiled and Charlie is acclaimed ruler. Now "Prince Charlie," he soon establishes Houses of Commons and Lords. He then announces that he must carry out a mission elsewhere, and names a Prime Minister who is to assume power while he is away. In fact, however, Charlie knows he must never return so that the country of Talyina, lacking its prince, will learn to govern itself.

NOTES

Humor is relatively uncommon among futuristic novels, but it is provided here in the figure of the Hoka tutor who switches from the role of an Oxford don to that of a Highland Scot, playing both to the hilt. Too, the reader delights in Charlie's astonishment at his constantly changing fortune, including Dzenko's staging of the first three feats and the unwanted rescue from Olaghi.

Each chapter title in this book is a literary allusion; some, however, are beyond junior high readers' backgrounds. A few are science fiction titles (e.g., "Stranger in a Strange Land"); most are not ("Songs of Experience: The Tiger" and "Wind, Sand, and Stars").

An underlying theory of cultural evolution is essential to the plot (see index, Part IV, for other novels incorporating that notion). The New Lemurians had moved technologically somewhat beyond the point at which democracy might have been expected to emerge. Therefore, Charlie may be viewed as a catalyst, bringing about social change already overdue. Superstition, religion, and sheer chance also contribute to resolving the situation.

Asimov, Isaac. **The Best New Thing**. Illus. Symeon Shimin. New York: World, 1971. 26p. Grades 1-3.

SUMMARY

This simple picture book for children stimulates one to wonder what, of the many things taken for granted today, may some day be the envy of space colonists. The story deals with two children, living with their parents on a low-gravity planet, who await a visit to Earth where the "best new thing" is lying on a grassy hillside and rolling down.

NOTES

This story and its fine illustrations may serve as the model for a creative project on the same theme for older students.

Asimov, Isaac. **The Heavenly Host**. New York: Walker, 1975. 79p. Puffin paperback, 1978. Grades 2-5.

SUMMARY

"In the universe peace, good will toward all intelligent beings,"—thus Jonathan amends the Christmas message at the close of this story. Jonathan's mother is a planetary inspector who is responsible for the certification of planets suitable for human colonization. The small group on Planet Anderson Two is very eager for such certification so that other humans may join them and convert the entire surface into an earthlike environment.

Jonathan accidentally makes contact with a young Wheel, the native life form which human colonists have dismissed as unintelligent. Nor are the colonists interested in reconsidering this assessment, since humans are required to abandon a planet if intelligent beings already live there. Jonathan and little Yellger work out a convincing demonstration, however, by assembling a large group of young Wheels, just entering their flying period, to form a five-pointed white star in the air just above the community Christmas tree.

NOTES

Briefly and simply told, this story describes a life form that resembles a wheel, grows to eight feet in diameter, communicates with telepathy accompanied by flashes of light, and pushes out fingerlike extensions along its rim when it wishes to roll. The colonists' interest in denying the Wheels' intelligence is explained—an example of bias motivated by materialism. It is worth noting that the Wheels are nearly as eager to deny human intelligence, since people appear bent only on destroying the Wheels' environment.

Ballou, Arthur W. **Bound for Mars**. Boston: Little Brown, 1970. 218p. Grades 7-9.

SUMMARY

Both the dangers and the excitement of space exploration are revealed in this adventure story which describes the journey toward our first space colony on Mars. Set three years after the rescue mission described in *Marooned in Orbit*, and including the same leading characters (along with others), this sequel begins at blast-off and concludes with a preliminary touchdown on Phobos, Mars' tiny satellite.

Among the most eager men in the crew is George Foran, a young technician who was only able to participate when the crew member for whom he was first alternate had an emergency appendectomy a week before blast-off. Foran, however, falls prey to the Antaeus syndrome, a mental imbalance brought on by suppressed homesickness for Earth. He manages to conceal his condition, and through an inspection box surrounding an antenna base introduces a message which appears to have come from outside the ship. Signed by the "Galactic Council Patrol," the message warns the ship that due to Earth's substandard civilization, space colonization will not be permitted. The ship is to circle Mars and return home, or face destruction. Colonel Sanborn soon satisfies himself that the message is a hoax and takes steps to identify the person responsible. However, when he realizes that his message has not had the desired effect, Foran goes amok and slips and falls to his death. The novel follows the crew's reactions to that tragedy and a brief geologic expedition to Phobos.

NOTES

Spaceship buffs will appreciate the detailed descriptions of equipment and maneuvers, as in Ballou's earlier novel. The four-page nontechnical glossary appended to the novel will assist the science-minded to check out the novel's accuracy, now that several years have passed. Although several races work cooperatively on the *Pegasus*, crew members also exhibit stereotyped expectations based on racial identity. Very little can be inferred about life on Earth at this (presumably) near-future time. Characters are sometimes wooden.

Ballou, Arthur W. **Marooned in Orbit**. Boston: Little Brown, 1968. 184p. Grades 7-9.

SUMMARY

A suspense story which dramatizes the dangers of space exploration, this novel describes the mission in which Major Ike Sanborn rescues two astronauts caught in orbit around the moon with a damaged spaceship and dwindling oxygen supply. It is a race against time.

NOTES

Although virtually no information is provided about the world which supports the Terran Space Corps, spaceship buffs will enjoy the detail with which this rescue mission is described, including actinic or Kresch drive, orbit calculations, and the final exchange of oxygen tanks while the men are hanging in space between the two ships. Characters are sometimes wooden.

Benford, Gregory. **Jupiter Project**. Nashville: Thos. Nelson, 1975. 192p. Grades 6-9.

SUMMARY

"Ultimately, there isn't anything *worth* fearing." This statement (p. 192) sums up the message of *Jupiter Project*.

Seventeen-year-old Matt Bowles is with his family on JABOL, the Jovian Astro-nautical-Biological Orbital Laboratory, more familiarly known as "the Can." He must cope with two sets of problems: 1) his continual overreaction to his arch rival, Yuri Sagdaeff; 2) the challenges associated with life on an isolated space station. Matt's most serious run-in with Yuri occurs on Jupiter's moon Ganymede, where efforts are under way to build an atmosphere. Matt and Yuri set out in a walker machine to check sensor packages scattered across Ganymede's surface. Yuri fails to replenish air and water supplies properly at one of the way stations, but Matt averts any need to call for help by walking in his space suit to another station nearby to obtain the critical supplies. While he is gone, Yuri radios headquarters and reports the error as Matt's doing. Of course, Matt cannot prove his innocence.

Such a blot on his record becomes very important to Matt when word comes that JABOL is to be shut down as an economy measure, with perhaps a skeleton crew to remain. Matt wants very much to stay on JABOL, but in addition to his supposed breach of safety rules, he must also accept responsibility for failure of the Faraday cups he had installed on two data-gathering satellites. In a pique, Matt sets off in a space shuttle to check the satellites and, all unknowingly, brings back electrically charged spores clinging to the faulty cups. Further, by tracing the spores to the tiny moon from which they had jumped into space, JABOL's scientists find alien artifacts with evidence that an alien spaceship may be en route toward Jupiter from beyond Alpha Centauri. After this momentous discovery, continuation of a full staff on JABOL is assured after all.

NOTES

Good luck as much as (perhaps even more than) good sense brings success to narrator Matt Bowles in this plot-centered novel with its large dose of adventure, touch of romance, and bit of armchair psychology. The technical information scattered throughout gains credibility when one notes that the author is a professor of physics. This novel is one of the very few that touches upon the possibility of general malaise as a consequence of technological development. Political and social influence on scientific pursuits are clearly, if a bit cynically, delineated. Jones's *Moonbase One* is a useful novel for comparison.

Berry, James R. **Dar Tellum, Stranger from a Distant Planet**. New York: Walker, 1973. 64p. Scholastic paperback, illus. by Ken Longtemps, 1974. Grades 3-5.

SUMMARY

Ralph Winston's unexpected telepathic contact with Dar Tellum of the distant planet Sidra coincides with a crisis on Earth. Ralph's father is trying to find a way to overcome the problem—a growing concentration of carbon dioxide which is holding heat and melting the polar ice caps. (The rising oceans have already flooded one city.) Dar Tellum tells Ralph that particular algae shot into the atmosphere will convert the carbon dioxide to oxygen. When the scientists are about to send up the wrong variety,

Dar Tellum and Ralph manage to switch two containers by telekinesis. However, since adults do not believe his tale of Dar Tellum, Ralph says he got the idea in a dream.

NOTES

Set in the immediate future, this story reflects no changes beyond the carbon dioxide problem. Ralph, telling his story in the first person, wants to let other kids know about his experience "in case they have one like it."

Biemiller, Carl L. **The Hydronauts**. New York: Doubleday, 1970. 131p. Grades 7-9.
Biemiller, Carl L. **Follow the Whales**. New York: Doubleday, 1973. 185p. Grades 7-9.
*Biemiller, Carl L. **Escape from the Crater**. New York: Doubleday, 1974. 203p.
    Grades 7-9.

SUMMARY

Survival is the keynote of this trilogy in which, a few thousand years after the pollution of the earth's surface by nuclear war, groups of humans have survived in underground hive cities. Some have more recently ventured forth into the oceans to produce food and other necessities.

In *The Hydronauts*, Kim Rockwell emerges as leader of a team of four young people trained for Warden Service. His comrades are Tuktu Barnes, of Eskimo descent; Genright Selsor, a black Ethiopian; and the girl Toby Lee, of Japanese descent. The team is assigned to the Hawaii Search Mission, an undertaking inspired by memories of Ury Kaane. Kaane is a Cryo; that is, he had been frozen into cryogenic sleep some 1,500 years earlier, before the nuclear war, and recently re-awakened when his crypt was discovered in an iceberg. He recalls a hive city in what had once been Hawaii. The hydronauts join the search for that city and locate a hatchery of creatures which appear to be a genetic cross between man and dolphin. Although ordered to destroy all life forms they might encounter because the world food supply is so limited, neither Kim nor his crew can bring themselves to obey. And, as it turns out, the Council of Cities shares their commitment to survival of human life in any form and orders the dolphin-humans spared.

The creatures have proved unable to survive by the time the second novel, *Follow the Whales*, picks up the action. The four hydronauts, meanwhile, have been assigned to whale duty, for whales provide dietary fat, meat, and even bone powder to nourish plants in greenhouses. While carrying out these duties, the hydronauts glimpse animals which look like sea otters three times normal size. They are assigned to locate these new creatures. Upon discovering and passing through an underwater tunnel, the team succeeds in finding The Kirl, which are humans in otter-like form. Volcanic activity then traps The Kirl and the Hydronauts by closing the tunnel entrance to their hidden crater.

In the third novel, *Escape from the Crater*, the hydronauts succeed in winning the trust of The Kirl. They learn that all The Kirl are genetic mutants except their leader, whose brain is that of the original Dr. Kirl transplanted into an otter's body. He has survived in this form for more than a thousand years, having created the species named for him. The problem of escaping from the crater turns out to be less a challenge than that of convincing the World Council that The Kirl should be accepted as fellow humans, for the council is again thinking in terms of destroying any competitors for the limited food supply. Dr. Kirl, however, succeeds in winning acceptance for his people, and the four hydronauts are instructed to train for their next expedition—to rediscover an undersea passage across the north pole.

NOTES

This trilogy is clearly an adventure story. Its fascination lies not in its literary characteristics, but in the future world it creates—man talking with dolphin and wearing a suit which permits him to breathe under water, shark and kelp farms, awakened cryogenic sleepers, and, of course, the genetic variations of humankind. A fascinating verbal or visual scenario can be developed from any of the three novels.

The second and third novels are comprehensible without having read their predecessors. The third book suggests that the setting is some time after the year 3000, although the exact century is unclear. Stylistically, the sarcastic banter among the four hydronauts detracts from the flow of the story and sometimes is based on race or sex stereotypes.

Bonham, Frank. **The Forever Formula**. New York: Dutton, 1979. 181p. Grades 7-10.

SUMMARY

The desire to prolong life, made possible through the drug Rejuvenal, has created a United States peopled mostly with Seniors 100 to 200 years of age. However, although they continue to live, the elderly also continue to age physically until finally they illegally seek death through suicide or else fall victim to Logardo's syndrome, thought to be caused by sheer boredom.

Just two weeks before the story opens, in the year 2164, Evan Clark has awakened after 180 years in cryonic suspension. Evan's father is known to have developed a formula called Substance 1000, believed to have been an improvement over Rejuvenal in that it could maintain physical youth as well as prolong life. The formula has been lost, but President Charlie Fallon hopes that Evan's brain, properly searched, will yield the formula. A group called the Juvies, on the other hand, convinced that all this is inhumane, want to prevent such an occurrence.

With the help of Eliza Tertia, a cloned nurse who seems to have been environmentally influenced somewhat away from her genetically programmed devotion to duty, ratcatcher Bill Tuggey, leader of the Juvies, manages to spirit Evan away from the hospital where he is held. Tuggey's group is about to erase Evan's memory of the formula when Fallon's men walk in and hear Evan recite it.

Within a few days the "Guppies," as young people call the emaciated elderly, are taking the "Big Shot" in droves. In their impatience, of course, Fallon's group has ignored any notion of testing the new drug. A few days later the elderly are dying by the thousands as the process of protein building caused by Substance 1000 goes wild in their bodies. Tuggey's group gains control of the government, which they plan to restore as a democracy, while Evan hopes to show that a cloned nurse can be made to fall in love.

NOTES

This is a science fiction tale complete with cloak and dagger mystery. The moral of the story, that life becomes pointless once one has run the cycle of raising a family and trying the various available recreations, is explicitly stated and not likely to be missed by even the least philosophical of readers. The technological wonders of the twenty-second century are fascinating in themselves: multisensory illusions, artificial eyes, telephones with hologram images, cloning, and artificial stimulation and erasure of memories hidden in one's brain. Students might compare this novel with *The Thursday Toads* by A. M. Lightner, in which prolonged life also escapes our grasp when scientists act without complete information.

---

*Bonham, Frank. **The Missing Persons League**. New York: Dutton, 1976. 157p.
  Scholastic paperback, 1976. Grades 5-9.

SUMMARY

Those with sufficient perseverance and ability may find a way to escape the destruction of this world and awake to a better. But as the story opens, Brian Foster has no inkling of such a possibility. His mother and sister have been missing for a year. Shortly after their disappearance his father quit his job with Solar Electronics and began inventing such items as a hand plow and a mercury-filled golf club. Neither is a very practical article, however, since the few grassy spaces in the world are off limits for the sake of the oxygen they produce.

At this time, late in the twentieth century, oxygen is so scarce that Brian's growth has been stunted. Oxygen tanks are placed around school buildings for those who become dizzy from such overexertion as walking fast. School is more a way to fill time than to learn. Nearly everyone takes tranquilizers to hold tempers within bounds and energizers to keep up daily routines. The air is severely polluted, and all but the highest echelon citizens live entirely on poor-tasting artificial food.

Brian, however, is very clever. He has dug out the soil beneath their basement-less San Diego home, secreting the dirt in the walls of the house. There he has rigged up a garden and begun to raise rabbits and chickens. His little farm under the house is reached through a trapdoor hidden beneath the refrigerator.

On the anniversary of his mother's and sister's disappearance, Brian places an ad in the "personals" column of the newspaper. Apparently this draws the attention of Lieutenant Atticus, who on his first visit discovers lettuce seeds and rabbit bones in the garbage. Brian is not at all sure why Atticus does not turn them in then and there.

The next day a new student, Heather Morse, enrolls at La Loma High. Soon Brian has enlisted her in the cause of tracing his mother and sister. Only later does Brian realize that Heather's parents are among the growing numbers of missing persons.

Meanwhile, Mr. Foster wants to drive to an area south of Tijuana to test his new golf club in the desert. Brian and Heather go along. Here, Brian's father disappears. There is nowhere for him to have gone but into an old missile silo which appears to have a cylinder lock, but no cylinder. How, then, could anyone get in? Yet splinters of the golf club are lying about, and Brian concludes that somehow his father has penetrated the entrance.

Brian finds that he and Heather are being followed by Lieutenant Atticus as they investigate what seem to be clues—a claim ticket for Brian's mother's ring and a letter purportedly from Charles Dickens. Unknown to Brian and Heather, these clues are intended to test their intelligence until they prove they are clever enough to be admitted to the group of missing persons who, it turns out, are to be placed in suspended animation until Earth again becomes habitable after 2,600 years.

NOTES

A mystery with science-oriented clues, this book's strongest literary feature is its plot, spun out in 35 unusually brief chapters. At the same time it is a dystopian projection of environmental pollution and uncontrolled population growth. Biblical and other literary allusions appear occasionally, e.g., "Knock and it shall be opened unto you" (Chapter 22) and "a better world than they had ever known" (Chapter 35).

The future portrayed here is dismal; one could develop a depressing scenario from Bonham's descriptions. On the other hand, the notion of surviving environmental collapse in suspended animation provides a fascinating, if slightly incredible, upswing at the novel's close.

Careful attention to information about dates reveals some inconsistency on the author's part. That is, one could argue for settings all the way from 1682 to 2290, based on Chapters 27 and 35. But Chapter 8 places the time after 1971, and Chapter 14 keeps it in the twentieth century. Note that the Scholastic paperback has been edited to remove a few swear words and mild references to sex.

---

*Bova, Ben. **City of Darkness.** New York: Scribner, 1976. 150p. Grades 8-11.

SUMMARY

After a winter caught in a jungle of gang warfare in the domed city of New York, Ron Morgan dedicates his life to the proposition that human beings must be treated as human beings unless we would see the downtrodden rise up to destroy their oppressors. The story begins in a United States in which all cities are sealed off because they are unfit for human habitation. New York is open only during the summer months as a sort of amusement park where people can experience motion pictures, be waited on in restaurants, and enjoy other forms of recreation no longer available in the Tracts which stretch endlessly across the land.

After a disagreement with his father, Ron runs away to New York City over Labor Day weekend, intending to return home two days later when the city is closed for the winter. He obtains $2,000 on his credit card, buys $300 worth of fancy clothes, and pays $20 to see a movie. There he meets Sylvia, an attractive girl about his age who offers to help him find a hotel room. On the street Sylvia is accosted by a fellow named Dino, whom she fears. Ron bests Dino in a fist fight, but is injured, so Sylvia helps him find a room and stays with him. In the early morning hours she slips away, taking all Ron's remaining cash with her. Not yet realizing he has been robbed and supposing that Sylvia needs protection, Ron descends to the street, only to be beaten unconscious and have his credit card and ID stolen by Dino and friends.

Sylvia had told an incredulous Ron that she and many others are permanently trapped inside the domed city. Ron is now one of those who cannot leave since any attempt to get past the gate without an ID will land him in "the Tombs." Sylvia again finds Ron and gets him to her dirty, dilapidated room. Then she tries to persuade Al, the leader, to admit Ron to their gang. Al is reluctant until Ron demonstrates his mechanical ability—ability which will keep the gang's electric generator, appliances, and guns in good working order during the winter. Moreover, Al soon arranges to trade Ron's talent to other gangs in return for scarce machine parts, food, and money.

Al tries to persuade the several white gangs to cooperate so they can fend off a black Muslim group. However, cooperation disappears as soon as fuel and food supplies run out. Dino and a rival gang burn down the building where Al's gang lives. Al is killed, but Ron helps Sylvia and young Davey escape. Davey, who Ron learns is

Al's and Sylvia's six-year-old son, is very ill with a cough and fever, so Ron sets off across the city to seek help from an older man he has befriended. Hiding by day and skulking by night to avoid hostile gangs, Ron needs five days for the trip. By the time he returns, Sylvia has turned to Dino for help and Davey is dead. Caught by Dino, Ron is locked in a dark room. He is then unexpectedly rescued by the black Muslims, who soon have him teaching his mechanical skills to their young people.

One day in late spring Sylvia comes to see Ron, bringing his ID card. The city is to be opened again for the summer, so Ron tries to escape. But Timmy Jim, the Muslim leader, tracks him down. He tells Ron that the city had originally been closed to get rid of the black people, and that is why he intends to invade the Outside. But finally, convinced that no one would believe Ron's story even if he told it, Timmy Jim lets Ron leave.

Realizing now that many Outsiders know about the people trapped in the cities, Ron is determined to make them understand the evil they have done. "Even if I have to make myself President, I'll make them change," he declares.

NOTES

A dystopian projection of the consequences of racial conflict, *City of Darkness* is a strong novel effectively written as to style and characterization. The story is not for the fainthearted, for this environment is more savage than any wilderness. Survival, violence, and tragedy, as well as the race issue, are among topics for discussion.

Bova, Ben. **The Dueling Machine**. New York: Holt, Rinehart and Winston, 1969. 247p. Grade 6 up.

SUMMARY

This adventure story is built around the machine which gives the novel its title. In a dueling machine, each contender in turn chooses a setting and weapon which are created with such vivid imagery that both feel they are in a real situation. In one simulated environment and then the other, the duelists battle until one of them seems to surrender or to die, although there is no real injury to either party.

Originally invented as a harmless way to work out anger and aggression, the dueling machine becomes a political tool when Odal of the Kerak Worlds faces Dulaq, Prime Minister of the Acquataine Cluster. Despite the machine's supposed safeguards, Dulaq becomes totally incapacitated. Odal proceeds to kill a local opponent of the Kerak dictator Kanus in a duplicate machine there. Dr. Leoh, inventor of the dueling machine, assisted by Jr. Lt. Hector H. Hector, Star Watchman, is unable to determine how Odal is overriding the machine's safety controls. Odal kills his next Acquatainian opponent in the machine, then plans to insult Leoh himself so as to force another duel and gain another victim. However, Hector intervenes to insult Odal, thus drawing the challenge to himself. By putting the incapacitated Dulaq back into the dueling machine, Leoh learns that Odal, a telepath, has been drawing other men into the simulated dueling scene and so throwing his opponent into a state of terror and shock. Leoh works out an electronic means by which Hector can draw in his own reinforcements and then, after Odal's defeat, adds new protective controls to prevent any further telepathic interference.

Kanus decides to capitalize on this change by letting Kerak duelists look foolish in a series of losses, lulling the Acquatainians into false security while he brings his military forces into position for an offensive. Having heard that Leoh is working on teleportation with the dueling machine so as to make it feasible for those of limited means to travel from overpopulated to uninhabited planets to colonize them, Kanus also directs Odal to attempt to transport soldiers by means of the dueling machine.

The plot thickens as Odal is forced to join Romis, Kerak Minister of Foreign Affairs, in a secret plot to overthrow Kanus. In the course of the teleportation experiments Hector and Odal inadvertently trade places. Odal, now thoroughly confused about his loyalties, agrees to return to Kerak to rescue Hector. But just as Odal steps into the machine on Acquataine, Hector is being forced into its counterpart on Kerak. Momentarily, the two minds become one, and thereafter Hector and Odal work together like a well-oiled team to bring Kanus to defeat.

NOTES

A tight, well-crafted plot. Bova's use of complete and interrupted episodes and gradual unfolding of plans and secrets to build suspense are worth examination. Characterization is less noteworthy, but Jr. Lt. Hector provides a bit of comic relief in his bumbling clumsiness. The technology of the dueling machine itself is of some interest—will it one day be possible to act out one's thoughts in so realistic a simulated environment? The dueling machine is one step beyond the simulated educational environments predicted by George Leonard in *Education and Ecstasy*; Leonard's simulations would permit one to relive an experience in ancient Rome, King John's England, or any other historical setting.

---

*Bova, Ben. **Exiled from Earth**. New York: Dutton, 1971. 202p. Dutton paperback, 1973. Grades 5-10.
*Bova, Ben. **Flight of Exiles**. New York: Dutton, 1972. 185p. Grades 5-10.
*Bova, Ben. **End of Exile**. New York: Dutton, 1975. 214p. Grades 5-10.
Complete trilogy in paperback, Berkley, 1980.

SUMMARY

This trilogy is a space age odyssey lasting for generations. In the first novel, we learn the cause of the journey. Earth is dangerously overcrowded. Most of its major cities are cement jungles in which violent gangs war with one another, outside the control of law. The rest of the planet has been brought to peace and stability under a world government.

Meanwhile, several teams of scientists are on the threshhold of a breakthrough in genetic engineering to create supermen. World government leaders are convinced that such a breakthrough will lead to violent disruption. Therefore, they undertake to exile all the leading geneticists, together with their families, to an enormous space station orbiting the earth. There, cut off from computer and laboratory facilities, the scientists are to live out their years with no possibility of carrying forward their research.

However, Lou Christopher, a computer programmer on the genetics project, is spirited away to a Pacific island to assist a group which claims not to fear the possibilities of genetic engineering. Lou soon realizes his new captors intend to create a population of mindless slaves and then take over the world. Having foiled that scheme, Lou is sent to the orbiting station. There he and an associate, Greg Belsen, persuade the exiles and the government that it would be better to seek a new earthlike planet among the stars than to vegetate on the space station, so they begin to convert the station to a starship bound for Alpha Centauri.

The scene shifts ahead 50 years in *Flight of Exiles*. Lou Christopher and Greg Belsen are in suspended animation, along with thousands of others. Their sons, Dan Christopher and Larry Belsen, are among those awake to operate the spaceship as it draws near the major planet of Alpha Centauri.

The ship's council must now decide between orbiting around this planet, which the data show is not suitable for human survival, until they genetically produce children adpated to that environment, or repairing the ship and searching for another, more congenial, location. Dan wants to stay; Larry, however, feels they should push on.

Dr. Loring, an astronomer, begins to search for another planet. One night when he is working late in the observatory, an unidentified person knocks him unconscious, erases his computer-recorded observations, and drops his body down an elevator shaft. Badly injured, Dr. Loring is put into cryosleep until one of the young people can be trained to operate on him. Both Dan and Larry accuse the other of having caused Dr. Loring's injury.

Valery Loring carries on her father's work. Since both Dan and Larry claim to love her, she reasons that neither of them will kill her. And if someone else aboard the spaceship is responsible for injuring her father, then Larry and Dan will cooperate to find the person who will certainly attack her. To tighten the web, she tells each what he least wants to hear—Larry, that she cannot find an earthlike planet; Dan, that there are two. Eventually Dan's insanity is revealed and he is put into cryosleep so that his nerve patterns can more easily be normalized. Since Valery has, in fact, found an earthlike planet, the crew refits the ship for another 50-year journey.

Again time shifts 50 years, perhaps more, to *End of Exile*. The ship has begun to fall apart. All the cryosleepers have died, and only about 50 teenagers survive. Unable to read, they do not understand that they are on a spaceship. Their only guide is a videotape by a man named Jerlet, who tells them never to be violent and never to touch the machines. One girl, Magda, acts as their priestess and interprets Jerlet's message. When Linc repairs a pump in the hydroponics section, thus saving half their food supply, he has also violated Jerlet's rule against handling machines. Encouraged by the power-hungry Monel, Magda then passes judgment; Linc must leave the group and find Jerlet.

Legend has it that Jerlet can be reached by climbing a long, dark stairway inhabited by rats. So Linc climbs the stairs and succeeds in reaching Jerlet, an elderly man who had retreated to the near-null-gravity section of the ship because of a heart condition. Jerlet is dismayed to realize that the servomechs (robots) and educational tapes have broken down, so that the genetically engineered geniuses he had helped to create are ignorant and superstitious. For weeks he teaches Linc—how to repair machines and the computer, how to put the ship into orbit, and how to use the space transmitter which will carry them to the planet's surface.

Jerlet, dying, is put into cryosleep. Linc returns to the others and, although neither Magda nor Monel believes him, he closes himself in the bridge and begins to head the ship into orbit around the intended planet. One by one, others of the teenagers join him; even Magda is finally won over. Monel sabotages one of the rocket burns required to achieve orbit, but Linc manages to work out a procedure to bring them close enough to the planet's surface so that, by turning off all the ship's life support systems, enough energy can be fed into the transmitter to carry the young people, even Monel, to the surface of their Edenlike planet.

NOTES

This trilogy consists of three independent plots held together by the story line of a generations-long trip across space and the science fiction ideas of genetic engineering and cryogenics. Even though an explanation is provided, it is a bit difficult to credit the breakdown of social control which purportedly occurs between the second and third novels, since the second voyage was supposed to last only 50 years. We wonder at the conclusion of the last book whether these unlettered youngsters will encounter weather conditions or other insuperable problems on their new home. They seem not, for example, to have taken seeds for food plants, tools, or the like.

Still, the novels are competently written and provide issues for discussion. Was the world government justified in exiling the scientists? Did the travelers make the right decision in striking out toward a second destination? What might happen in a fourth novel?

Bova, Ben. **The Weathermakers**. New York: Holt, Rinehart and Winston, 1966-1967. 249p. Charter paperback, 1979. Grades 7-10.

SUMMARY

Weather control serves as the battleground between young, impetuous, and self-assured Ted Marrett and bureacratic officials who want to move more cautiously to be certain that any experiments will not produce damaging weather conditions in other parts of the world. Jeremy Thorn, narrator of the story, provides money and administrative talent so that Ted, fired from his position with the Weather Bureau, can refine and market his accurate, long-range weather predictions. But Ted's real goal is weather control. He realizes that the only way to get a crack at that is to return to the Weather Bureau, share everything he has learned, and let his former boss take the credit. Soon, however, the military recognizes potential utility in weather control. Determined to avoid so necessarily restricted a focus, Ted proposes Project THUNDER, promising that no hurricane will hit the East coast. The inevitable occurs, however, and four incipient storms brew simultaneously when available air power can deal only with three. In a last gamble for success, Ted directs a massive weather change over most of North America, thereby forcing Hurricane Omega back out to sea. And Ted, rather than Jeremy, also "wins the girl."

NOTES

Young meteorologists as well as students generally interested in predicting and altering the future will enjoy the technical information which is woven into this novel, though not to a point which would interfere with the story. Bova makes clear that good luck, as well as genius, plays an important role in Ted's success. This novel, when compared with *The Weathermonger*, sets off science against psychokinesis. Both books are interrupted from time to time by descriptions of weather in the making which might be compared scientifically and as literary devices.

Bova, Ben. **The Winds of Altair.** New York: Dutton, 1973. 135p. Grades 5-9.

SUMMARY

Does man have a right to extinguish animal species for his own survival? In this circumstance the author's answer is "no."

When gravity field drive opened the universe to man, every nation was assigned a star whose planets it might colonize. The first starship launched by the United Federation of North America in the year 2100 or so reaches its destination, Altair VI, only to find that the atmosphere is composed of deadly methane, the water filled with ammonia, and the animals hostile. Even robots become corroded so rapidly as to be unusable.

The scientists think they have a solution when they succeed in planting electrodes in the brains of Altair's animals and then in using teenagers aboard the starship to establish contact with those animals to direct their actions. Soon several six-legged wolfcats are guarding ape-like creatures as the latter build equipment which converts methane to oxygen, thus all unwittingly sealing their own doom.

Jeff Holman, the central character in the novel, controls the wolfcat Crown. So closely does Jeff identify with the animal that he soon becomes convinced the humans have no right to wipe out Altair's native species as they make the planet fit for human habitation. An earthquake and tidal wave destroy the oxygen machines, wiping out the work of a year. When Jeff's father and three others go down to the surface to survey the damage, they are attacked by a hungry wolfcat family. Jeff must add his intelligence to Crown's strength to protect them. The scientists begin to see the situation from Jeff's viewpoint and finally decide to return to Earth and use their technology to clean up their home planet.

NOTES

Young people will be fascinated with Jeff's experience through the senses of Crown, the wolfcat. This mental contact, made possible by electronics, is both like and unlike psychic possession (*see* "Possession" in Part IV to locate novels for comparison).

The theme, preservation of a species and a way of life, is handled differently than in Stoutenburg's *Out There*, with which this novel may be compared and contrasted. Racial and sexual discrimination come in for brief comment, providing a counterpoint to the central theme. Alternative decisions, not mentioned in the novel, might have been considered by the expedition's leaders at the close of the story; students might list and discuss some of these.

---

*Bulychev, Kirill. **Alice: Some Incidents in the Life of a Little Girl of the Twenty-First Century, Recorded by Her Father on the Eve of her First Day in School.** Trans. and adapted by Mirra Ginsburg; illus. by Igor Galanin. New York: Macmillan, 1977. 64p. Grades 3-6.

SUMMARY

Alice is an intrepid adventurer, albeit only five years old. Her adventures are described in a series of stories. In "Bronty," she befriends the brontosaurus who hatches from a frozen egg found in Siberia. In "The Tuteks," she inadvertently discovers a building left by an extinct people on Mars, and scratches her father's "picture" into the stone while waiting to be found. This "picture" is the source of eternal confusion for scientists, who take her art work for an alien artifact. The third story introduces a six-legged kangaroo-like animal who can talk. In "About a Ghost," Alice rescues a professor caught partly materialized in a faulty experiment with transmission of matter. Next, all the world is looking for the space travelers whom Alice innocently brings home in her strawberry basket. Finally, she steps into a time travel machine and meets a science fiction writer back in 1977.

NOTES

Translated from the Russian, these six lighthearted stories in a rather utopian future will be good for reading aloud. Any of them, especially stories two through five, will inspire young writers to create and illustrate their own futuristic adventures. A question to consider: is the heroine's name chosen as an allusion to Alice in Wonderland?

Bunting, Eve. **Science Fiction Series**. Mankato, MN: Creative Education (dist. Children's Press, Chicago), 1978. Grades 3-8.

This series was not available for examination but is listed for the information of teachers needing easy-to-read material for classroom use. Readability level is grade 3. Titles are:

The Day of the Earthlings, 25p.

The Robot People, 25p.

The Space People, 27p.

The Undersea People, 26p.

The Mask, 35p.

Island of One, 35p.

The Followers, 35p.

The Mirror Planet, 35p.

Available with read-along cassettes. *See also* easy reading series by Harriette Abels.

Butterworth, William E. **Next Stop, Earth**. Illus. by Paul Frame. New York: Walker, 1978. 80p. Grades 3-5.

SUMMARY

Coming back with a shipment of valuable haloconite, mined and purified on the distant and ugly planet Mega Sixteen, 12-year-old Charley Wilson is awakened from deep sleep. He finds the robot malfunctioning and the computer unable to indicate whether or not his parents are still aboard or were killed and jettisoned due to an asteroid shower. Charley's younger sister Julie wakes up briefly, but is so frightened that the computer puts her back into deep sleep. Charley realizes that he must make his way to the control room and the main computer, but the robot, Helper Two, bars his way. Quite by accident Charley succeeds in distracting the robot and reaches the control room. Just as the computer runs out of instructions, Charley's father appears in the control room door, still dizzy, but able to give Charley necessary directions.

NOTES

A suspense story which suffers some from the obviously limited vocabulary and sentence structure. Students may want to discuss the challenges and dangers of space travel for children.

Campbell, Hope. **Legend of Lost Earth.** New York: Four Winds Press, 1963, 1977. 154p. Grade 8 up.

SUMMARY

A semi-fantasy, this novel proposes the idea that we can only find what we are prepared to perceive in our world. At the same time, it dramatizes the psychological as well as the physical consequences of destroying our environment.

Eighteen-year-old Giles Chulainn is not satisfied with his world, Niflhel, on which drearily uniform streets and buildings are obscured by a never-ending fall of factory soot and ash. Perhaps that is why he accepts an unknown girl's invitation to a meeting of the Earth Worshippers—a group, barely tolerated by the government, which teaches that man did not originate on Niflhel, but escaped thence from polluted Earth.

Giles soon learns that his apprentice-master as well as the girl with whom he has been paired for three years belong to the Watchers, spies for the Society of Protectors. These two want Giles to become a Watcher and to spy on the Earth Worshippers. Hoping thus to save the green-eyed girl Lir Regan, who is the Bard of the cult and carrier of all their traditions, Giles decides to pretend to be a Watcher. Shortly thereafter, a Classification law is passed naming Earth Worshippers as "contrary"; arrests and trials begin immediately. Searching for Lir Regan in order to warn her, Giles stumbles into a machine which whirls him into unconsciousness and then opens onto a warm, verdant Earth inhabited only by birds and animals. Giles is delighted but returns to Niflhel, still seeking Lir Regan. When he finds her, the two of them carry her elderly uncle to Earth, this time by psychic powers rather than with the machine. Finally, Giles returns once more to Niflhel to lead the two hundred Worshippers by a third route, through a rock tunnel, to their long-awaited Earth.

NOTES

Niflhel and Earth are not two separate planets, but somehow parallel, Giles is told. People of Earth had escaped pollution not by traveling to another planet, but by going underground. When they had finally emerged, men perceived only the drab, ugly world in which Giles had grown up. Perhaps they could not see beyond the screen of their own limitations, or perhaps Earth had rejected them by way of retribution. This almost mystical conception of the relationship between the two worlds gives the novel its fantasy quality. The nature of parallel reality as explained here may be compared with that in other novels (*see* index, Part IV).

Borrowed bits from Celtic and Scottish literature on the one hand, and the unrelieved, dismal monotony of Niflhel on the other, combine to create a sense of unreality, of surrealism. Nevertheless, the characters discuss seriously the "history" of Niflhel, thus contributing to its futurism. Characters are one-dimensional, much like mythological figures. Given these distancing factors, students might search for those qualities in the novel which succeed in keeping a reader involved.

Carlson, Dale. **The Human Apes.** Illus. by Al Carlson. New York: Atheneum, 1973. 135p. Grade 6 up.

SUMMARY

Imagine that another sentient species developed from *Homo sapiens'* own ancestors; further, that this species long ago tried and rejected technology except as an instrument to accomplish their transformation into disembodied intellects to whom technology would no longer be necessary. Then suppose that this species, disguised by genetic manipulation as ape-like beings, have hidden themselves away among the Virunga Volcanoes of Central Africa. With these notions, Carlson creates a utopian society of 150 primates who have found means to remove their aggression, step up their powers of memory and thought, stop the aging process indefinitely, and establish instantaneous communication with several cultures in outer space.

Todd, Diana, and Johnny have come to Africa, as part of a scientific expedition led by Todd's and Diana's fathers, to observe gorillas in their natural habitats. Todd is the one who is first contacted by the human apes and who ultimately decides to join them. The novel traces Todd's growing involvement with the primate community, his attempts to persuade Johnny and Diana to join him, and the consequences of his decision—turmoil for his friends and family and near discovery for the human apes. Finally, however, Diana and Johnny come to respect his choice. Todd's father, of course, cannot believe what Diana blurts out in her hysteria upon seeing Todd after his physical transformation, and therefore believes that his son has died in a jungle accident.

NOTES

Although not actually set in future time, *The Human Apes* depicts a society more advanced than our own, with promise of further advancement to come. Carlson uses the "Intourist guide" technique common in much earlier utopian writing. Here is an ideal blend of technology and living in tune with nature. Quite philosophical conversations and reflections slow the movement of the story line, but are necessary to reveal Todd's character and to do justice to both positive and negative aspects of his final choice.

---

*Carlson, Dale. **The Mountain of Truth.** Illus. by Charles Robinson. New York: Atheneum, 1973. 169p. Grade 7 up.

SUMMARY

"To know one's necessity is to find one's own Truth." This is the basic precept of the Order of the Children of the Mountain of Truth, a group founded by Michael Jordan when he and his brother Peter go to summer camp in Tibet just a few years from now. There Michael is drawn telepathically to a hidden lamasery, where he is trained by the aged Dalai Lama himself.

The order grows each summer as young people at the camp are tested for admission. Telepathic skills are required, since Michael believes that trained psychic powers must be combined with technology to solve the world's problems and eventually to establish telepathic contact with other intelligent beings in the universe.

Each fall a few young people decide to stay at the lamasery, rather than to return home. In each case, the parents are informed that the missing individual fell in a mountain climbing accident but that the body has not been found. Meanwhile, the members of the order are free to develop their mental skills undisturbed. They also learn to sublimate physical love (heterosexual and homosexual) to a psychic sense of community.

When fourteen young people have "disappeared," including Michael himself, Michael's father persuades several parents to join him in an expedition to learn the truth about the purported accidents. The first chapter ("The End") opens with two paragraphs that let us know that the parents will be disappointed with the outcome of the expedition. Then we return to the beginning of the expedition to follow the parents as seen through the eyes of the viewpoint character, Peter Jordan. In subsequent chapters, Peter leaves the parents behind and climbs to the lamasery, where he waits for the drawbridge to lower across the chasm which separates him from his destination. While waiting for his brother to admit him, or for the sun to descend to the point at which it triggers the drawbridge mechanism, Peter recalls his experiences during his summers with the order.

At last the drawbridge falls and Peter crosses the chasm. But the lamasery has been destroyed by fire and Michael, who is alone, has been horribly disfigured in the blaze. The other members, having lost faith, must have fallen and died in leaving the mountains, disbanded across the world, or perhaps become disembodied souls— Michael does not know. He waits, serving as Dalai Lama through a regent, hoping the others will eventually send children to him for training.

In the last chapter ("The Beginning"), the parents arrive to find Peter again on the ledge opposite the lamasery entrance. Peter keeps the secret of the order, including what he has just seen. Facing the fire-blackened rocks and the impassable chasm, the parents accept the loss of their children.

Years pass. Peter never returns to the Mountain of Truth, although he reads of good things happening in the world from time to time and wonders whether they are brought about by those who are acting in accordance with their personal necessities as the order requires.

NOTES

The central idea in this novel is that of a monastic group devoted to reforming the world by controlled use of psychic powers. Several of Michael's teachings echo beliefs popular with young people during the several years just preceding the novel's publication. Since the Order of the Children of the Mountain of Truth begins apart from society and intends to de-emphasize technology, it suggests a pastoral utopia. However, the novel does not fully exemplify that genre, both because the order also speaks of eventually transforming society from within, and because its intent is not fully realized.

The order does not believe in God, but rather in the power of human capacities fully realized. Nevertheless, its rituals focus attention on the light of the setting sun. Some allusions suggest Michael is a Christ figure, but other elements contradict that symbolism. The ambivalence of the novel's conclusion will certainly engender debate as to the author's meaning.

Carlson, Dale. **The Plant People.** Photos by Chuck Freedman. New York: Watts, 1977. 92p. Dell paperback, 1979. Grades 5-8.

SUMMARY

The theme of this story is revealed in that each person who escapes the fate of turning into a plant is a "preserver," someone who cares for living things. The story begins with a mysterious fog filled with dancing pinpoints of light. The fog passes through the isolated desert town of Cactus. Some hours later many people, including Mike Ward's parents, become unnaturally passive and peaceful. But there are no physical symptoms of change, so when Mike and the school teacher persuade officials in a neighboring town to send a policeman to investigate, he sees only an unusually peaceful town. However, plantlike veins soon appear on the skins of the afflicted people—all but a dozen persons in the whole town—and they begin to absorb food from plants through their skins, eventually being transformed into cacti.

By this time the outside world is alarmed; indeed, the affliction begins to strike major cities. Convinced that aliens are using this means to conquer Earth, scientists race to find a defense. The remedy is simple, they discover, but just as the TV announcer begins to describe it, the picture fades from the screen to be replaced by a fog filled with tiny, dancing lights.

NOTES

A horror story set in the immediate future, with most of the stylistic flaws typical of fare for reluctant readers, this story leaves the reader anticipating the extinction of the human species. However, students may imagine other possibilities to write about or to dramatize. They may consider whether the photos included in the book make the story more, or less, convincing. They might also examine the logic of Mike's explanation for the fact that some people are affected immediately while others are not, as well as the validity of the term "osmosis" as applied here.

Christopher, John. **Empty World.** New York: Dutton, 1977. 134p. Grades 7-10.

SUMMARY

Survival in the face of disaster is no easy task. Ironically, it is the death of his parents, brother, and sister in an auto crash which has temporarily hardened Neil so that the death of one person after another in the Plague does not have the impact it might otherwise have had.

The Plague had begun in India and affected only the elderly. It began with a few days' fever, followed by several days' good health, but concluding with an incredibly rapid aging process and death. The disease spreads rapidly around the world and to ever younger victims. Neil goes through the few days' fever. He has about concluded that everyone in Winchelsea and Rye is dead when he discovers two youngsters, about six and three years of age. Believing he has only a few days before the aging process begins in himself, Neil hopes to set up a place for the children and teach Tommy enough to keep himself and his sister alive. After a whole day spent provisioning a farmhouse for them, he returns home to find that the aging process has already begun in them.

After the children die, Neil spends days in despair, but finally realizes he has somehow escaped the second and fatal stage of the illness. Taking an auto, he sets out toward London. He meets Clive, who has fitted out a traveling van with luxuries, including a Rembrandt painting. However, Clive has been driven insane by the situation; during the night he steals a ring from Neil, slashes to ribbons the upholstery of the sports car Neil has been driving, and leaves.

After a few weeks in London, Neil finds a balloon with a message inside giving the address where another survivor is apparently waiting. When Neil reaches the house, he finds the young man, about his own age, has only within the last 24 hours given up hope and hung himself.

Finally, Neil finds two girls and joins forces with them. However, Billie resents Neil's intrusion, especially when it becomes clear that Lucy and Neil are developing a romantic attachment. One day Billie and Neil go out to gather supplies and she attacks him with a kitchen knife. In the final scene, after Lucy has dressed Neil's wound, they hear a keening sound. It is Billie. At first determined not to let her in, they soon realize they cannot spend the rest of their lives with the memory of her unanswered cries.

NOTES

Despite the humanity of opening the door to Billie (the author has referred to this as an "upbeat ending"), *Empty World* overall is a chilling picture of the immediate future—surely one of the most depressing novels in this bibliography. For all that, it is a story of coping. Very well written, it offers opportunity to discuss each of Neil's choices, especially that final decision to let Billie rejoin himself and Lucy. A more optimistic post-plague situation is depicted in *The Girl Who Owned a City* by O. T. Nelson.

---

*Christopher, John. **The Guardians.** New York: Macmillan, 1970. 168p. Collier paperback, 1972. Grades 5-10.

SUMMARY

This novel is a call for freedom from mind control and exploitation. Set in twenty-first century England, it postulates a society in which the majority of people are packed into crowded Conurbs. Their work week is only 20 hours long, but their leisure time is filled with mindless pursuits designed as an escape valve for aggression. Outside the Conurbs, the gentry and their servants live in the County where, although some modern technology is discreetly used, the overall impression is that of upper class, late Victorian England.

Rob Randall lives in London Conurb with his father, his mother having died a few years earlier. In the opening chapter, Rob's father, an electrician at the Stadium where the old Roman games have been updated with modern technology, is severely injured by "accidentally" touching a live wire. He dies the next day.

Rob is assigned to a boarding school where the students are very harshly treated. The schoolmasters and the food are bad enough, but the torturous hazing of newcomers by the older boys is more than Rob can stand. He decides to run away—no easy matter in this highly routinized society.

Having taken some of his father's mementos, Rob discovers that his mother had been born in the County, where she must have been a servant. Perhaps he can hide out in the County, somehow getting food from the farms. Fortunately, the general belief that the fence on the border between Conurb and County carries a lethal electric current turns out to be false, so Rob succeeds in crossing. Hungry, his feet blistered, Rob is found by Mike Gifford, who helps him. Mike's mother is persuaded to take Rob in, introducing him as the son of a cousin in Nepal who sent him to England to complete his schooling.

Rob has much to learn about speech and manners, including how to treat the servants, but he is determined to fit in. Ironically, Mike falls in with a group of young men who wish to revolt against the authoritarian system and erase the lines which place gentry, servants, and Conurbans in separate groups.

Their revolution is quickly put down, but Mike and several others are missing. Rob, who had not joined the rebels, is called for questioning by Sir Percy, Lord Lieutenant of the County. There Rob learns that the real power is in the hands of a few "guardians," and that Mike, if caught, will be subjected to a brain operation which will take away any desire to rebel against the system. Sir Percy then tells Rob that his real identity has been known all along; nevertheless, Rob is invited to join with the guardians. He accepts, but is caught between his friendship for Mike and his obligation to Mike's parents; between the safety of his place in Mike's family and sympathy for the view of the revolutionaries—among whom, he gradually realizes, his father may have been included.

Rob's final decision comes clear when he realizes that Mike's own mother accepts the necessity of the brain operation for her son; indeed, she tells Rob, her husband had had the same operation in his youth. The story closes as Rob is crossing the border back to the Conurb to join the rebel group.

NOTES

A young reader's *1984*, *The Guardians* is a classic dystopia, the title perhaps borrowed from Plato. One wonders just how present-day society evolved into the class structure described here, but clearly the control and exploitation depicted are seen by the author as extrapolations of trends in our own time. Characterization is well handled, the plot well knit, the style economical, with sentences of varying lengths and structures well used.

Students might discuss how it happened that Rob was motivated to undertake so "unusual" an act as running away in the first place. (Sir Percy indicates in the closing chapter that this very issue might be worth discussing at the next meeting of the Psychosocial Committee.) However, Rob is determined to conform. Why, then, does he not report Mike's activities? Is it out of obligation to Mike, as Rob says, or fear of being unmasked, as Sir Percy supposes? Finally, does Rob make the right decision?

Christopher, John. **The Lotus Caves.** New York: Macmillan, 1969. 154p. Collier paperback, 1971. Grades 5-8.

SUMMARY

This novel is a space adventure with a touch of fantasia. When Marty's best friend, Paul Miller, is sent from the moon station back to Earth for health reasons, Marty teams up with Steve du Cros. Their first escapade is to paint dozens of Christmas balloons to resemble their school principal, fill them with warm air, and let them rise until trapped by the dome of the Bubble which is their city on the moon.

The second undertaking, however, is the main focus of the novel. The two boys find a crawler in which the previous user has left a key which will override the usual eight-mile limit. Careful to check supplies and leave a message for their parents, the boys cross the moon's surface to First Station, the original moon base, now abandoned.

They find the diary of Andrew Thurgood, who had been presumed dead 70 years earlier, when he had set out in a crawler and never returned. Marty and Steve decide to find a location mentioned in Thurgood's diary where he reported having seen—incredibly—a giant-sized, swaying flower.

The boys crash through into a series of caves filled with an array of fantastic plant forms—and with air, fruits, and other foods. There they meet Andrew Thurgood, still young, but hopelessly devoted to the Plant, which has created all the wonders in the caves. By appealing to Thurgood's memories of his early life, Marty and Steve beguile him into helping them escape. Thurgood disappears back into the caves while the boys decide to keep its existence a secret so it will not be destroyed by overly zealous scientists.

NOTES

The Lotus Caves is one of those science fiction novels which is more fiction than science. It takes its title from a reference to the Odyssey in which the lotus-eaters ate fruit that made them so happy they forgot everything else—the fruit and other edibles in the cave seem to have the same effect. Another reference: "The Pearl," title of the closing chapter, likens Thurgood to the pearl formed about a bit of sand by an oyster, as the Plant has filled the caves for Thurgood's pleasure. The story is well told but, except for the few opening chapters which describe the moon station in 2068, is scarcely a realistic future-world image.

---

*Christopher, John. **The Prince in Waiting**. New York: Macmillan, 1970. 182p.
   Collier paperback, 1974. Grades 6-9.
*Christopher, John. **Beyond the Burning Lands**. New York: Macmillan, 1971. 159p.
   Collier paperback, 1974. Grades 6-9.
*Christopher, John. **The Sword of the Spirits**. New York: Macmillan, 1972. 162p.
   Collier paperback, 1976. Grades 6-9.

SUMMARY

Human passion and intrigue may cause plans to go astray, as this trilogy demonstrates. Luke Perry, first person narrator, is proud and ambitious. At first the son of a mere captain, he is named Prince in Waiting when his father is chosen Prince of Winchester.

Luke's father had been previously married, and has an older son, Peter. Peter's mother, in attempting to kill Luke out of ambition for her own son, brings about the death of Luke's mother instead. Inconsolable, Luke's father nevertheless carries his responsibilities as prince. He subdues neighboring Petersfield, and, violating long custom, declares it part of his domain rather than restoring its independence—just punishment for their having used machines in the battles. For machines were (incorrectly) thought to have caused the Disaster which even now, in the twenty-third century, leaves part of the land smoldering with volcanos and steam and shaken by earthquakes from time to time, and has led to the birth of misshapen animals and humans, or polymufs.

Luke's father is treacherously killed by Prince Jeremy of Romsey. Peter leads the Winchester soldiers to victory by re-entering the city through a secret tunnel whose location had been revealed to him by his Christian wife. Luke flees to the

Sanctuary of the Seers, priests who have kept scientific knowledge alive and hope to win the people from their hatred of machines after the cities have been united under a single leader. The Seers have chosen Luke to be this leader.

In *Beyond the Burning Lands*, Peter recalls Luke to court, largely at the behest of his Christian wife, but wrests Luke's pledge of loyalty to himself and his heirs. His lady is pregnant, but drowns in her bath. Luke escapes the mourning castle by joining a group of envoys to a city which, a peddler tells them, can be reached via a pass through the burning lands. There Luke kills a monster, the bayemot, and is betrothed to the Princess Blodwen as a reward for his heroism. When he returns to Winchester, however, Luke finds himself accused, along with the local Seer and his acolytes, of having killed Peter's wife with electricity. Although the Seer is guilty of having committed this murder on Luke's behalf, Luke knew nothing of it. Luke challenges Peter and kills him using the "sword of the Spirits" (fashioned by the technology of the Seers), carries out the death sentence on the Seer and his assistants, and becomes Prince of Winchester.

In the final volume, Luke re-establishes Winchester's control of Petersfield and brings Romsey under his control. He returns to find that Blodwen has come to visit Winchester. However, Luke's friend Edmund falls in love with Blodwen, and she begins to return that love. Blind with jealousy, Luke imprisons them both, thereby arousing his enemies to join in revolution. Again he escapes to Sanctuary, where he and his loyal dwarf Hans learn about Sten guns. The two then go to Blodwen's father, King Cymru of the Wilsh, demanding his help in punishing Blodwen for her dishonorable behavior. Cymru's people make 250 Sten guns under Hans's direction. They cross the burning lands, win two battles, and lay siege to Winchester. The Seers bring a mortar and Luke begins to break an opening in the city wall, but turns back when the Christians lead the citizens to fill the breach with their bodies.

Luke is accepted as Cymru's son and the Seers openly study and teach as scientists in the land of the Wilsh. Eventually, we are told, all civilized lands must bow to the superiority of their knowledge.

NOTES

A simpler way of life following disaster—we expect a pastoral utopia, but this Britain is no utopia. Language, dress, and customs remind us of feudal Britain, but the author (in a lecture in Berkeley, California, 1978) has compared the situation rather to that of the Greek city-states, constantly warring among themselves. We find here the motifs of technology vs. anti-technology, scientific knowledge withheld from but also used to deceive the general populace in the name of religion, and widespread geologic disaster.

Luke never directly admits his errors, although he does remark that he "may have" acted on impulse, misjudged, etc. He also mentions advice he ignored. Using these devices, Christopher manages to show Luke's failings without bringing him to confessions that would be out of character. Luke is an example of tragic hero with tragic flaw—still a prince, but an unhappy prince of a foreign city, at the story's end.

*Christopher, John. **The White Mountains**. New York: Macmillan, 1967. 182p. Collier paperback, 1970. Grades 5-9.

*Christopher, John. **The City of Gold and Lead**. New York: Macmillan, 1967. 159p. Collier paperback, 1970. Grades 5-9.

*Christopher, John. **The Pool of Fire**. New York: Macmillan, 1968. 162p. Collier
    paperback, 1970. Grades 5-9.

SUMMARY

What begins as a quest for freedom becomes a race for sheer survival as a small
band of rebels tries to find a way to drive the alien Tripods from the earth. Will Parker,
who narrates the trilogy, is nearly fourteen years old when the story opens a century
hence. At the next Capping, Will is to receive his Cap from a Tripod. The Cap will be
fastened into the flesh of his shaved head, eventually to be hidden as his hair grows
back over it. However, as he observes the change in his recently Capped older cousin
Jack, Will begins to wonder whether he wants this mark of adulthood after all. Too,
he worries that he may be one of those few for whom the Capping does not work,
leaving them Vagrants, wandering aimlessly about the countryside, incoherent, fed
and clothed out of citizens' generosity.

One day a Vagrant wanders into the village. It turns out that he is not a Vagrant
at all, but wears a false Cap and seeks boys who question the Tripods' right to impose
the Cap and are willing to run away to join a rebel group in the White Mountains in
southern France. The Cap, he explains, is the means by which the Tripods keep men
docile and obedient. Will resolves to run away, so the supposed Vagrant provides him
with a map and compass.

The night Will slips away he is followed by his cousin Henry. The two boys have
shared a mutual and hearty dislike, but Henry wants to run away, too, so the pair sets
out together. They manage to cross the English Channel but are immediately apprehended. Their escape is accomplished with the help of a third boy whom they nick-
name Beanpole, and after several more adventures, the trio reaches the rebel group
in *The White Mountains*.

The City of Gold and Lead finds the three young men training to enter the
annual athletic Games in Germany, since the winner of each event is taken to the
Tripod city as a slave. If any of the boys can thus gain entrance to the city, he is
to find out as much as possible about the Tripods and then somehow get this information back to the rebels. Will, Beanpole, and Fritz Eger are sent to compete (Henry
is left behind), but only Will and Fritz win their events and are taken away as slaves.
They learn that the familiar Tripod is only a machine, and that the "Masters" are
three-legged, green creatures twice the size of men. They have invaded from another
planet and have established three gold-domed cities on Earth. The cities are filled
with a greenish atmosphere poisonous to humans, and equipped with artificial gravity
so strong that the human slaves cannot stand erect under its pressure (hence the title
word "lead"). The physical situation is so harsh that human slaves do not live more
than a couple of years, even though strong athletes when they arrive. Will's Master
is unusually interested in the ways of humans and has read about "pets," which is
how he regards Will. One day he sends Will on an errand, dons a mask, and enters
Will's cubicle, where he finds a book whose margins Will has filled with notes about
the Masters—totally inappropriate behavior for one who is Capped. However, having
already learned by accident of a vulnerable spot in the Masters' bodies, Will manages
to kill his Master. Then he escapes the city, carrying back to the rebels the knowledge
that four years hence more Masters will come with machines to change all of the
earth's atmosphere, thus killing all human life.

The Pool of Fire describes the group's efforts to destroy the three alien cities.
They manage to disable a Tripod and capture a Master, whom they keep in a cell
with the necessary atmosphere. Quite by accident they find that alcohol will

paralyze a Master, who cannot detect it as he seems to detect other possibly harmful substances. By introducing alcohol into the water supply, they overcome two cities. The third is bombed from balloons, although Henry gives his life to place the last bomb so that it will break the dome of the city. A "pool of fire" is each city's energy source. Since the Tripods have been destroyed, their new spaceship decides not to land. When the nations then meet to form a World Council, old national rivalries emerge. The novel closes as Will, Beanpole, and Fritz agree to dedicate their lives to restoring world unity.

NOTES

Scarcely the most probable vision of the future, the Tripod trilogy nevertheless succeeds in suspending our disbelief. Primarily a good adventure yarn, the novels nevertheless are well written with good characterization and cohesive plot—the latter even though the author remarked to an audience in California that he had no idea when the first book was published as to how the Tripods' downfall would be accomplished.

Several questions are worthy of student discussion, all hinging on the over-riding necessity of driving out the Tripods. In the cause of freedom, the boys are lured from home without regard to their parents, and both boys and rebels steal food and other supplies from the countryside. The boys more than once escape imprisonment, although admittedly their detention was unjust; they steal a hermit's boat, leaving him trapped on his island; and they take advantage of a Master's kindness. Finally, when the issue has become survival of the human species, the rebels capture a Tripod and use him as a "guinea pig" to find out what substances can be used to poison him, and then they poison a city's entire water supply. Some, but not all, of these actions elicit at least a feeling of regret in the characters, but all are moral choices that might engender debate.

This trilogy may be compared with *The Delikon* by H. M. Hoover in which even well-intended alien control is overthrown by revolution. Village life and Will's skepticism are similar to the opening situation in Engdahl's *This Star Shall Abide*.

Christopher, John. **Wild Jack**. New York: Macmillan, 1974. 147p. Collier paperback, 1978. Grades 5-8.

SUMMARY

The comfort and control of life in a city is placed against the risk and freedom of life in the Outlands. Early in the twenty-first century, after the earth's natural resources had been depleted, civilization had broken down. But a small group of nuclear scientists established a limited number of walled cities, each with its own nuclear power source. Other survivors of the Breakdown live as savages in the Outlands.

Clive Anderson, son of a councillor in London, is spirited away to an island reformatory on a false charge. He and two other boys escape and make their way to a wild shore where they are captured by the so-called savages and taken to Wild Jack, whose name is used by nurses to frighten children into good behavior. After a short period, Kelly and Sunyo opt for Wild Jack's band, but Clive returns to the city. There he very nearly becomes a tool in a plot to bring about his father's downfall. Clive releases the homing pigeon Wild Jack had given him and the latter, taking this as a sign that Clive is in trouble, rescues him.

NOTES

It is not surprising that the story seems incomplete; it is the first volume of an unfinished trilogy. The author says his attempted completion was not successful. He notes that the book was written with controlled syntax for students whose native language is not English. Nevertheless, this first person narrative avoids the stilted quality associated with American controlled-vocabulary readers.

Wild Jack is vaguely reminiscent of Robin Hood. Since the author no longer plans to complete the trilogy, students may want to flesh out this particular image of the future and to spin their own tale of political skulduggery and group conflict.

Corbett, Scott. **The Donkey Planet**. Illus. by Troy Howell. New York: Unicorn/ Dutton, 1979. 89p. Grades 4-7.

SUMMARY

Dashes of science fiction, mystery, and humor are combined in this story. Eks, head of the Space Center, sends Jason Scully and Frank Barnes to trade samples of aluminum for samples of quundar from the planet Vanaris, where donkeys are the only means of transport.

The chief of police, Gru, is leader of the Isolationists and has the ambition to rule not only Vanaris, but all the inhabited planets in the universe. For a moment, it appears that Gru will prevent Jason and Frank from returning home, but they succeed in transmitting themselves to Earth, leaving Gru foolish and discredited in front of his followers.

NOTES

One of the few humorous science fiction stories, *The Donkey Planet* is intriguing both because it involves instant transmission of matter and because Jason and Frank deal with the villain Gru in a nonviolent, but effective, manner.

Del Rey, Lester. **The Infinite Worlds of Maybe**. New York: Holt, Rinehart and Winston, 1966. 192p. Grades 6-9.

SUMMARY

A quest for utopia directs the plot of this novel, with the unfolding maturity of the protagonist a secondary focus. The final stopping place is a plane where science has solved most of the problems of physical disease, but the overriding goal is "the freeing and the elevation of the human spirit."

Bill Franklin's father has developed a theory that for every major choice made, an alternate plane springs into being where the rejected choice is carried forward. Some of these planes have short life spans; others continue in tandem with our own world. Mr. Franklin develops a machine for moving from plane to plane and Bill, together with young Professor Neal Adams, follows. Brief views of dystopian and utopian planes provide opportunity to reflect upon the features of an ideal world. The dystopias are a simian world, where the two humans are nearly sacrificed in a religious ceremony, and a global ice age, where Bill is regarded as a god to be kidnapped from village to village. The two utopias have different appeals: Neal stays in "the shining world" of highly advanced technology; Bill goes on to be reunited with his father in a plane which shares with our own a continuing struggle to improve the human mind.

NOTES

The notion of nonlinear time is explored here, as in most time travel and parallel world stories (*see* index, Part IV). For older students, *Man and Time* by J. B. Priestley (London: Aldus Books, 1964) provides a profusely illustrated nonfiction resource on man's understanding of time.

The device of setting several alternate worlds side by side in a single novel prohibits detailed description, but encourages comparison. Characterization is not a strong point of the book.

Del Rey, Lester. **Prisoners of Space.** Philadelphia: Westminster, 1968. 142p. Grades 5-8.

SUMMARY

Dave Harmon and Jane Larkin, the first children born on the moon, are too weak to live comfortably on the earth's surface because scientists did not at first realize all the steps necessary to build the body in a low gravity environment. Since there is talk of closing down the mining base on the moon as ore reserves dwindle, the two teenagers may be forced to spend their lives on an orbiting space station.

However, they find a chittering, furry little creature wandering in the tunnels beneath the lunar surface. Eventually we learn that Fuzzy is a baby Mantrin, one of several who came from Mars with Dave's father (thought to have died on a space mission), and hotly pursued by their physically similar enemies, the Banton. The latter are defeated, however, and plans are set in motion for a new expedition to Mars.

NOTES

Prisoners of Space is an example of "space opera," or adventure with scientific trappings. Even a decade ago, when this was written, several of its assumptions surely were already dubious. Students may enjoy evaluating the book from a scientific standpoint. Jones's *Moonbase One* offers a somewhat more realistic picture of moon colonization.

Dickinson, Peter. **The Devil's Children.** Boston: Little Brown, 1970. 158p. Grades 7-10.
Dickinson, Peter. **Heartsease.** Illus. by Nathan Goldstein. Boston: Little Brown, 1969. 223p. Grades 7-10.
Dickinson, Peter. **The Weathermonger.** Boston: Little Brown, 1968-1969. 216p. Grades 7-10.

SUMMARY

That simple life of the past had its own vices—intolerance, violence, illness, and suffering—along with the virtues of pure air, unspoiled nature and the like, is shown in Dickinson's trilogy. *The Devil's Children* is set a month after "the Changes."

Nicola Gore's parents have not come to find her. Nearly everyone is gone—some victims of sickness or violence, but most just fleeing as a madness—a hatred of machines and anyone who operates them—strikes all Englishmen. Despairing of her family's return, Nicky attaches herself to a caravan of Sikhs who had emigrated to England after the war. Unaffected by the madness themselves, the Sikhs accept Nicky as their equivalent of a "miner's canary," able to warn them against doing things which might make them victims of a violent mob.

The group settles on a large farm and trades ironwork for vegetables and lambs from a nearby village. When a passing gang of robbers takes over the village, holding its children as hostages, the Sikhs drive off the interlopers. Finally, the Sikhs arrange to send Nicky across the English Channel to France, where they hope she will find her parents.

About five years later, feudal life has become firmly established in England. A foreign witch has been stoned and left for dead, but Margaret hears the little hill of stones groan. Soon she, her cousin Jonathan, the hired girl Lucy, and Lucy's simple-witted brother Tim hide the American "witch," eventually spiriting him away on a tugboat called the "Heartsease." When Margaret's pony, Scrub, is washed overboard in the storm-tossed river, Margaret jumps on his back and eventually returns to assure Aunt Anne and Uncle Peter that Jonathan is safe and will certainly return when the Changes are over.

The third volume, *The Weathermonger*, is set shortly after *Heartsease*. Jeff had been the village weathermonger, able to control the weather with his spells, but his error is to take an interest in the hated machinery. Jeff and Sally escape to France when the villagers try to drown them for witchcraft. A French general helps the two young people return to England to trace the cause of the Changes. At first driving a Rolls Royce, and finally on foot, they reach a tower where, five years earlier, Mr. Furbelow had discovered the sleeping Merlin and botched the job of waking him. Merlin, Furbelow suggests, is a mutant who had intended to remain asleep until the entire species would evolve to mental and physical powers more like his own. But that time has not yet arrived. Jeff and Sally contrive to see Merlin, and Sally explains to him (in Latin) that an error has been made with resulting damage to his mind. Merlin then puts himself back to sleep—not because of what is happening to England, for he believes machines are contrary to nature and prevent people from realizing their intended selves, but because of the damage to himself. England begins to return to normal, one sign of which is petrol fumes.

NOTES

This trilogy is unusual in several respects. First, the books were published (and, presumably, written) in reverse chronological order; that is, *The Devil's Children*, published last, tells of the early months of "the Changes"; while *The Weathermonger*, published first, brings them to a close.

Secondly, the trilogy borrows conventions of the pastoral utopia—a system break and return to a feudal mode of life—but human relationships are cool, even hostile, rather than idyllic. All three novels convey the notion that the situation, confined as it is to England, must certainly be only temporary. Therefore, Dickinson does not write in the tradition of the pastoral utopia, which peals forth a clarion call to return to the "good old days." Rather, he shows us that those days had their faults, too. Perhaps he believes that we should not, or simply are unable to, turn the clock backwards. Or perhaps a reader might argue that Dickinson is simply exercising his imagination to spin a good yarn, that he is ambivalent toward machinery, and that in any event his attitude toward technology is merely incidental to the story.

A third unusual quality in these novels is the crossover between futurism and fantasy. *Devil's Children* and *Heartsease*, taken by themselves, portray a future world in which a madness of unknown origin has turned the English sour on machinery. But, in *The Weathermonger*, the figure of Merlin, even though described as a mutant, introduces a mythic element which is difficult to reconcile with futuristic fiction as considered in this bibliography. Jeff's weathermaking, too, although telekinetic, depends on a surprisingly scientific understanding of weather patterns, clouds, and winds. (Compare Bova's *The Weathermakers*.) Therefore, the trilogy might be compared with genuine pastoral utopias on the one hand, and on the other, with other novels which blur the boundary between fantasy and reality (consult the index on both themes; *see also* "Technology–Negative Attitudes" in Part IV).

Dickson, Gordon R. **Alien Art**. New York: Dutton, 1973. 162p. Grade 7 up.

SUMMARY

Perhaps there comes a time when the price of progress and wealth is too high too pay. The planet Arcadia must make such a decision by voting on renewal of a mortgage which would permit commercial and industrial development to move apace. The ultimate choice is affected by what appears initially to be a wholly unrelated set of events.

Cary Longan, backwoodsman, has come to appreciate the art objects created by Charlie, a giant-sized, intelligent otter native to Arcadia. Cary takes several of Charlie's smaller pieces to Lige Bros Waters, an art trader, but Waters can make little of them. Nevertheless, he agrees to look at Charlie's life-sized statue of Cary if the latter can get the piece to the city when Lige stops back in ten days. For this venture Cary needs to buy equipment, so he persuades Mattie Orvallo, a 19-year-old girl who has learned that the key to survival is to put money above all else, to loan him the necessary funds.

Hauling the enormous statue on rafts, a travois, and an oxcart is difficult enough, but becomes dangerous when they have a run-in with several "loopers," off-planet interlopers representing the company which hopes Arcadia will vote to renew its mortgage. Two of the loopers wound Cary so that he dies a few days later. Charlie's statue then becomes a symbol of Arcadia as a frontier world, inspiring the planet's "woodies" and farmers, and even Mattie, to vote against renewing the mortgage.

NOTES

Beauty—even meaning—is in the eye of the beholder as various people consider and either admire or reject Charlie's statue. Charlie himself is a virtual outcast among his own people because he tries to bridge the gap between them and the human newcomers, yet by so doing he succeeds in winning respect from humans who earlier had trapped the otters for their fur. The novel may be studied from this standpoint of alien-human contact, and Charlie's people compared with Biemiller's Kirl or Tofte's Thrulls.

From another viewpoint, however, Dickson has written a parable on the theme of commercial and technological overdevelopment. The novel might be analyzed as an analogy of the human situation, especially in areas which still have qualities of primitive or frontier existence.

Dorman, Sonya. **Planet Patrol**. New York: Coward McCann & Geoghegan, 1978. 161p.
    Grades 7-9.

SUMMARY

An episodic adventure story, this novel follows the experiences of Roxy Rimidon
from training to rank of corporal in the Planet Patrol, the officers who are called by
Councilmen to handle any serious disorders in the ten dominions of Earth or the
colonized planets. Roxy's field test is to locate a dog lost in wintry forests of Asia.
Her first regular assignment is to patrol the Interdominion Games, where athletic
rivalry is likely to erupt into violence. Next she investigates the murder of a Patrol
officer in Cuba Dominion.

After arguing for the right of the colony planets to have their own patrol, Roxy
is sent to Vogl to help in that effort. There she is attuned to a disembodied living
brain, but a sect called Dust Bowlers breaks into the laboratory and destroys
"Domingo" before Roxy has accomplished her mission. Nevertheless, she is promoted
to corporal in recognition of having undertaken so difficult a task as working with
Domingo.

NOTES

Roxy is certainly a "liberated woman," and her story is filled with futuristic
motifs, including space colonization, medical advances, and a new form of government.
However, it is not so much her own ability as it is fortunate circumstances that see
her through most of her assignments.

Dwiggins, Don. **The Asteroid War**. Chicago: Children's Press, 1978. 63p. Grades 4-7.

SUMMARY

An adventure story based, the author tells us, on NASA's expectation that
humans in a 10,000-person space station will undertake mining of the asteroids within
the next hundred years, this narrative pits humans against aliens in a battle over depos-
its of the isotope Grissonium on Ceres. Neil Youngblood and his companions first kill
the giant space spiders unleashed by the enemy and then overpower the alien intercept fighters. Still the alien vessel will not abandon its determination to destroy the
human space colony, so Armando Vivas uses a weapon given him by his grandfather.
This instrument, called a gravitron, is connected to an Aztec legend that their people
had come to Earth through a "black wormhole." The weapon sends Armando, Neil,
and three of their companions, including the robot Tenfour, through a black hole
along with the alien spaceship. Together they reach the planet where the Aztecs
had originated.

NOTES

The actual printed text is about 45 pages long, a skeletal plot designed to appeal
to students who are not overly fond of reading. Illustrations are black and white drawings and pseudo-photographs, many of them obtained from government sources and
aerospace firms. The material on outer space origins of the Aztecs recalls some of
the material in von Däniken's *Chariots of the Gods?*

Earnshaw, Brian. **Dragonfall 5 and the Empty Planet.** Illus. by Simon Stern. New
York: Lothrop, Lee & Shepard, 1973. 96p. Grades 2-5.

SUMMARY

A lighthearted space mystery, this story finds the rather antiquated starship
Dragonfall 5 landing on the Empty Planet. There Tim and Sanchez are to attend
school for four weeks while their parents, Old Elias and Big Mother, collect a few
of the planet's mysterious Stones for delivery to a museum on Arkel X.

The first day the children play jet polo and then learn from infiller cassettes
while sleeping. The second day they take a field trip to investigate Empty Planet's
walking trees and plants and one of its mysterious circles of enormous Stones. While
the rest of the group eats and sings songs on the grass within the circle of Stones,
Sanchez and his friend Mike slip away to find a group of elusive walking trees. Suddenly there is lightning, the Stones seem to make music of their own, and when the boys
return, all the picnickers have disappeared.

With the help of telepathic little creatures called Minims, the boys learn from
the walking trees that their friends have inadvertently triggered the mechanism of the
Stones so that they, like the Great Ones who originally built the Stones, have been
transported to the planet's moon of frozen hydrogen. *Dragonfall 5* is called upon
to effect the rescue.

NOTES

This brief story may be a bit far-fetched, but it is quickly read and includes
several interesting ideas, among them the learning tapes, space age games, and the
Stones (reminiscent of the dolmens of Europe). The children's relationships are
handled well; in particular, the boy who teases Sanchez and Tim about their rickety
old starship is one of the group which is rescued by that same ship, yet Sanchez
refrains from "rubbing it in."

Two other books in this series, *Dragonfall 5 and the Space Cowboys* and
Dragonfall 5 and the Royal Beast have not been summarized or indexed because
they do cross the line into fantasy. *Royal Beast*, however, includes an illustration
and "explanation" of an airborne anti-grav machine.

Eldridge, Roger. **The Shadow of the Gloom-World.** New York: Dutton, 1977. 191p.
Grades 6-8.

SUMMARY

Dreamers may find solutions to problems which seem insoluble to the more
practical majority. Among the cavern people, Fernfeather is such a dreamer. He
has dreams and tells about them; he wonders what lies beyond the rock; he protests
the law by which his mother must be sent away to her death in the outer caverns
to balance the new life just born, keeping the population at 250. Following a forbidden tunnel, he stumbles upon the secret birth rites of the women folk. For
these crimes, he is sentenced to spend some days in the choke-rooms. Finally, blamed
for the rock-shake which then threatens to collapse their world, Fernfeather is permanently banished to the Gloom-World.

Beyond the wall of blue fire he meets Harebell, a girl who had been banished
some months earlier. She shows him the machines and food supplies she has already

discovered. But Fernfeather wants to explore further, to see whether the voice of the Oldens, which also comes from a machine, is truthful when it speaks of emerging into light. Harebell tells him that she has already followed the route described, but upon emerging from the caverns had found only gloom and poisonous yellow clouds. Nevertheless, Fernfeather is not to be dissuaded from his own investigation.

Afraid to be alone, Harebell follows Fernfeather. They reach the Badlands at the surface, but travel beyond them to the forests, only to be taken captive by the misshapen folk of this upper world. The Elected, leaders of these forest dwellers, are persuaded to believe Fernfeather's tale of a people under the earth because they have ancient charts showing an underground retreat built to escape the Scorching when men had burned each other. When Fernfeather promises that his leader can make fruitful those patches of land which are still barren, the Elected agree to let him lead his people forth from their crumbling prison.

NOTES

Life in this underground city is primitive by comparison with Martel's Surréal. Fernfeather's people have lost all knowledge of the machines which mysteriously provide them with heat and light, or of the unseen computer which advises them. Nor do they even realize there is a world above them. The novel's English author says this idea came to him when he was riding the subway; this may account for the metal rails running through the tunnels of his underworld, which is probably to be thought of as having been converted or expanded from a subway system.

Characterization—both development and motivation—is well handled. The quasi-religious nature attributed to the invisible technology may be compared with that in the last volume of Bova's exile trilogy. Older students who may have seen the film *Logan's Run* will note obvious similarities in plot.

---

*Engdahl, Sylvia Louise. **Enchantress from the Stars**. Illus. by Rodney Shackell. New York: Atheneum, 1970. 275p. Atheneum paperback, 1970. Grade 7 up.

SUMMARY

Elana's textbook says "the human peoples of the universe have similar histories . . . the same patterns emerge on every home world" (p. 16). This assumption underlies Elana's story, in which three levels of culture come into contact.

Andrecia, a feudal world, is about to be taken over by a people new to star travel who are invading from another planet. The even more advanced Federation sends agents of its Anthropological Service to prevent that takeover in the interests of protecting the right of all peoples to develop in their own way. The agents must accomplish this task, however, without disclosing their origin to either the natives or the invaders of Andrecia.

Elana is not assigned to this mission, but she stows away on the shuttle which takes her father and her future husband to Andrecia. Elana turns out to be useful, however, when her father devises a plan in which she presents herself to two woodcutter's sons as an enchantress and helps them learn psychokinesis, or "magic." The young men are to use their "magic" to conquer the "dragon," which is actually a land-clearing machine, because Elana's father believes that if the invaders see their machinery stopped by something they cannot explain scientifically, they will leave Andrecia in a panic.

What her father had not foreseen, however, was that Elana and Georyn would begin to fall in love, and that Elana would decide to accompany Georyn in his quest against the dragon. As a result of Elana's naive impetuosity, both she and Georyn are captured by the invaders to be taken to their planet as specimens for scientific research. The methods will be painless, but so effective that Elana will be unable to resist disclosing the Federation's existence to this less developed people. So she is prepared to commit suicide rather than break her oath. Still, in a desperate last attempt to fulfill the mission of her team, Elana confides in Jarel, the invaders' doctor, telling him something of her predicament in order to obtain Georyn's release. She herself takes an opportunity to run toward the "dragon," intending to be crushed by the rocks falling from its scooper, but Georyn astonishes everyone by stopping the rocks in midair. This psychokinetic feat has the intended effect of frightening the invaders off. Elana and Georyn say a sad farewell, and the Andrecian natives are left to follow the natural course of cultural development.

NOTES

Three viewpoints alternate in this novel, each break marked by three asterisks or a new chapter—Elana (first person), Georyn (style of a medieval folk tale), and Jarel. Sometimes they overlap so that the same event is presented through one, then another, character's eyes. Students might compare these three styles, note when each is used, study the different perceptions two observers hold of the same event, and consider the effectiveness of the author's choices. Although the flow of the narrative is slowed a bit by the characters' philosophical reflections, readers should be attracted by the alternations of style, convincing characterization, and use of telepathy and psychokinesis.

Miss Engdahl has written that she developed and wrote her theory of cultural evolution before she expressed it in novel form. Students could characterize and compare each of the three levels described here. They might analyze how cultural differences affect one's understanding of and interpretation of the same event. Important, too, are the philosophy and decisions regarding interference with other less developed cultures.

All three groups in the novel have originated on the third planet of a yellow star. Is any of these our own Earth? Note the foreword: ". . . whether this is a tale of the past or of the future is anybody's guess." Nevertheless, in relation to Earth at this moment, both Elana's people and Jarel's people clearly represent future stages in Engdahl's evolutionary line.

Elana's next adventure is told in *The Far Side of Evil. Enchantress from the Stars* may well be compared with *Ice Crown* by André Norton, in which a girl on a similar scientific mission becomes romantically interested in a "native" and makes the choice opposite to Elana's.

---

*Engdahl, Sylvia Louise. **The Far Side of Evil**. Illus. by Richard Cuffari. New York: Atheneum, 1971. 292p. Atheneum paperback, 1971. Grade 7 up.

SUMMARY

Can humans, even in **very advanced** civilizations, truly judge what is best for another people? Or is there a higher power which somehow brings good results out of evil and error? These are the questions Elana asks herself in the course of this novel.

Elana, just graduated from the Academy which trains agents in the Anthropological Service to study the less developed Youngling worlds, is sent to a planet in its Critical Phase. The Service knows that at a certain point in its cultural evolution each planet develops technology which could bring about its own destruction. At that point the culture must reach out and travel to the stars, or it will destroy itself in nuclear war. But what factors influence the move toward space?

The planet Toris, recently discovered by the Federation, offers the Service a rare opportunity to explore that question. Elana is but one of several anthropologists sent to observe events there, but sworn not to intervene or to reveal the existence of the more advanced Federation. Another agent, Randil, although well versed in Critical Phase theory, is less well prepared for field work. Influenced in part by his love for Kari, Elana's Torisian roommate, Randil comes to believe that he must intervene to save the planet. To this end he calls down a shuttle from their starship and announces himself to the Neo-Statist government as an ambassador from the neighboring planet of Juta, which is actually uninhabited. Through this ruse, he hopes to arouse the Torisians to travel into space, thus averting nuclear war, while he slips away with Kari.

Bound by her oath to keep secret the Federation's advanced technology, Elana tries to blow up the shuttle and, having failed, tells the guard the ship has been sabotaged. The Neo-Statists are immediately alarmed because they have conceived their own purpose for the space shuttle—since it cannot be detected with radar, they plan to load it with nuclear bombs and wipe out their Libertarian adversaries on Toris. Therefore, they torture Elana to find out what she really knows about the sabotage. She resists with psychic powers, so the Neo-Statist commander decides to torture Kari in her presence. Not knowing their connection, the commander permits Randil to witness Kari's torture, at which point Randil finally recognizes the kind of people with whom he is dealing. He manages to activate the shuttle's self-destruct mechanism, though at the cost of his own life.

With all this outside interference, Toris is no longer a suitable location for studying the Critical Phase. However, the explosion which destroys the shuttle also takes several Torisian lives. Believing that the shuttle is from Juta, all Torisians unite in an effort to travel through space to wreak vengeance on that planet. Thus Toris turns away from the path to self-destruction.

NOTES

Although this book takes place after *Enchantress from the Stars* and has the same central character, it is an independent plot rather than a sequel. Having been trained to see events through other people's eyes, Elana sometimes interrupts her first person narrative to tell Randil's story. Besides changing viewpoint, the narration also switches tense between past and present (e.g., p. 225). Ostensibly, the present tense episodes indicate the process of "recording" by which Elana mentally stores her experiences for later high speed transfer to another person or to a computer. With this stylistic device, of course, these scenes are given heightened impact.

As in *Enchantress*, the theory underlying the story, the Critical Phase, is brought forward as remembered passages from a textbook (pp. 87-88). Other issues which the characters consider include the difficulty of understanding a different culture, the nature of human equality which transcends different levels of cultural advancement, and the principle of nonintervention vs. the humanitarian impulse to keep people from hurting themselves. Many of the qualities of a spy story combined with the fascination of telepathy carry readers through the introspective and philosophical passages.

Engdahl, Sylvia Louise. **Journey between Worlds.** Illus. by James and Ruth McCrea. New York: Atheneum, 1970. 235p. Grades 6-9.

SUMMARY

Important constants reside in the hearts of people, but at the same time, "if you don't believe that human beings will keep growing and changing and moving on, you don't believe in the future at all." This theme is forcefully presented in *Journey between Worlds*.

Some time after the twentieth century, Melinda Ashley receives an unexpected present for her high school graduation—an opportunity to accompany her dad on a business trip to Mars. Mel had expected a short summer trip, not a half year involving travel across interplanetary space. Moreover, Dad, who has had to travel a great deal for his firm, Tri Planets Corporation, does not know that Mel plans to go to college with Ross and, after the first year, to marry him.

However, between Ross's proprietary attitude and her dad's enthusiasm, Mel finds herself an unwilling passenger on the S. S. *Susan Constant*, named for one of the ships which had brought European settlers to the first permanent colony in Virginia. Aboard ship she meets Alex Preston, who is returning to his native Mars after a year of graduate school on Earth. Mel is patronizing in her attitudes toward "colonials," including Alex, because she is wholly unable to understand why anyone would want to live inside a plastic dome for an entire lifetime, except perhaps in the interests of science. From this point forward, Mel recounts her gradual discovery, guided by Alex, that she is not afraid of space, but of change and uncertainty. They are married, and Mel becomes a space age pioneer, following in the footsteps of her namesake ancestor Melinda Stitwell, who had traveled to Oregon in a covered wagon.

NOTES

This first person narrative holds no surprises—the conclusion is inevitable from the moment Mel and Alex first meet. The novel may serve as a bridge from romance to science fiction for some readers. The stereotype of male equals protector and female equals protected virtually overshadows the woman pioneer image.

---

*Engdahl, Sylvia Louise. **This Star Shall Abide.** Illus. by Richard Cuffari. New York: Atheneum, 1972. 246p. Atheneum paperback, 1979. Grade 7 up.
*Engdahl, Sylvia Louise. **Beyond the Tomorrow Mountains.** Illus. by Richard Cuffari. New York: Atheneum, 1973. 257p. Grade 8 up.

SUMMARY

These novels deal with the conflict between scientific knowledge and religious faith. They are set on a planet inhabited by the only humans who survived after the earth's sun entered its nova phase, destroying the Six Worlds in the solar system. The planet is hostile; although its atmosphere is safe, its soil, water, and plant life contain poisons. It totally lacks metals, apparently having been mined to depletion by other space travelers, long since departed.

Noren lives in one of the villages, where there are few machines and the people are unaware of their off-planet origins. He has just finished school. He wants to claim a farm and marry Talyra, but feels he must tell her honestly that he doubts the Book of Prophecy—that he believes it was concocted, along with the High Law, by the Scholars in order to protect their privileges of knowledge and power. Talyra sorrowfully decides she cannot marry a heretic, and Noren recklessly declares his views in public. He is condemned to be taken to the City by Technicians, but escapes. Ultimately, however, he is recaptured and taken to the Scholars, who engage him in a series of duels of the mind.

Gradually Noren learns that the Book of Prophecy is true, though told in symbolic language. He learns that the Scholars are scientists, confining technological information to their sealed city until they find a way to synthesize metal, which will be needed desperately when the machines brought from Earth finally break down. Having accepted the necessity for this system, Noren publicly recants his heresy. Only then does he also learn that only those who are bold enough to question the Scholars' authority and be convicted of heresy in a village may themselves become Scholars. Only they may learn the true history of their people's origin and journey through space. With this requirement the Scholars hope to insure that the people who hold the knowledge and power will be persons of a type to share it willingly when it is possible to do so.

In *Beyond the Tomorrow Mountains*, however, Noren realizes that the portion of the prophecy which promises that all men will share the Scholars' secrets when the light of the Mother Star reaches them may be false because the scientists may fail in their attempt to synthesize metal. Yet he sees Scholars whose integrity he trusts attending rituals where the words of the prophecy are read. Noren very nearly causes his own death, along with those of Talyra and another young Scholar, before he realizes that such things as love, the need to maintain life, and the existence of an ultimate truth are matters of faith. At this point, he accepts the robe of High Priest, prepared to take his turn in leading the rituals. Through this act, too, he finds that he has become free to marry Talyra.

NOTES

For the serious-minded young person this pair of novels provides an exceptionally absorbing adventure into the why's of life, although the reader who wants a fast moving adventure story should look elsewhere. Thoughtful readers will be made aware of the realities and assumptions that lie behind appearances, especially as they consider Noren's heresy, which turns out to be a mark of the inquiring mind. But this awareness is incomplete if readers do not move on to the second novel, in which Noren moves to a higher level of faith.

The second volume is the strongest of the novels in this bibliography in proposing evolution toward a new religious understanding fully compatible with science. (The second volume, it should perhaps be noted, calls for enough maturity on the part of the reader to maintain separation from the extended period of depression which accompanies Noren's inner struggle. It also includes passing references to sexual relations and to human cannibalism.)

Character development and style are superb. While the several characters are presented as real people, they also serve as representations of various philosophic-religious views, thus making these views more readily comprehensible. In particular, Noren is a person who must come to faith through doubt; Talyra, one born with faith which never wavers.

Fairman, Paul W. **The Forgetful Robot**. New York: Holt, Rinehart and Winston, 1968. 163p. Grades 4-8.

SUMMARY

This novel carries no strong theme, but is a mystery narrated in lighthearted, fast-paced style by a robot—albeit a very sophisticated robot, a Wellington model 69S named Barney. Larry and Janet find Barney in a junkyard where he has been accidentally buried by a dump truck after his memory banks had been tampered with and his batteries had run down. They take him home to Granddad Ravencraft. Barney is not sure who owns him, but he is certain that Larch and Slezak, who arrive to claim him, are not the right people. He is right, of course. Larch and Slezak need to get to old Mars for nefarious purposes of their own, and they recognize the Ravencrafts' plan to further cultural understanding through Shakespearean drama as an ideal cover. Granddad believes they are en route to Colony City in New Mars, but the two schemers have switched the computer tape to bring the ship down near the supposedly uninhabited ancient ruins of Zark in Old Mars. There they hope to pick up a stash of jewels stolen from the old city.

Their plans are foiled, however, when they and the Ravencrafts (and Barney, of course) are captured by two henchmen of Roger Gardner, former curator of the Space Museum in the St. Louis Complex. Gardner has established contact with the Shadow People of Zark and has persuaded himself that his mission is to arm and train these people to protect their planet from foreign exploitation. The arms are to be delivered soon from Venus; the price, jewels and silver from Zark. Gardner also holds as prisoner Professor Dixon, Barney's true owner, who had come to Zark on a scientific expedition some months earlier. Barney's first efforts to save Dixon and the Ravencrafts fail, but at the last moment he succeeds in turning a killer robot named Mildred against Gardner and his assistants.

NOTES

Although this story does not pretend to offer a weighty theme or poetic style, the author uses Barney's supposed naiveté effectively to twit the human species (e.g., pp. 67, 97). On the other hand, Barney himself is anthropomorphized; his responses are explained in computer equivalents (loyalty equals "electronic affinity," hostility equals "negative reaction," dream equals "vague functional images from a residue of power leaking into the command unit"). One might debate the feasibility of a robot like Barney—or is he indeed a human character with machine trappings? This space opera offers several opportunities for science-minded readers to discover impossible predictions, most notably the existence of intelligent aliens such as the Shadow People on Mars, green-shelled Venusians, silicon-based natives of Jupiter, and the like.

Fisk, Nicholas. **Escape from Splatterbang**. New York: Macmillan, 1978. 94p. Grades 5-7.

SUMMARY

Understanding the balance of nature is the key to rescuing Mykl and Amina from the planet Aaron VII, more informally known as Splatterbang. That name refers to the flamers which shoot up from the planet's surface when a ship lands. On this

occasion, the flamers are so numerous that Mykl's parents, space traders, dash back to
the ship. They do not realize that their son, quite against orders, has descended to
the surface. So Mykl is left behind.

Fortunately, the planet is equipped with a Settlement, a domed shelter complete
to a super-computer named Ego. Mykl finds another left-behind, the Romni girl
Amina. Together, having donned eco-suits, they explore the planet. It is Amina who
intuitively discovers the planet's life cycle. The flamers eat metal, then cook the plants
so they will be eaten by the ugly little creatures who in turn nourish the flamers with
their excrement. But the planet's metal supply is running out, hence the wild attack
on any metal objects which approach the planet's surface.

The first rescue attempt fails because Mykl, not willing to listen to Amina,
tells a Gunship to land. That ship and its several crew members are consumed by
flamers as Mykl and Amina watch. When Mykl's parents come to rescue him, however,
they manage to use Amina's discovery to avoid another disaster.

NOTES

A brief adventure story, quickly read, *Escape from Splatterbang* has two interesting features. First there is the food chain. Students might imagine other food cycles
and networks—and then perhaps create stories related to those circumstances. Do note
the author's acknowledgement (verso of title page) to a middle school student who
helped create the life cycle used here. (*See* "Balance of Nature" in the index, Part IV,
to locate novels for comparison.)

Secondly, some students may be interested in how Mykl solves his problems—
sometimes with Ego's help, but on other occasions through stream-of-consciousness
(pp. 63-64) and a dream (pp. 77-78).

Gypsies are most unsympathetically portrayed. *See* Lightner's *Space Gypsies*
for a more balanced view.

Fisk, Nicholas. **Grinny: A Novel of Science Fiction.** Nashville: Thos. Nelson, 1973-
1974. 124p. Grades 6-9.

SUMMARY

Grinny is a mystery horror story with science fiction trappings. Three children
try to uncover the identity of a previously unknown Great-Aunt Emma who arrives
quite unexpectedly one day and is immediately accepted by the entire family. Beth
is the first to become suspicious, and the first to discover that Great-Aunt Emma's
skeleton is a metal framework rather than bone, moreover that she has no blood
and that her skin closes and heals in a matter of moments after an injury.

Grinny, as the children call her, exerts mind control over the adults, but not
over the children because she needs to study them. Her objective is to determine
whether the planet Earth is a suitable home for her own species, and whether its
younger inhabitants will be useful as slaves. However, the children note that Grinny
is afraid of electricity and then discover that they can unnerve her completely by
playing "Eyes Right," that is, by looking off just to the right of her rather than
meeting her eyes, and at the same time projecting negative emotions. Grinny believes
that her mission has been satisfactorily accomplished, and tells the children what she
has been trying to do. But she has underestimated them, for the children use what
they have learned to force her to report Earth as unsuitable. Immediately, her artificial body is viciously dismantled by her flashlight-like servant, and Grinny, who also

now resembles a flashlight, is carried off by a waiting spaceship. The children hope
that she will not return.

NOTES

Told in the form of a diary, this suspenseful, fast moving, and rather brief novel
is set in present-day, rather than future, England. Grinny is the most blood-chilling
alien in this bibliography. Perhaps this effect is heightened by the otherwise ordinary,
familiar setting, since the telepathic octopoids of Sutton's *Lord of the Stars*, for
example, are certainly as fearsome. (*See* "alien" headings in Part IV to locate novels
for comparison.)

A secondary theme is rejection of technology at the expense of humanity: we
note that Grinny comes from a planet which is overdeveloped and overpopulated.
Her species' solution, like that of the Pollutians in Bill Peet's *Wump World*, has been
to invade and conquer other worlds.

Goldberger, Judith M. **The Looking Glass Factor.** New York: Dutton, 1979. 136p.
Grades 4-7.

SUMMARY

Hannah Markus finds that she can say no to a fascinating project, recognizing
that this is not the right place or time to demonstrate her courage. Hannah lives at a
time when twenty-sixth century buildings have an antique air. And as an accidental
result of genetic experiments, humans now share the planet with intelligent, speaking
Cats—*Felis sapiens*.

The Cat scientists Agnes and Putney Brancusi have undertaken research on
"merging" after reading notes left to Agnes by her human friend, Margo Krupp.
Merging is a process by which one merges with something nonliving—for example,
a wall. The Brancusis call Hannah away from school to help them extend their research
to humans. Hannah gradually learns to merge and, when she finally disappears totally
into a wall, discovers an exhilarating sense of freedom—a sensation that merging
apparently does not create in Cats. Margo Krupp, who had been thought dead in a
space shuttle accident, contacts Hannah and the Brancusis to let them know that the
experience of merging has become so essential to her that she had merged with a
spaceship. Now she can barely restrain her yearning to merge with the entire universe
long enough to warn them to abandon their research. Hannah, although realizing
the study of merging is too important to be abandoned, decides that her most important task at the moment is to remain a child.

NOTES

The notion of merging is indeed fascinating, and is based on what we know
about the space between the protons and electrons that make up so-called solid objects.
A less esoteric aspect of the novel is Hannah's consideration of what is important for
her at a particular point in her life, a decision students might relate to present-day
choices in their own lives.

Grohskopf, Bernice. **Notes on the Hauter Experiment; A Journey through the Inner
World of Evelyn B. Chestnut.** New York: Atheneum, 1975. 135p. Grades 5-8.

SUMMARY

The peace—and imprisonment—of a totally regulated environment contrasts with the annoyances and human interaction of our everyday world in Grohskopf's novel. For nearly a month, Evelyn B. Chestnut records her daily experiences and impressions in a wholly enclosed school where 12 boys and 12 girls follow a regimented routine obviously designed to reduce distractions and maximize learning. None of the students knows how he or she arrived in the school. No adults are visible, although films and tapes are narrated by adults, papers and tests are returned through a chute thoroughly corrected with copious notes, meals appear on conveyor belts in the cafeteria, and signals for various activities carry them smoothly through each day. As Evelyn observes, it is like a school of the future. Evelyn and Drucy find a loose tile in the kitchen and make good their escape. At that point, we learn that they have been guinea pigs in an experiment. Ultimately, however, we find that it is all a story written by the aspiring young author Evelyn B. Nussbaum, alias Chestnut.

NOTES

This "diary" is set down in the first person in "teen-age." Although finally revealed as imaginative, and therefore not actually set in future time, the school is "like the future." Educational technology and conditioning techniques may be compared with those in more strictly future-time novels.

Harrison, Harry. **The California Iceberg.** Illus. by James Barry, New York: Walker, 1975. 128p. Grades 3-6.

SUMMARY

A series of problems with weather and technology provides the plot for this episodic adventure. Todd Wells flies to Chile to meet his father, captain of the atomic tugboat Stormqueen, which in this year 2000 is towing five icebergs from Antarctica north to drought-ridden California. During the months-long voyage, Todd must keep up with his schoolwork by computer. He sees how the icebergs are propelled by water-jet motors and guided by cables, one of which needs repair soon after his arrival. Then, during a severe storm, a cable breaks. Todd loads oxygen on the helicopter and then finds himself stranded with the crewmen after the copter crashes on the berg. Rescued, he next becomes involved as the men unfasten one of the underwater motors in need of repair. At long last, he sees one of the bergs come to shore in the harbor at San Diego.

NOTES

Young scientists will be intrigued with details about the towing of the icebergs and the operation of the tugboat. However, little else in this novel is futuristic. The only woman included is Todd's mother, who stereotypically stays home and worries. Although an Indian, Screaming Owl, supervises the construction of the towing arrangements, there is no other evidence of nonwhite characters. The notion of towing icebergs captures the reader's attention, but controls on vocabulary and sentence structure, an episodic plot, and sometimes stilted drawings detract from the story.

Harrison, Harry. **The Men from P.I.G. and R.O.B.O.T.** New York: Atheneum, 1978.
141p. Grades 5-10.

SUMMARY

Eleven hundred new members of the Patrol, "the warriors and policemen of
space, the mighty men who stood between the civilized planets and the chaos of the
galaxy," hear two stories of Special Assignments intended, no doubt, to inspire them
as they embark upon their own careers.

The message of the first story is that things are not always what they seem.
Bron Wurber appears to be a crude pig farmer when he disembarks from a space
tender on the outskirts of Towbri City, but in fact his pigs are carefully bred, highly
intelligent (for pigs) members of the Porcine Interstellar Guard (P.I.G.). His task is
to find out what is responsible for the haunted quality, and more important, recent
deaths on Ghost Plateau. Having set his pigs to defend him from two 1,000-pound
flesh-eating marsupials, Wurber moves on to prove that the mysterious murderer on
the plateau is a giant hovercraft controlled by the treacherous Sulbani. These aliens,
abetted by a human conspirator, are mining uranium and shipping it into their own
sector of space.

The second story appears at one point to describe a dystopia created by capitalist
competition run wild, but the situation turns out to be the result of a microorganism
which has indirectly caused paranoia in all inhabitants of the planet Slagter. Henry
(Hank) Venn appears to be a salesman of robots and soundie comics, but is actually ·
on special assignment with Robot Obtrusion Battalion Omega Three (R.O.B.O.T.).
He is sent to Slagter to locate a missing Galactic Censustaker. The computer on
Hank's ship has located the censustaker's ship, buried nearby, and is already tunneling
through to it. Meanwhile, the Slagterans kidnap Hank's robot double, whom Hank and
the computer follow by means of dozens of spy-eyes and other surveillance devices,
thus locating the beef slaughterhouse in whose control center Censustaker Sergejev
is held prisoner.

The real question, however, is why such hostility is exhibited by everyone here.
The answer lies with an antibody formed in response to a small microorganism. As
the antibody reaches too high a level, after about 15 years, the individual becomes
paranoid: he begins to behave as though everyone is out to do him ill. Now, of course,
that situation can be ameliorated.

NOTES

No graduating class would be regaled with 140 pages of anecdote in a single
afternoon, but then, none of this book is intended to be taken seriously. One of the
infrequent examples of humor among futuristic novels, these stories also include
several fascinating bits of technology, such as the mutated pigs, robots, spy-eyes,
and soundie comics. The book is not really a single novel, but a loosely joined pair
of short stories.

Hendrich, Paula. **The Girl Who Slipped through Time**. New York: Lothrop, Lee and
Shepard, 1978. 128p. Grades 6-8.

SUMMARY

The lesson of this novel is that if we use our resources wantonly, "sure enough, one day it's all gone, and it's too late to bring back things the way they was before." It is the year 2040. Much of the earth's surface has been laid waste in the Eco-War, when eco-destroyers tried to gain control of the world with mutant jackrabbits, killer bees, and giant grasshoppers.

Paramecia Foster-Picard, usually called "Para," is traveling across the Great Wasteland in an Air-Cushioned Vehicle with her father, Dr. Jason Picard. While he is talking by telecom with Para's mother, Dr. Athena Picard, Para takes off across the desert in a pique.

Attracted by what appears to be an oasis, she stumbles through a mist into an incredibly different world where her poly-aluminized jumpsuit with automatic temperature controls, her science-oriented language, and her attitudes toward nudity and religion are equally out of place. It is Kansas in 1934, just before the great dust storm.

She finds a home with Shandy McShamus Twigg and his adoptive Granny Twigg. From them she learns respect for the natural harmony of living things and disgust for people like bounty hunter Jake Murty, organizer of periodic animal kills. She finds that Granny is from another planet, an Indianlike psychic wanderer who has been unable to return to her home, or to die.

When Para finally regains her own world, she carries coyote and rabbit babies with her. She then learns that Shandy became, in his own time, a well-known naturalist, and was her great-great-grandfather. Most importantly, Para now understands her parents' passionate concern with replenishing the earth's population of plants and animals.

NOTES

Time travel permits the author to contrast an exploitational with an ecological attitude toward natural resources. This technique might be compared with, for example, Stoutenburg's *Out There*, in which an old woman's recollections and, later, characters' attitudes make the same contrast; or with Lightner's *Space Ark* or her *Thursday Toads*, in which the consequences of thoughtless interference teach the importance of the balance of nature.

Paramecia, first person narrator, spins out an intriguing plot with varied syntax and adequate, if not memorable, descriptions. She reveals some of the stereotyped characteristics of today's typical teen, despite her rational scientific assumptions about religion, reproduction, and ecology.

---

*Hooker, Ruth. **Kennaquhair**. Illus. Al Michini. Nashville: Abingdon, 1976. 159p.
    Grades 5-8.

SUMMARY

Kennaquhair focuses on the theme of cooperation and nonviolence. Six children, completely garbed in shiny suits, gloves, and gas masks, happen upon one another as they follow roads through the wasted countryside. Quite by accident they discover a valley which has been sheltered from the devastation—a valley where an elderly man and his dog have a cabin, water, and crops. Gradually, Olmun wins the children's trust and teaches them how to survive in the valley. Continually he warns them never to fight. But eventually Olmun leaves in search of his own family, never to return. He tells them to close up the passage through the rocks with dynamite if he does not return in two weeks. The children grow careless, even selfish, and eventually quarrel about whether or not to close the way in and out of the valley, as Olmun had instructed. Afterwards, one of the children nearly drowns and in cooperating to rescue her, they all realize the wisdom of Olmun's advice.

NOTES

Consisting of a simple plot with a profound message, *Kennaquhair* is a pastoral utopia following upon, presumably, nuclear war. The title of the novel, the blurb indicates, means "don't know where." The children—as the illustrations show, though the text never indicates in any way—represent at least two ethnic groups. Small day-to-day details create a sense of reality. Since so many characters of about equal importance are treated in so short a story, none of them is developed in great depth.

---

*Hoover, H. M. **Children of Morrow**. New York: Four Winds Press, 1973. 229p.
　　Grades 6-9.
*Hoover, H. M. **Treasures of Morrow**. New York: Four Winds Press, 1976. 171p.
　　Grades 6-9.

SUMMARY

The place of one's birth and childhood always holds some measure of magnetism, but "home" is with people like oneself, as Tia and Rabbit discover.

During the twenty-first century came the decade known as the Death of the Seas, followed by suffocation of 93% of all living things. In the 2300s, enormous earthquakes lowered parts of the California coast seven to twelve feet, correspondingly raising the Chilean Andes, and devastating Japan.

A century later, two colonies of survivors exist—one in the mountains inland from San Francisco, the other in the vicinity of San Diego. The northern group, Base, is descended from military personnel caught in a missile silo. Their way of life is primitive and brutal. The southern colony survived in an underground installation called LIFESPAN, built by Simon Morrow, a corporate executive, for his family and about 200 technocrats, all carefully selected for survival. Despite his precautions, Morrow's society nearly collapsed due to lack of discipline and the results of eating still-poisoned seafood, but was again pulled together by his descendant, Simone. Like many Morrowans by that time, Simone was a highly intelligent telepath—the telepathy apparently a by-product of that same food poison which also caused sterility and birth defects in the small population.

For some time the Morrowans had explored their world, bringing back great treasures of lost civilizations and searching for other survivors. They are now quite certain that they are alone on Earth, so their current Elite, Ashira, elected by the Council of Ten, cannot account for the telepathic images she begins to receive. Even after a few years of such contact, although Ashira realizes there must be two telepathic children, mistreated for their difference, in a primitive settlement somewhere, there is no way the Morrowans can locate them. The children are Tia, age 12, and her younger half-brother, known as Rabbit. Eventually Ashira learns that these children are the second generation result of an unauthorized experiment by a Morrowan geneticist who had happened upon the village during an earlier exploratory expedition.

The situation becomes critical for Tia and Rabbit when Otto, the cook, threatens them. Tia bites him and Rabbit, unaware of the consequences, wishes him dead, a wish which his undisciplined telepathic power immediately brings to reality. The Major, the village's brutal leader, believes it was Tia's bite that killed the man, and decides Tia must be killed. However, the children escape. Ashira directs them telepathically toward the seacoast, where the Morrowans rescue them.

At this point the sequel, *Treasures of Morrow*, continues the story. Tia and Rabbit reach Morrow and are educated in both technology and history. They learn to control their telepathic powers. However, the time comes when the Morrowans send an expedition to Base, including the two children. The Morrowans set up a fence to protect themselves in the middle of the village, observe, and decide that the people of Base are no threat to Morrow. However, they inadvertently collapse the tunnel to the defunct, buried missile which has served Base as its religious symbol. As the Morrowans drive their amphibious vehicles down river toward their sailing ship, the people of Base ambush them, intending to recapture and kill Tia, whom they regard as a witch. In the ensuing confrontation, Rabbit shoots a flare gun, setting fire to the woods. Tia argues that the three vehicles should backtrack and dig a fire-break across the fields to prevent the fire from burning the village. Ashira, pleased with Tia's ability to overcome desire for revenge and to feel compassion, carries out Tia's wish. Finally, still watched sullenly by the people of Base, the Morrowans set off toward home.

NOTES

These novels, produced with careful thought, describe a future situation with a plausible history. The setting dramatizes the consequences of environmental destruction. The descriptions of the Death of the Seas might be compared with Paul Ehrlich's 1969 scenario, "Eco-Catastrophe," in Toffler's *The Futurists* (New York: Random House, 1972). Students might also expand upon the design of LIFESPAN, described in greater detail in *Children of Morrow* than in *Treasures*.

The evolutionary changes at Morrow demonstrate that even tragedy may have a positive result. The second novel, juxtaposing the Base and Morrow cultures, is a piece of futuristic anthropology. The ethical standards of Morrow are thrown into relief, but recognition that Base has done what it must to survive is also apparent. Most striking in this regard is Ashira's warning to Tia not to destroy the people's belief in their missile, fear-ridden though such a belief may be, unless she offers something better which Base is able and willing to accept (p. 116). Character development is well handled, especially as Tia and Rabbit learn trust, discipline, and self-acceptance in the second novel. A prologue and background comments throughout the second volume make it thoroughly readable without the first.

---

*Hoover, H. M. **The Delikon**. New York: Viking, 1977. 148p. Avon paperback, 1978. Grades 5-10.

SUMMARY

An alien species fails in its attempt to help humankind mature into a "complex social being" with a grasp of cosmic order because it does not recognize that short-lived humans are unwilling to sacrifice for a long-term goal they will never see and cannot comprehend. The Delikon had crushed—nearly destroyed—the earth after Earth's spaceships had damaged alien worlds. Then the Delikon ruthlessly imposed their rule on Earth. One of their techniques is to select attractive, intelligent human children to be educated for governorships in the several sectors of Earth. These children live for ten years with a Delikon tutor, then go on to an academy for further instruction.

Varina, presently tutor to Alta and Jason, is the central figure in this novel. Like all Delikon based on Earth, her body has been restructured to resemble human form. Her round, cinnamon eyes are the only obvious clue to her species. Although a child in appearance and in the Delikon life span, Varina is 307 Earth years old. She has had a long tour of Earth duty, and it is time for her to resume her own form through chemical restructuring, and then to return home. Her last assignment is to take her two charges for their last lesson—a view of the caves of cosmic order, a museum of Earth's history, followed by a short camping holiday under the protection of Cornelius, a human bodyguard. However, the group is caught by rebels under the leadership of one of Varina's former pupils. This Aron, now governor of sector nine, tries to explain to Varina that human beings need human goals which they can work toward within a single human lifetime. He also, however, makes it possible for Varina and her companions to escape.

Not only the rebels' bombs and guns, but the Delikon's warrior drones are dangers to the group trying to make its way back to the Delikon palace, for the drones at first doubt Varina's identity in her altered form. When at last they reach the goal, Varina finds the Delikon spaceship gone, and only one of her species remaining—the queen Sidra, abandoned midway through her restructuring. The rebels peacefully take over Kelador, but Varina is aware only of Sidra. When the queen finally emerges, she sings a pavane which causes the entire building to collapse upon her. As last we see Varina, some years later, she is running toward a landing spaceship, hoping that she will finally be able to go home.

NOTES

Occasionally authors presume to know thoughts of alien beings, but this novel is unique in that an alien so different from ourselves is the sole viewpoint character. This device permits Hoover to comment on several human qualities. The larger question, however, is why the Delikon's plan failed. Does Hoover mean that it was inappropriate to humankind because it merged individuality into social consciousness? Was it just badly managed by the Delikon because they underestimated human individuality and the significance of humans' short life span? Or are we to suppose that short-sightedness is a flaw in human mentality, such that we fail to work toward goals more than a lifetime away? Does the author communicate an answer, or is the reader to decide?

Hoover's style approaches poetry. Many compound and complex sentences are written separately; or to put it conversely, many sentences begin with "and" or "for" to avoid lengthy compound and complex constructions. Students' attention may be drawn to the repetition in the last chapter of sentences from the first chapter. The typeface and page shape and design are notably well suited to the mood of the story. Characterization, too, is effectively developed.

From a futurist standpoint, the novel is unique among those in this bibliography because it deals with beneficent intervention by an alien species—at least beneficent intent over the long term. It shares with Karl's *The Turning Place* the notion of brief, destructive war with aliens—due in Karl's book to competition, in Hoover's to human damage to other planets. The Delikon themselves have several insectlike physical characteristics which, along with the terms "queen" and "drone," may offer clues to the social consciousness they wish to teach us, although both Varina and Sidra demonstrate individuality of thought and personality.

---

*Hoover, H. M. **The Lost Star**. New York: Viking, 1979. 150p. Avon paperback, 1980. Grades 6-10.

SUMMARY

Two thematic elements interact in *The Lost Star*: a search for honesty in facing oneself, and for mutual trust in relating to others. Lian, daughter of two astrophysicists doing research on the planet Balthor and already published in the field herself at age 15, crashes due to a storm as she brings supplies from a spaceport. Rescued by the archaeologist David Farr, Lian soon becomes deeply involved with the work at the "dig" and wonders whether she really wants the career she had chosen when she was nine.

The archaeologists, human and nonhuman, have been at work for six weeks, unearthing what they surmise to be the home of an extinct people. Lian, meanwhile, is trusted by the awkward low-intelligence gray creatures called "lumpies," who lead her inside their hill. Gradually, with Lian's help, the scientists discover that the entire structure, which has become covered over with soil and vegetation, is a highly sophisticated spaceship. The lumpies prove to be highly intelligent, telepathic beings who have pretended stupidity for self-protection. Housed in their ship is the Counter, an artificial intelligence embracing "the essence of the best minds of seven generations of Toapa"—the lumpies' true species. Originally, the Counter had tried to provide everything the Toapa needed, leaving its people unable to cope with the floods which repeatedly filled the ship, covering and filling it with debris. As the scientists proceed and the crablike tolats clear the dome, solar energy is converted to power to reactivate the Counter. The Counter then begins to plan to help its people regain their lost knowledge, but this time also to retain their independence.

NOTES

The gradual revelation of the lumpies' abilities and their history introduces an element of suspense, as does the early hint that Lian may wish to turn from astrophysics to some less austere field of study—a decision which would inevitably lead to confrontation with her parents. Lian's steps toward maturity arise naturally from the circumstances in which she finds herself. She is a well delineated, believable character, though possibly a bit idealized.

One might attempt to describe and to draw each of the alien species—sentient and animal—found in the novel. The difficulties of interspecies understanding, as well as the variety of attitudes demonstrated by the human characters, provide rich resources for discussion, with many implications for readers' own lives. Other novels which describe the difficulties of establishing communication with intelligent aliens are: Karl's *The Turning Place*; Morressy's *The Drought on Ziax II* and *The Humans of Ziax II*; Norton's *Breed to Come* and *Iron Cage*; and Yep's *Sweetwater*.

---

*Hoover, H. M. **The Rains of Eridan**. New York: Viking, 1977. 183p. Avon paperback, 1979. Grades 6 up.

SUMMARY

How are trust and companionship built? Dr. Theodora Leslie has been a loner for some years and has been entirely alone on the planet Eridan for a month. But she is awakened by sounds of violence and, after a plane leaves, she finds the bodies of the man who is second in command of the expedition and his wife. A lone survivor is their daughter, Karen Orlov. Unreasoned fear has spread among the people at Base One, from which Karen has come. It is hope of finding the cause of a similar, if less severe, fear at the other two camps that has brought Theo into the wilderness to study the native animals.

Uncertain now as to the situation at her own Base Three, Theo sets out to walk back, taking Karen along. On the way, they find a large, apparently dead, life form, dehydrated and nearly buried in sand, and surrounded by a number of the crystals which the scientists have been collecting with the assumption that they will have high commercial value. Photos of the new species are taken.

Theo and Karen continue on foot toward Base Three, but are overtaken by rains. Their small tent is not adequate shelter for long; soon Theo risks signaling the base to send an aircraft to their rescue. Fortunately, Base Three is still under control, although the fear symptoms are widespread.

Returning to the base, however, they find that 20 staff members have been eaten by a large beast which broke into the dining room, leaving only empty husks of bodies. Other scientists have observed large beasts which may be the predator and show startling resemblance to the dehydrated form Karen and Theo had seen in the cave. Eventually, Theo realizes the form, enormous though it is, must be cryptobiotic, that is, able to survive dry periods in a dehydrated state and to revive during rainy seasons. The base's equipment keeps out the animals, but not the mounting fear.

As she works to try to find the cause of this fear, Theo comes upon tapes of two of the dead staff members, geologists who had tried to tell everyone that the so-called crystals are a protein substance. Next she realizes that the crystals house a virus which is causing the epidemic of fear. Both Theo and Karen are immune, apparently because each had at one time licked a crystal to test its taste. From Karen's blood an antibody is isolated to inject the entire staff.

As important as this need, however, is the growing feeling of both Theo and Karen that they want to stay together. Fortunately, Theo's request to adopt Karen is granted. Since Vice-Regent Madame Koh of the Aurora Corporation decides to abandon the work on Eridan, however, the two will soon travel to another planet.

NOTES

The risks of settling on planets whose biology is not fully understood is the futurist theme in this novel. However, the fascination of scientific investigation and the developing friendship between an orphaned teenager and a young career woman are equally important. The style parallels the growth in that relationship from uncertainty to mutual commitment: after the poetic prologue, the style is at times quite abrupt, but as the girl and woman come to know one another better, the sentences flow more smoothly. A minor note is the determinant role given to commercial enterprise in space exploration.

Despite the dangerous "cave bears," Eridan is a beautiful planet, a striking contrast to the Earth Hoover describes in the Morrow books (*see* pp. 40-41). Moreover, the novel offers splendid models of the "liberated woman."

Hoskins, Robert. **Jack-in-the-Box Planet**. Philadelphia: Westminster Press, 1978. 153p.
 Grades 7-9.

SUMMARY

This novel, an adventure story about perseverance in the face of difficulties,
opens with Will Harlowe imprisoned in his own home. The skeletons of Will's parents
are visible outdoors in their air car, where they had perished 12 years earlier of a
virus unleashed in germ warfare. Will cannot break the locks his parents had programmed, and the robots, including the toys (hence the book's title), treat Will like
the young child he had been then.

Will has two contacts, an old man named Ernst and girl named Margret, with
whom he speaks by telecommunication. Finally the household mechanisms begin
to break down and Will escapes. But Ernst, believing he is dying, has shut off his
communicator, and Margret turns out to be a fat, middle-aged woman who comforts
herself in her loneliness by eating sweets.

On the way back home from Margret's place, Will's air car is shot down by a
small group of invaders from Earth. These scouts have become stranded on an island,
but are trying to reach Grid Central, from which they can contact other would-be
settlers on overcrowded Earth. Knowing it was Earth people who had unleashed
the germs which had killed his parents and virtually wiped out New Paradise, Will
escapes. He then discovers another group of survivors with whom he teams up to
foil the plans of the Earth scouts. With help from other colonial planets, the rebuilding
of New Paradise is begun.

NOTES

Although characterization is rather shallow, and such touches as the parents'
skeletons a bit macabre, the story is of interest. The people of Earth, in an attempt
to escape the crowding and pollution on their planet, wage war on their own colonies
rather than seek empty planets or expel alien beings. The use of a computer and robots
for household management and child care is described in some detail.

Hughes, Monica. **Crisis on Conshelf Ten**. New York: Atheneum, 1977. 144p. Grades
 5-8.

SUMMARY

The author demonstrates her faith in the power of persuasion as opposed to
violence. Kepler Masterman, son of the Moon Governor, accompanies his father on
a trip to Earth, where the senior Masterman hopes to persuade the U.N. to grant
autonomy and representation to the Moon. Ultimately, he expects that the Moon
settlers, "Sellenites," will have a fairer share in the fruits of their labors.

While his father pursues that diplomatic mission, Kep, unable to cope with
Earth gravity, visits a cousin in the underwater complex Conshelf Ten. Although life
there is not quite as austere as on the Moon, Kep finds the same resentment against
corporate exploitation. A few of the ocean dwellers have even left the Conshelf
complex and had themselves surgically altered and provided with gills, enabling them
to live in the water. While Kep is still trying to find out about these gillmen, he is
framed for sabotaging a pressure valve in his uncle's living quarters, then for releasing

three million fish just ready for marketing. Escaping conviction only because his hand had been injured, making it impossible for him to have turned the valve to permit the fish to escape, Kep soon finds out that the gillmen plan to blow up a group of oil rigs in an attempt to force the U.N. to accord them fairer treatment. Kep is certain their scheme will not only lead to retaliatory measures, but will also jeopardize any chance Moon might have of obtaining better conditions through democratic means. He talks to the gillmen, but when persuasion fails, he risks his life by rising through a hundred feet of ocean with a message to the U.N. strapped to his body. Kep is rescued by the gillmen themselves, his message is transmitted to the U.N., and both Sellenites and Conshelfers win support. Kepler briefly considers staying in Conshelf Ten, but realizes that the Moon is home.

NOTES

Occasionally this first person narrative suffers from awkward language, but the plot is fascinating and skillfully developed. Kepler's comparisons between Moon and ocean living demonstrate both similarities and sharp contrasts. In both environments, for example, loss of oxygen is a constant danger. Both situations reduce the pull of gravity. On the other hand, water is literally worth its weight in gold on the Moon, while it envelops the Conshelfers whenever they venture from their bubble homes. And of course, the more familiar lifestyle on *terra firma* reveals unexpected strangeness when seen through the eyes of "moon-baby" and "water-baby."

---

*Jackson, Jacqueline and William Perlmutter. **The Endless Pavement**. Illus. by Richard Cuffari. New York: Seabury Press, 1973. 48p. Grades 5 up.

SUMMARY

In this story of machine takeover, foiled by the curiosity and courage of young Josette, Home-a-rollas move endlessly in one lane while the School-a-rolla, Assembla-rolla, and other vehicles circle in the other. Each morning at nine the School-a-rolla stops even with Josette's Home-a-rolla so she can scoot across to school. For Josette, like everyone else, was bolted into a rollabout as soon as she could sit up, and remains in her wheeled machine thereafter, even to sleep at night. Humans exist only to repair automobiles, which rule the world.

One day, though, Josette sees a bit of green pushing up through the endless black asphalt which stretches to the horizon. As her Home-a-rolla passes the little plant every few days, Josette watches it grow and, eventually, produce a round, red fruit. Josette's father had told her about fruit one night when the screen which broadcasts the great auto races broke down. So she crawls out from her rollabout, hoists herself over the fence, plucks and bites into the fruit. But she is captured by the great autos and taken to the Great Computer-Mobile, which she disables by throwing her fruit at its dashboard. Thereupon all the machines are still and the people are free to lurch and crawl out of their rollabouts and over the fence onto the endless pavement.

NOTES

The anti-technology theme of this picture book will certainly provoke discussion, especially since it is so sharply delineated. The relation of this theme to the style and coloring of the illustrations, page layout, and typeface is noteworthy. Satire is applied to patriotism, religion, schools, and police. (For example, the school closing recitation on page 9 is a play on Ecclesiastes 1:6.) The publishers suggest grades 3 to 6 as the appropriate audience; as part of a future studies unit, however, grades 5 to high school will make better use of the book.

Two other books, not set in the future, nevertheless resemble *The Endless Pavement* in format and theme and might well be compared with it. *Machine* by Lore Shoberg (New York: McGraw-Hill, 1973) follows the growth of a tiny robot as it incorporates features of everything it sees, from an electric toothbrush to the treaded wheels of a steam shovel. When the populace wants to make a king of the now-mighty machine, the boy who owns it reduces the monster to its original size and form by mutilating the computer card which had been delivered with it. The second book, *The Ultimate Auto* by Patrick McGivern (Illus. by Susan Perl; New York: Putnam, 1969) recounts the consequences of one auto too many on the crowded streets of New York City. (*See* "Technology—Negative Attitudes" in the index, Part IV, to locate other novels that deal with or debate that theme.)

Jakes, John. **Time Gate**. Philadelphia: Westminster Press, 1972. 174p. New American Library paperback, 1978. Grades 7-10.

SUMMARY

This novel focuses on travel backward and forward in time, including the consequences of a major alteration of history. Secondarily, it follows a young man's growing independence from a domineering older brother.

In the year 1982, 18-year-old Tom Linstrum assists his brother Calvin in the government-funded time travel project initiated by their father, who has died. The time gate has been used only for archaeological investigations of the past, with great care taken to avoid altering the course of history. Young Donald Koop, however, a fanatic conservative, decides to use the device to go back a few months in time to assassinate President Archibald before the latter's disarmament proposals can be completed. Koop succeeds, leaving the time project crew the only persons who can remember a reality in which Archibald was not killed. Koop then transports himself to the year 3987 A.D., where he wanders in the desert and goes completely mad.

Accompanied by a robot newspaper reporter known as Sidney Six, the Linstrum brothers and Gordon White, meanwhile, trace Koop's actions and seek him out in 3987 A.D., where Koop is killed by the police. This world is, however, a dreary landscape where all the world's population live in 19 cities. Since the fertility rate has dropped to 4%, extinction of the human species is but a matter of time. Doktor Phlonykus, Chairman of Federal Earth, attributes this situation to failure to achieve disarmament after President Archibald's assassination in 1982.

The older Linstrum returns to 1982 and prevents the assassination—again Donald Koop dies—but 3987 does not improve. Therefore Doktor Phlonykus decides to return to the year 2080 to prevent detonation of the doomsday weapon. Although he dies in the attempt, Tom Linstrum, White, and Phlonykus's daughter Mari succeed. The year 3987 is now a near-utopia, and the three scientists—together with Mari, who no longer has a family in 3987—return to the year 1982.

NOTES

The nature of time, the plausibility of time travel, and the consequences of altering history, were that possible, are intriguing topics which are perhaps handled a bit glibly here. Why Donald Koop should exist in both 1982 and 3987 when no one else has a double is a perplexing, though not insoluble, logical problem which is not explained in the novel. *Man and Time* by J. B. Priestley (London: Aldus Books, 1964) will prove a useful, though difficult, resource for pursuing this question. The pursuit of Koop melts into the attempt to prevent doomsday, so the one element which carries through the novel is the rather stereotyped conflict between the Linstrum brothers.

Jones, McClure. **Cast Down the Stars**. New York: Holt, Rinehart and Winston, 1978. 186p. Grades 5-9.

SUMMARY

This novel is woven around the conflict between the head and the heart, or between what one ought to do and what one wants to do. As the story opens, Glory is already Second Starcaster of Solstice Tower and is destined to be First Starcaster and First Reader—a unique combined honor. Yet her grandfather Sun in Winter, who is also the village First Councillor, has transferred to her his displeasure with Glory's mother and father, his daughter and son-in-law. They had led many young men and women to their death some years earlier by breaking through the serpent wall, only to be attacked by barbarians. The gap in the wall has never been rebuilt.

Now, six barbarians are captured at the border. When the stars are cast and read to discover the significance of this event, they direct that the gap in the wall be rebuilt. Sun in Winter leads a group from Solstice and calls for help from other villages. When they reach the break in the wall, Honor, Second Geomancer, determines where the missing section should be built, and Glory reads the stars to ascertain the time to begin. But Sun in Winter ignores their findings. All goes well until the barbarians attack. Afterwards, the defeated people must await more workers and new supplies to begin building again. Meanwhile, Glory has found that part of the serpent wall is hollow and that a gem lies in a rock monolith there. Entranced with its beauty, Sun in Winter takes the gem. Crops are poor that year, but the gap in the wall is finally mended. The people set out for their home villages, but find that crops have failed nearly everywhere. Sun in Winter's own party barely escapes freezing and starvation in a land which has always been fertile and mild. The Wise Ones tell Sun in Winter he must return the gem because the serpent wall had been built by the spirits long ago to control the climate, and the gem provides power to the wall. Some weeks later the climate changes as proof that Sun in Winter has succeeded in replacing the stone. The book closes with a promise that he will return to Solstice, and that Glory will find love with Second Geomancer Honor.

NOTES

A first person narrative notable for well-constructed, varied sentences, this novel probes its theme in two directions. On the one hand, Sun in Winter fails as leader to the extent by which his heart rules his head. He spoils his daughter with the result that she and many others are killed and the serpent wall breached; he gives in to the impatient builders who insist on rebuilding the gap before the time appointed by the stars, again leading to great loss of life; finally, he covets and takes the gem stone, causing drought and then a harsh winter.

On the other hand, First Reader and First Starcaster are seen as having done well when they change the star positions so as to avoid predicting Sun in Winter's death. In this case the ruling of heart over head seems affirmed, although the message is softened by an implication that they were acting by their faith in the spirits.

Readers will be fascinated with the author's focus on astrology—no other futuristic novel deals with that topic in depth. However, it is difficult to be sure that this is a futuristic story. Before the novel begins there had been a highly scientific civilization to the south. That civilization had been destroyed when extensive testing of weapons caused land to break up and slip into the sea. At the same time, Glory's people had lived to the north of this civilization, apparently at their present level of advancement. The scientists, or "spirits," had moved north to escape the destruction of their own land, built the serpent wall, lived among Glory's people for a time, and then gradually died out. Since this does not bring to mind a likely extrapolation from a situation on Earth today, it may be that the author has created a world purely of fantasy.

Jones, Raymond F. **Moonbase One**. New York: Abelard Schuman, 1971. 144p.
Grades 5-8.

SUMMARY

A story of survival in space with a dash of mystery, *Moonbase One* also proposes the notion that fear is overcome only to the extent that it can be subordinated to larger concerns. The moonbase is an experiment to determine whether some 200 persons can survive and become self-sufficient. Three months after the base is established, its hydroponic farms are destroyed by an explosion which is found to be sabotage. When discovery of water-containing rocks revives hope of success, the saboteur arranges the destruction of fuel cells essential to the water extraction process, thus endangering the colony again. The colonists close portions of the base and double up in their living quarters so that they can take electric wiring from the closed air domes and string cable to the water-processing plant, thus obviating a need for fuel cells. This plan nearly fails when wire runs short, but is saved when one of the boys in the story suggests that they check an abandoned moon station; there a plentiful supply of wire is found.

Meanwhile, the saboteur confesses his guilt, explaining he had become desperate to return to Earth and saw no way he could do so without either admitting cowardice or forcing the base to close. He is returned to Earth, his actions a well-guarded secret. This decision is based on the fact that he had been included in the expedition with the full knowledge, since he had not passed the prerequisite psychological tests, that he would somehow create a genuine emergency situation to test the colonists' resourcefulness.

NOTES

A plot-centered story, *Moonbase One* provides some scientific information about life on the moon which readers might check for accuracy. The novel clearly delineates the dangers of space colonization, drawing a parallel to the situation of settlers at Jamestown and Plymouth Rock. Benford's *Jupiter Project* is a good novel for comparison on that same theme.

The decision to send a psychologically unsuited person with the colonists results in the death of a worker and in loss of self-respect on the part of an otherwise highly competent scientist. Students might debate the wisdom or morality of that decision.

---

*Karl, Jean E. **The Turning Place: Stories of a Future Past**. New York: Dutton, 1976. 213p. Dell paperback, 1978. Grade 7 up.

SUMMARY

True progress comes through those who remain open to new experience, absorbing the incredible while maintaining a sense of inner unity and direction. A series of short stories develops this theme. Karl begins by imagining the "Clordian Sweep," by which intelligent aliens destroy nearly all life on Earth. She extrapolates the consequences of that event, one of which is a startling increase in psychic powers.

"The Turning Place," first of the nine short stories which comprise the book, probably occurs in the last decade of this century. Twelve persons wander inside a cylindrical force field which soon intensifies so that they cannot get out again. Suddenly the force field expands until it moves out of sight. Their communicators bring no response. What has become of their families and friends?

Some time has elapsed before the second story, "Over the Hill." Pockets of survivors live in small, fertile areas. When a young woman reaches her family's land and her brother takes the woman to wife, it is Carpa's turn to strike out in the hope of finding a new home.

Still later, 85-year-old Velta Akbar broadcasts the story, "Enough," of her discoveries in Pre-Clordian Sweep archaeology. Again some time elapses before Casselia Sorchum demonstrates the telepathic powers which have emerged in Earth people and wins an "Accord" from the now apologetic Clordians. By the time of the "Catabilid Conquest," the sequestering which young teenagers undertook to control their powers of telepathy, or focus, is already old-fashioned. Still, the twins Vana and Chory want to have a sequestering and stow away on their parents' spaceship bound for the planet Frod. They bring back a new ability to bounce with the help of mental energy. In the last four stories, this psychic power is refined to permit teleportation to ever more distant and difficult places, where the several characters meet ever more unusual forms of intelligent life.

NOTES

The nine stories are separated by indefinite, but apparently long, periods of time. Taken together, they simulate a series of fictionalized historical vignettes, concluding with "notes on sources" by way of strengthening credibility.

Some of the stories are in first person, others in third; some are narratives, others cast as surviving documents with concomitant changes in style. Therefore, they exemplify a single author's deliberate use of style to create different effects. No clues are provided as to passage of time, and no connections are made between characters from one story to another—only the "historical" sequence of the stories assists a reader to construct the history of Earth after the Clordian Sweep. The book probably needs to be read twice to be fully understood, but is well worth that investment of time. The overall structure may be related to the important advice to "learn everything and then jump to the unexpected" (p. 207), since that is what happens at the end of each chapter.

Syntax is masterfully used. Various sentence constructions and fragments are brought into play so as to control the flow of the story. The first paragraph of "Accord" (page 59) is a case in point.

In addition to these literary topics, such subjects as psychic powers, teleportation, and cultural evolution are important in relation to future studies. (*See* the index, Part IV, for comparison novels on these topics. *See* Part IV and notes on Hoover's *The Lost Star* for comparable novels which involve alien beings.)

---

*Kestavan, G. R. **The Pale Invaders**. New York: Atheneum, 1976. 178p. Grades 6-9.

SUMMARY

At the time of The Upheaval, as a result of social unrest, misuse of technology, and overpopulation, the "townz" had fallen to ruin and gangs had stolen food and killed innocent victims. The details are unclear, but the Founder of Gerald's village had gathered several children and sought out the valley where Gerald now lives, 70 or 80 years later. But can they—or ought they—forever avoid the technology which had brought benefits as well as disaster? Can they regain the good, yet avoid the bad associated with machines, money, and the like?

The only man alive in the village who remembers the Old Days before the Upheaval is Great-Grandfather Paul, dubbed "Old Carz" because he speaks so often of "carz" which carried people along "roads." Ostracized by the villagers, Old Carz lives in a hut up on the hillside. Correctly guessing that Gerald will be the boy chosen to learn the Reading and Writing, Old Carz tells Gerald that he is beginning to write his memories of the Old Days. But before he can give the few sheets of paper to the boy, the old man is "left" without supplies as winter sets in.

Meanwhile, however, Gerald is beginning to piece together, bit by bit, some understanding of those times. During these same months, strangers come to the area seeking a black stone called coal. Just when Gerald has the opportunity to find and interpret Old Carz's manuscript, the village is visited by a half dozen paler-skinned people who bring an enormous machine which can clear land of large trees. Thinking to show the villagers the power of machinery to help them, the "invaders" bring their machine forward. But Father Dennis springs to attack the machine and is killed. Both villagers and strangers are horrified, but with Father Dennis's death, leadership falls to Father Alan, who has always believed Old Carz's tales. After discussion with the villagers, he indicates the "invaders" will be permitted to mine coal in the Forbidden Area. In exchange, the miners are to use their machines to clear land for farming, as well as to pay money. As the book closes, one of the miners meets with the Fathers and Grandfathers to explain how money is used and how they might invest it in livestock and seeds to insure their continued prosperity after the coal mine has been depleted.

NOTES

Gerald, first person narrator, finds himself torn between fear of knowing and desire for more knowledge. He finds his best allies, not in the two older men who already know the Reading and Writing, but in Susan, a girl about his own age, and in Father Alan, both of whom refuse to deny the obvious evidence that Old Carz was not a madman making up fanciful tales.

The conflict over knowledge is paralleled by that over technology. Since there are two groups of people (the villagers are apparently English, the miners Welsh), each presenting a different viewpoint, students can dramatize these roles to debate the issue. One should not overlook the fact that the question is not really resolved at the close of the novel.

Kestavan is the same writer as Kesteven (real name G. R. Crosher). We have used the names as they appear on the books but, because of Library of Congress cataloging, the novel may be cataloged under Kesteven in some libraries.

Kesteven, G. R. **The Awakening Water**. New York: Hastings House, 1977. 160p.
  Grades 6-9.

SUMMARY

This novel explores the tension between restrictions necessary for survival and freedom needed to make life worthwhile. In 1997, fighting and bombing had caused widespread destruction. By drugging food or water, the Party had subdued the populace for 30 years.

Watford Nine John, age 13, is one of the young men in a House occupied with raising food. But one hot afternoon he spies two girls beyond the fence. He drinks water from the spring they show him, and after a couple of days avoiding the drugged water of the House, finds himself thinking and speaking more quickly, and aware of details he had never noticed before.

John runs away when Matron is called to deal with his strange behavior, and joins a group of Lost Ones, young people who are hiding out in ruined buildings. His group has strict rules—one of their number is banished to an Island for stealing food from the farmhouses. As they grow older, the Lost Ones pair off and are helped by Old Potter to go beyond the Marsh, there to establish a family free of the Party's interference.

However, John's group is captured by the Party. They find that at least one faction in the Party is convinced that people like themselves, who have learned to solve their difficulties democratically and honestly, are ready to be resettled in new villages in the hope of rebuilding a society which will not repeat the mistakes of 1997.

NOTES

Perhaps a bit shy on plot, *The Awakening Water* is well written as to diction and sentence structure. It is unclear whether the disaster of 1997 was limited to England, or was more widespread. Also left for the reader to decide is the question of whether or not it will prove to be too soon to release the people from the control imposed by tranquilizing drugs. The astonishing discovery that the Party shares the goal of the Lost Ones is quickly accepted by John and Janet, who recognize that the excitement of hiding is no substitute for the opportunity to build a new life in a village settlement.

Key, Alexander. **The Forgotten Door**. Philadelphia: Westminster Press, 1965. 126p.
  Scholastic paperback, 1968. Grades 5-8.

SUMMARY

This novel focuses on human attitudes toward an alien boy who can leap like a deer and read minds. Little Jon accidentally falls through a door long sealed off and forgotten. Thus he slips through from his planet to the state of Georgia, losing his memory in the process. Only gradually, with the help of the Bean family, does Jon realize his own origins. At last, hostility of fearful neighbors reaches so high a pitch that when Jon returns to his world, he takes all the Bean family with him.

NOTES

Although set in present time, *The Forgotten Door* will round out any discussion of attitudes toward intelligent, especially superior, alien beings. Key shows us at least three responses: fear and its accompanying hostility, desire to exploit Jon's telepathic abilities, and sympathetic understanding. Further, although we can form only a general impression of Jon's utopian planet, his astonishment at much of what he sees here serves both as critique of our society and as an example of the difficulty of translating from one language to another where underlying concepts are not shared.

---

*Key, Alexander. **The Golden Enemy**. Philadelphia: Westminster Press, 1969. 176p. Grades 6-10.

SUMMARY

On the book jacket, Alexander Key is quoted as saying

If, in all I have written and hope to write, I am able to perpetuate one small thought that will help to raise the moral level of man, so that at least the wolf does not continue to rank above him, then my work will have been worth the effort.

The theme that man must live in brotherhood with animals if he hopes to live in peace with his fellow man is well explicated in *The Golden Enemy*.

Many generations have passed since Earth was destroyed in war followed by a shift of the earth's axis and consequent floods and earthquakes. Boy Jaim's people live in four agricultural communities whose members eat no meat and have no weapons. One day their utopian existence is threatened by a gigantic golden bear, sole survivor of the time when men killed animals merely for sport. The bear is intent on destroying the communities' food supply, for he knows that a cosmic cloud is coming, and that lacking food and lacking foreknowledge which would send them into deep earthen shelters, his old and hated enemies will die. The only possible stumbling block to his revenge is Boy Jaim, who, because he has extraordinary telepathic powers, may tap into the Pool of Knowledge and so learn the nature of the coming danger.

When the bear stampedes their goats and destroys their granary, the people turn to poisoned arrows to kill the bear. They try out the poison on goats and thus rekindle the lust to kill which still lies dormant within them. Only Boy Jaim, the best archer of all and best able, because of his telepathy, to locate the great beast, refuses to join the hunt. Instead, he hopes to communicate with the bear and learn the nature of the calamity he already senses. But when the bear kills Jaim's dog, the boy, too, becomes a hunter. He leaves his cousin L'Mara at the village, since she can talk with Jaim telepathically.

Jaim wounds the bear, but is almost immediately sorry when the animal, mad with pain, crashes away toward the Barrens. Perhaps he can put it out of its misery, or even wrest from the dying creature the secret which will save his people. When he catches up with the bear next morning, it is near death and suffering from thirst in the unnatural searing heat of the sun. Jaim gives it water and pulls out the poisoned arrow. As the bear recovers, it finally communicates with Jaim, forcing him to relive scenes of human cruelty to animals and finally of the war which had nearly accomplished man's self-destruction.

Horrified, Jaim nevertheless also sees the cause of the great heat and warns L'Mara to send the people, who are standing in a small lake because of the heat and anticipated earthquakes, to safety before freezing winds descend. The bear then offers Jaim the protection of his great body.

NOTES

The unilinear plot holds the reader with its elements of mystery and telepathy. Preceding each chapter and at the novel's conclusion, however, we find two or three pages which follow a separate narrative in which a young herder whose dog has been killed by an unknown wild creature undergoes a change of heart from hatred to compassion much as does Jaim in the concluding chapter. The herder is descended from men who had fled Earth generations earlier; he picks out a particular star and wonders whether it is Earth—the reader, of course, knows that it is. Do these interludes disrupt or enhance the flow of the main plot? If the plot is enhanced, then how?

The Pool of Knowledge of events past and future, open only to an animal or a person with psychic ability, may provoke discussion, along with Key's harsh indictment of man's desire to kill. The bison in the U.S. and several current examples in Africa are among specific instances students may want to investigate, even as they debate vegetarianism and abandonment of virtually all weapons as appropriate correctives.

Boy Jaim's community is a pastoral utopia, the classic return to a simple lifestyle after a system break, although new technology has emerged, as when solar energy is used to power anti-gravity air sleds. Characterization and style, especially the juxtaposition of sentence structures, also deserve attention.

---

*Key, Alexander. **The Incredible Tide**. Philadelphia: Westminster, 1970. 159p. Grade 6 up.

SUMMARY

A survival story, *The Incredible Tide* poses faith and morality against materialism and immorality. Magnetic weapons have caused flooding of large parts of the earth's surface. Two communities survive: Industria, remnant of the model city of the New Order; and High Harbor, a community of several hundred youth and but a few adults loyal to the ideas of Teacher. Teacher has not been found in the several years since the flooding. His people believe he is on an island somewhere in the ocean, but in fact he is in Industria under an assumed identity. There he is joined by Conan, who is rescued from his island by Industria's survey ship.

Teacher realizes that another large section of Industria is about to slide off into the sea. Having attempted to warn the citizens, he escapes with Conan, hoping to sail to High Harbor. Shipwrecked in a storm, the two are joined by the woman commander of the survey ship, which has also been sunk while pursuing them. Together, they build a new ship and again set out for High Harbor.

Meanwhile, the New Order's Commissioner Dyce has been meeting with the rebellious youth of High Harbor, hoping to persuade them to take control of the community and to join the New Order. Dyce is not above loosing a virus on the island to help get his way. However, Conan arrives just in time to save Teacher's people from the New Order and from the tidal wave which crosses the ocean after the predicted disaster at Industria.

NOTES

One of the few futuristic novels to present a positive viewpoint of religious faith, this story is one of the few juvenile novels to make use of a device quite common in science fiction for adults—a Stalinist government model. The members of the New Order are, for the most part, overcome with a lust for power. But, as Teacher notes, they also have been able to rebuild their society under nearly impossible circumstances. Mental telepathy and the ability to enter into a bird's body are psychic elements which will interest readers.

Key, Alexander. **The Magic Meadow**. Philadelphia: Westminster, 1975. 124p. Grades 4-7.

SUMMARY

"People can do anything if they really believe they can and try hard enough" (p. 15). In this instance, five hopelessly crippled orphans and their nurse transport themselves into the future—into a utopian world of natural beauty where cities no longer exist and young people float in the moonlight in anti-gravity air boats, singing to the resplendent dawn. Upon arrival, they contact the inhabitants through telepathy. And gradually they regain use of their crippled bodies.

NOTES

Although bordering on fantasy, this novel depicts a future to encourage and inspire any young reader.

Kurland, Michael. **The Princes of Earth**. Nashville, TN: Thos. Nelson, 1978. 190p. Grades 6-10.

SUMMARY

The recurring motif in Kurland's novel is that of individuality vs. conformity. Adam Warrington, the novel's protagonist, has been facing that conflict for some time as the story opens.

Adam is a graduating senior in a 30-floor high school on the planet Jasper in the Reformation Group, a bit of the universe which prides itself on its high moral standards. Like all high school seniors in the Confederation of Human Planets, Adam learns of an opportunity to be tested for entrance to the Imperial University System. At first disinterested, Adam pursues the test idea after being denied graduation on false charges. Adam's intent is to attend Hapsburg Agricultural College on Jasper—those who fail the university test must be admitted to a college or university on their home planet. But Adam passes and the school officials argue that only failure on the test requires that they admit him to college.

So, with his father's blessing, Adam leaves Jasper. Aboard the spaceship, he is rather like a country yokel in the big town. His first shock is the sight of a girl's legs, since skirts on Jasper cover the ankles. The young lieutenant who thus startles him, however, later becomes the object of Adam's mild romantic interest. Also aboard ship, Adam meets humans quite unlike those he has known before, as well as several alien species. He learns about the Humanate Congress, whose members want to isolate humans from other species. A group of these persons try to commandeer the spaceship but, with an assist from Adam, are foiled. Again, when the ship reaches the spaceport, Sol Terminus, Adam helps Nancy avert disaster for a windjammer whose pilot is Prince Michael of New York. Finally, Adam is kidnapped in a case of mistaken identity. He and Prince Michael's daughter are taken to an asteroid inhabited by a small, monastic cult which conforms to its own rules, but certainly not to usual norms of behavior. Their rescue, helped along by Adam, closes the book.

NOTES

A first person narrative enlivened by flashes of dry humor, this novel is primarily an episodic adventure story. Adam is an engaging character, though perhaps a bit immature for his age. So many strands lie loose at the conclusion that the book fairly cries for a sequel.

The contrast between Adam's conservative home planet and the empire is clearly delineated. To expand the dimensions of the conformity question the author describes the Humanate Congress, the followers of Mother Hubbard on the asteroid Aegle, and the elite ruling class—all viewed by the naively inquiring backwoods (or back-planet) mind of young Adam. Adam's father, too, is an interesting blend of conformity and independence.

Other topics for discussion are information control, space travel through null-E (Einsteinian) space, and the imperial government. The university entrance exam is fascinating—one speculates on the purpose of each portion and on other testing possibilities with advanced technology. Students may enjoy reconstructing the quotations which are mangled in the "tomato" conversation (pp. 144-47) and writing similar conversations of their own.

Larson, Glen A. and Robert Thurston. **The Battlestar Galactica Storybook**. Adapted by Charles Mercer. New York: Putnam, 1979. Grades 5-8.

SUMMARY

This is a retelling of the initial television episode of *Battlestar Galactica*. Even as the Cylons and humans are holding a peace conference, the Cylons mount a sneak attack on the battleships and home planets of their human enemy. Commander Adama manages to save his ship and a ragtag collection of 22,000 space ships carrying survivors. Their goal is to reach the lost human colony called Earth, but to do so they need a supply of the fuel Tylium. This they obtain from the planet Carillon, but only after a narrow escape from the insectlike Ovions, allies of the Cylons.

NOTES

Flashy because of its 100 photos from the television show, the book will attract readers. The text is little more than a plot outline, interspersed with uninspired dialogue. Nevertheless, because of its tie to television, the book can serve as a jumping-off point for comparing portraits of the space age in the several media.

*Lightner, A. M. **The Day of the Drones**. New York: Norton, 1969. 255p. Grade
    7 up.

SUMMARY

Discrimination based on skin color is a theme which captures the reader's attention, but willingness to reach out for new knowledge despite dangers is the major issue
in this novel. Amhara, who has a quick mind and a black skin, progresses to ever higher
levels in the training for Medics. But advanced education is closed to her cousin
N'Gobi, whose skin is such a pale brown that by law he should probably have been
killed as a baby. Still, N'Gobi wants to learn, so Amhara secretly brings books with
her when she visits home during vacations. And it is N'Gobi who discovers a strange
rope tied around a duck's leg and recognizes that somewhere else on the face of the
earth there must be another pocket of human survivors of the nuclear war brought
about 500 years earlier by white men.

Reluctantly the Wasan, leader of the Afrians, brings from its hiding place a
solar-powered helicopter, hidden away and taboo ever since the Disaster. Amhara,
N'Gobi, and three others set off to trace the route along which the duck may have
migrated, testing each landing place for lingering radiation. Eventually they reach
what had been England, where they find a blue-eyed white man tied to a rock, awaiting his execution by giant bees. They free the man, who speaks ancient Anglic, and
eventually visit his village. There they find a social pattern resembling that of bees.
The work is done by small women, while their taller counterparts bear the children.
Men do no work and are executed if they cannot father healthy children or if they
incur the queen's displeasure. Amhara enters a sacred cave filled with books, but is
discovered by the queen and barely escapes with a single precious volume of Shakespeare's complete plays, most of which had been lost to her culture. All the Afrians
and the white man they had rescued manage to reach their helicopter, but not before
N'Gobi has been fatally stung by the giant bees. As the novel closes, the survivors
await the decision of the Wasan and the Council as to their fate and the opportunity
to reach out to the white colony.

NOTES

Both black and white survivors have taken harsh measures to overcome the
genetic problems created by radioactivity and to insure their survival. The requirement
that light-skinned babies in Afria (Africa renamed) be killed arises from the tradition
that the Disaster had been caused by white people; however, this requirement has
been relaxed over time. The white survivors in England have kept careful genetic
records to determine who will be permitted to have children.

Ironically, although the white people have a cave filled with books containing
pre-Disaster knowledge, it is only the Afrians who have regained enough science to
be able to understand many of these books. Thus the decision to be made by the
Wasan and the Council is not a simple one, and students might well debate that
choice and project various sequels.

Lightner, A. M. **The Space Ark**. Illus. by Denny McMains. New York: Putnam, 1968.
    190p. Grades 5-8.

SUMMARY

Motivated by a desire to save a valuable species of animal from extinction, the characters in this novel face successively three dangers of a space age future: environment, greedy human beings, and equally greedy intelligent aliens. Ecology and nonconformity are recurring motifs.

When a periodic review of stars indicates that the sun of the planet Shikai is about to nova, destroying the planet in that explosion, a frantic evacuation begins. Johnny Dincum's uncle Rol arrives unexpectedly with a rather battered spaceship equipped to remove animal species, especially a breeding group of the valuable keratoros, unicornlike bearers of a golden horn which is periodically shed and regrown. Such a horn, particularly after it has been carved by one of the monkeylike chi-chis who are also native to Shikai, brings a price of about two million credits. However, only Uncle Rol knows the secret of growing Shikai grapevines off-planet, and lacking those leaves, the keratoros will die.

First, the ship, now popularly dubbed "the ark," lands on the uninhabited planet Emma, only to find that the animals are attacked by small, night-flying reptilians with bloodsucking habits. Next stop is the planet Barbaryos, no longer a home for pirates, but nevertheless the setting for a nearly successful theft of the best male keratoro in the small herd.

The third landing place is another uninhabited planet, promptly dubbed Flora. Quite unexpectedly, the space ark has discovered the original home of one of its travelers, a rock-shaped, intelligent, telepathic insect called Queenie. Accidentally picked up as a mineral sample by a survey scout, Queenie was eventually given to Johnny Dincum ("Dinkie"), who managed to keep her alive. However, as a result of her travels through space, Queenie is now so different from her own kind, the planet-bound Varoni, that she helps the humans resist the insects' telepathic control. At last, Fauna Control directs the ship to safety on Terra (Earth), where the inhabitants now "realize in full the great value of all animal life."

NOTES

This novel follows two others (*The Rock of Three Planets* and *The Planet Poachers*), now out of print. Although this fact is obvious from several references in *The Space Ark*, the novel is fully understandable on its own.

Dinkie, narrator of this plot-centered novel in four episodes, is committed to saving animal species from extinction. He describes the possible dangers of colonizing space and encountering alien beings with psychic powers. As one group vies with another, greed is set off against altruism; yet both motives come together in the person of Uncle Rol and, in a different fashion, the girl Tariri.

Most readers will catch the obvious references to Noah's ark, but several literary names (e.g., Queen Mab) and chapter titles (e.g., "Never Scrutinize a Gift Planet") may escape notice if not drawn to students' attention.

---

*Lightner, A. M. **The Space Gypsies**. New York: McGraw-Hill, 1974. 216p. Grades 7-9.

SUMMARY

Lightner explores the juxtaposition of a present-day ethnic group with a space age setting. Unresolved friction between the Romany and the Gaje is a thematic element.

Having completed his study of mining, Kalia has been waiting two years for his family to return to Helios. Fearing they have perished in the far reaches of space, he accepts an invitation to lift off with another Gypsy family headed by Pani.

The first stop is a ten-year Gathering of the Rom. Here young Kizzy comes aboard, with the intent that she will eventually wed one of Pani's sons. Resentful, Kizzy does a poor job in the hydroponics room; the plants begin to fail and the ship's air turns unhealthy. Although the situation is soon corrected, Pani decides to revitalize their oxygen supply on Olympia, even though he knows the planet is inhospitable to Gypsies.

Here they encounter hostility and resistance as they work on their ship and help another Gypsy family stranded at the port. When Pani's ship lifts off, it carries Kizzy's dog, which had been sold to pay their debt for repair parts, and later had run right back to her mistress. Also aboard as a stowaway is the blond Gajo Tom Gresham, eager to travel in space. The deep-space patrol does not yet know about Gresham, but does catch up with them to recover the dog, Putzi.

Changing course to elude further pursuit, the *Stallion* makes its next planetfall on Secundus. Here Kizzy finally accepts a new pet to replace Putzi, a native bearlike creature called a wiskit. Angry at the inhabitants because they kill wiskits for fur, Kizzy tells fortunes in which she predicts destruction by fire, thus causing a near riot. Her customers assume her prophecy means their sun will nova, or self-destruct. However, the real danger is volcanic activity caused by giant worms. The worms, no longer held in check by their natural enemy, the wiskits, are multiplying rapidly. While investigating this phenomenon, the Gypsies find evidence of the death of Kalia's family. Pani adopts Kalia as his son, the people of Secundus learn how to control its volcanoes, and the Gypsies blast off once more.

NOTES

A plot-centered, episodic story held together by use of first person narrative and the unknown fate of the narrator's family, this novel assumes that minority groups will continue to be ostracized even when man can travel through the universe. Romany values of honesty and loyalty are explained. The sequence on the planet Secundus is a memorable illustration of the consequences of disturbing the balance of nature.

Lightner, A. M. **The Space Olympics.** New York: W. W. Norton, 1967. 211p. Grades 5-8.

SUMMARY

Lightner juxtaposes a present-day institution with a space age setting. Sportsmanship and honesty are secondary motifs in the novel.

Tyros Vann throws rocks and his dog, Wolf, retrieves them while they herd sheep on the planet Permia, at 1.25 times earth gravity. There Tyros is discovered by Barnum Winkle, space trader and self-appointed scout for the recently revived Olympic Games. Having persuaded Ty to compete as a discus thrower, "Wink" continues along his trading route, recruiting other young athletes. Of these, we read most about Devra, native of the water planet Oceanos. Since only a few small islands and mountains dot the watery surface of Oceanos, settlers there have developed underwater and underground living space, as well as sophisticated water craft and an excellent fish cuisine.

At last "Wink" and his team reach the planet Arcadia, where the games will soon begin. During training, Ty meets Endean Vort, a scaly-skinned native of Arcadia who may not participate in the games because he is nonhuman. Here, too, Ty is enraged when the young man Fredolph offers him a large sum to permit the local favorite, Valencourt, to win the discus throw. It seems that large amounts of money have been bet on the outcome of the games.

The games begin with the traditional ceremonies of the eternal flame and parade of the athletes. Devra wins all of the swimming events by a wide margin, and Ty makes the finals for the discus throw. Although Valencourt exceeds his own previous record, Ty, tossing from a handicap position nine paces back (since he is from a higher-gravity planet), surpasses even that mark to receive a gold star-burst.

His celebration is short-lived, however, because Fredolph has ferreted out and now shares with the judges the fact Ty was born and lived his first several months on the planet Gravus, with 1.4 times earth gravity. Although recognizing that the error was unintentional, the judges impose a stiffer handicap and award the star-burst to Valencourt.

Ty runs out into a violent storm, encounters Endean Vort, and accompanies him to his home—an astronomical observatory in the mountains, where it has just been determined that a large meteor will strike Arcadia and cause a tidal wave. All other communications having broken down, it is Ty's toss of a message tied to a rock across a vast canyon which warns the citizens to evacuate the danger area and, incidentally, leads to Ty's regaining his coveted award.

NOTES

This plot-centered, third person narrative may be read quickly and touches upon a broad range of adaptations to the various circumstances of multiple worlds. Modifications in the Olympic Games to suit the situation (e.g., variations in gravity) may lead to a discussion, or chart, of future changes required in other present-day institutions such as scouting, team sports, or schooling. Life on an ocean world is described in enough detail to permit comparison with such novels as the Hydronaut trilogy by Biemiller or Hughes' *Crisis on Conshelf Ten.*

Lightner, A. M. **Star Circus.** New York: Dutton, 1977. 169p. Grades 5-8.

SUMMARY

A science fiction mystery combination, *Star Circus* revolves around a small creature, resembling one of Earth's precursors of the horse, known as the Chalicothere. Actually, this small creature can be expected ultimately to grow to a height of some ten feet. Moreover, it turns out to be a symbiont, for living in a recess in Calico's skin is an ugly wormlike creature which is telepathic and also the more intelligent of the symbiotic pair.

Gratia, advance scout for Pa Jory's circus, finds the horselike creature on the inhospitable surface of the planet Furioso and names it Calico, in reference to the fossil earth creature it seems to resemble. Calico quickly learns tricks and becomes a major attraction at the circus when it performs on Furioso's sister planet Halcyon. One of Calico's abilities is signaling "yes" or "no" in response to questions, so she soon has a separate tent where she gives answers to customers' questions. However, when Calico signals to Colonel Dagan that the new settlement at Glorianna will not succeed, and that prediction turns out to be true, the government wants to take Calico from the circus people.

In studying Calico, the government people discover a huge wormlike creature hidden in a slit on Calico's shoulder. Thinking it is a parasite they operate and remove it, but the boy Jono senses that the worm must be put back or both horse and worm will die. Restored, Calico returns to the circus and preparations are made to blast off. Colonel Dagan tries to prevent their departure by releasing the bloodsucking creature called Blob, only to be consumed by it himself. Nevertheless, when spaceship *Barnum* blasts off, Calico and Jono are left behind to prepare to serve as Halcyon's emissaries to Furioso.

NOTES

The author leaves it to the reader to speculate on the nature of the symbiotic relationship of "horse" and "worm." Students may be interested in the Galactic Law regarding intelligent species and their planets (pp. 150-51) and might debate whether Calico is an intelligent species, as suggested.

---

*Lightner, A. M. **The Thursday Toads**. New York: McGraw-Hill, 1971. 189p. Grade 7 up.

SUMMARY

This novel deals with the consequences of interference with the balance of nature. Colonists on Thursday Planet (named for Dr. Cyril Thursby) find themselves and their livestock threatened by the large, ugly, red—and very poisonous—toads native to the planet. Dr. Thursby's first attempt to eliminate the creatures by releasing sterile males is abandoned when one of the colonists is bitten in the process and dies. His second approach, however, is successful; he releases toads infected with a virus imported from another planet.

Meanwhile, some of the scientists have discovered natives living on the few islands across the Heat Barrier. Actually the descendants of humans who must have crash landed generations earlier, these people have among them many males who have lived to the age of 200 years, but still look youthful. Eventually it is learned that these individuals had been bitten by the poisonous toads in a rite of initiation after which, although many of the young men died, those who survived live long, healthy lives. By this time, however, all the toads have been killed, so the only hope of creating some sort of chemical to bestow long life lies in the often unsuccessful anti-toad serum which Thursby had been developing, or in the bloodstreams of the natives or of Gillian Abbott, one of the few scientists to have survived a toad bite. Gillian, first person narrator who has changed from a skinny, clumsy youth to a tall, strong young man as a result of his encounter with the toad, decides to leave the planet before he becomes a human guinea pig.

NOTES

Gillian's awkwardness provides a touch of humor unusual in futuristic fiction. The theme of the novel is clearly set forth; it may well be compared with others listed under "Balance of Nature" in Part IV. Another point for discussion lies in the dangers of space colonization. Students should note the allusions in the chapter titles.

Mace, Elizabeth. **Out There**. New York: Morrow, 1975. 181p. Grades 5-9.

SUMMARY

Out There (same title as Stoutenburg's novel) focuses on persistence, even when the goal is unclear, and on resourcefulness, confidence that one will think of something when the time comes. The setting is Britain, the time indefinite. A Terrible Disaster involving war, illness, and geological disturbances has returned peoples' way of life to that of an earlier time and altered geography to the extent that some lakes now cover parts of ruined towns and cities.

The boy is in Class 7 in School, where there is much to learn—all of it dull—and the slightest misbehavior is punished by the Rodman. Indeed, sometimes quite innocent boys and girls feel his lash. But now the boy is old enough to go Out There "to find a name and a place for life." He must take with him his older, but simple-witted, brother. The shining promise of adulthood is rapidly destroyed, however. The boys and their classmates reach Reception, where each is given a number to serve until a name is earned. The boy is to be called Eleven—thereafter shortened to Leven—and the brother, Thirty. Because Thirty cannot do much work, the two are assigned to a quarry mine.

At the mine the sadistic Overlooker known as Leatherjack torments the several children who toil to haul slate from shafts supported by rotting props, the slate serving no apparent purpose. Here Leven comes to know Susanna, an unkempt rebel who has found a copy of Arthur Ransome's *Swallowdale* and become entranced with the resourcefulness shown by those children of long ago. Here, too, Leven meets Will, an example of "corruption and truth walking in one body," who alternately emulates and detests Leatherjack. Susanna and Leven have already discussed running away when two sisters who are trying to make their way northward take temporary refuge in the mine. When Will booby-traps the mine so that Leatherjack is buried in a cave-in, he unknowingly kills the older of the runaway sisters as well. Feeling responsible for the younger girl, Leven and Susanna decide to run away with her, whom Leven christens "A.B." from Ransome, taking Thirty with them. Will sets out separately. Their destination is a vague location somewhere to the north, known as Colony—perhaps Scotland. There, according to rumor, people "don't use others like no-good machines."

Thirty is shot to death, probably due to Will's connivance. Nevertheless Leven, Susanna, A.B., and Will travel on. Susanna stops at the first homelike place they find. Will sets off to join a group of clever men on the northernmost coast of Scotland who are reportedly trying to "find the way back to the stars." Only Leven and A.B. reach the Colony, where A.B. is adopted into a family from her home area of Britain, and Leven decides to become a keeper of "Swallowdale sheep waiting like white stars for his hands, on the green universe, the mountain."

NOTES

In Mace's dystopia, human relationships are governed by greed, suspicion, and sadism. The book's original English title, *Ransome Revisited*, symbolizes the importance of Arthur Ransome's *Swallowdale*, which tantalizes Susanna and Leven with the thought that somewhere things may be better, if only they will dare to strike out. The "somewhere" which is found at the close suggests that the alternative to dystopia is pastoral utopia.

With so proactive a theme, one might wish for a style less repetitive and abstract, for a more cohesive plot, and for characters who grow a bit wiser from their experiences. For example, Susanna, always the model of determination and resourcefulness, lapses almost gratefully into dependence at the first available refuge. On the other hand, each character presents a different and intriguing blend (as said of Will) of "corruption and truth walking in one body."

A similar feeling of finding the best among a set of very limited choices is common to this novel and *No Man's Land* by Watson. Both are 1975 British books, both with the Greenwillow imprint, both dystopian. However, *Out There* is apparently a situation of autonomous local control, while *No Man's Land* depicts a nationally planned welfare state.

MacGregor, Ellen and Dora Pantell. **Miss Pickerell Meets Mr. H.U.M.** New York: McGraw-Hill, 1974. 160p. Archway paperback, 1980. Grades 3-6.

SUMMARY

In a lighthearted vein, Miss Pickerell demonstrates that even the fainthearted can muster courage to stop a computer takeover of the world. It was bad enough when a computer telephoned Miss Pickerell to demand that she pay $490.96 for a $0.69 pair of knitting needles for which she had already paid cash. But when every house in Square Toe City has been painted dark brown, every family is limited to one animal and, finally, all animals over eight years of age are to be killed by order of a computer, then Miss Pickerell goes into action.

She tries her friend the Governor first, with little success. Then she accompanies Mr. Humwhistel and Deputy Administrator Blakeley to a meeting of scientists in the City of Progress where traffic lights do not work, the river is a morass of trash and oil, and one dump truck fills an excavation as quickly as another empties it. Just as the scientists conclude that the Highest Universal Monitor, Mr. H.U.M., is already carrying out its program to destroy the world, Miss Pickerell's nephew Euphus, assisted by his teacher, changes the computer program cards in Square Toe County, thereby averting disaster. Once assured that Euphus had not done anything wrong and that the mad scientist who had programmed Mr. H.U.M. was not anyone she knew, Miss Pickerell enjoys the party held in her honor.

NOTES

Although *Mr. H.U.M.* is the most futuristic of the Miss Pickerell books, the series is more properly regarded as fantasy. Nevertheless, this quickly read volume may be useful to compare with more serious and realistic novels dealing with machine takeover.

---

*Malzberg, Barry. **Conversations.** Indianapolis: Bobbs-Merrill, 1973. 89p. Grade 8 up.

SUMMARY

In the final analysis, the theme of this novelette is nihilistic. On the one hand Dal, the narrator, declares: "I will tell the truth and I will know the truth and I will change the world." But after the Elders have fallen and the towers have been opened, life changes very little, and Dal is "happy after a fashion" (pp. 84, 89).

Dal lives in the twenty-second century in a 40-story Domicile which encloses 6,000 living units. His group consists of his Group mate, Narn, and two other couples. Dal has formed a friendship outside his group; he has been meeting from time to time with Lothar, who tells him of the past which neither the Elders nor the teaching simulator will discuss. Lothar is spoken of as crazy and finally is sentenced to Exile, but before he leaves, he gives his scrapbooks about history to Dal. Others in the complex know about the history, too, and finally the Elders lose their power.

NOTES

The Domicile is a dystopian society within which one is conditioned to seek comfort from and give comfort to one's Group, reporting any difficulties in frequent interviews with the Elders. The scenes are disjointed and the narrator is sometimes even out of touch with himself, speaking and acting in ways he does not expect or understand. As a consequence, the book is indexed under "Surrealism" in Part IV.

Mark, Jan. **The Ennead.** New York: Crowell, 1978. 306p. Pocket Books paperback, 1980. Grade 8 up.

SUMMARY

This novel brings a message of nihilism, of failure with perhaps a bit of comfort in the traditions of one's people or in contact with a genuine, if abrasive, human being. The story takes place in the nine-planet system for which it is named. Deformed creature that he is, Isaac can hope to remain on the forbidding planet Erato only at the sufferance of his adopted brother, Theodore. He has nowhere else to go. Thinking to gain Theodore's gratitude, Isaac arranges for a woman sculptor to be brought from the overpopulated planet Euterpe. But Eleanor, the sculptor, turns out to be headstrong and singularly unattractive. Moreover, she strikes up a romance with Moshe, a gardener and a Jew. She violates nearly every legal and social restriction, of which there are many, bringing Theodore's anger on herself, Isaac, and Moshe. The latter is taken for deportation. Finally, throwing away his last hope of survival, Isaac helps Eleanor escape into the mountains.

NOTES

Isaac is an anti-hero in this surrealistic novel. Scenes shift, attitudes change, people seem deliberately to misunderstand one another. If this is the sort of self-demeaning and dishonest behavior which will be required to survive on a colonial planet, there will be few space pioneers. Students might discuss the author's purpose in the novel, and the relationship between style and intent. Finally, the significance of Moshe's rebellious demonstration of his Jewish heritage might be explored, as well as Isaac's conscious choice against survival.

---

*Martel, Suzanne. **The City Under Ground.** New York: Viking, 1964. 159p. Archway paperback, 1970. Grades 4-7.

SUMMARY

In this adventure story in the year 3000, the underground city of Surréal, near present-day Montreal, is experiencing a frightening loss of electrical power. Bernard 6B12 works his way through the narrow underground tunnels and discovers that the electric lines have been tapped; apparently others survived the war which destroyed the earth's surface a thousand years earlier. Bernard is trapped when he collapses a part of the tunnel in the face of the onrushing enemy; his brother Eric rescues him.

Meanwhile, Eric's friend Luke has found an opening to the now livable surface of the earth and has met Agatha, member of still another group living outside. Luke takes one of the new Upsilon ray machines to help Agatha's people survive a smallpox epidemic, but falls and injures himself so that his older brother, Paul, must come to his rescue. Paul, though threatened with loss of his citizenship, persuades his father and ultimately the Council to establish contact with Agatha's people.

NOTES

A well-constructed picture of life underground, noting the many restrictions necessary in such circumstances, this novel is a tale of survival and willingness to take risks. Technology is well-advanced in Surréal and life is orderly and pleasant. This novel might well be compared with Eldridge's *Shadow of the Gloom-World*, in which a group has been driven underground in similar circumstances, but has somehow lost all understanding of the machines which keep them alive and so live in fear under quite primitive circumstances.

McCaffrey, Anne. **Dragonsong**. New York: Atheneum, 1977. 262p. Bantam, 1977.
Grade 6 up.
McCaffrey, Anne. **Dragonsinger**. New York: Atheneum, 1978. 264p. Bantam, 1978.
Grade 6 up.

SUMMARY

Self-fulfillment, following one's own drummer, is the theme of these novels. In this case, the major barrier to be overcome is the community conviction that the occupation of Harper is inappropriate for a girl.

Nearly a thousand years have passed since colonists from Terra first settled Pern, the third planet circling Rukbat. Their one great danger is Threadfall, which occurs over a period of several years when the Red Star comes close—once every two centuries. Protection is provided by dragonriders astride beasts native to Pern—they destroy the hungry threads while other people remain indoors.

Menolly is the daughter of Sea Holder Yanus of Half-Circle Sea Hold, a small, isolated fishing community. She has learned all the old songs from their Harper, Petiron, and teaches the children after his death until a new Harper can be found. But then her family is ashamed, even cruel to her, and she runs away. Nearly caught in a Threadfall, she is rescued by a dragonrider and taken to Benden Weyr, his home. With her come nine fire lizards, small versions of the great dragons, whom she unknowingly Impressed at their birth, so that they will never be long parted from her. The small creatures have limited telepathic powers, far less than the mighty and intelligent dragons. But they have learned to sing with Menolly, so she comes to the attention of the Masterharper of all Pern. When it is discovered that she is the apprentice whose compositions old Petiron had sent to the Masterharper, Menolly is invited to Harper Hall, where all the Harpers in Pern are trained.

The second novel opens with Menolly's arrival at Harper Hall, where she faces jealous girls and demanding, sometimes harsh, teachers. The entire novel covers scarcely more than a week, at the end of which Menolly is advanced from apprentice to journeyman and, more important, accepts her own talents on an equal footing with the male students.

NOTES

Without the foreword to *Dragonsong*, one could scarcely regard these as futuristic novels. The people of Pern, for all that their ancestors arrived in a spaceship, have no space age technology, neither are we told how they may have lost it. Furthermore, their legends and ballads do not, apparently, speak of that arrival or recall earlier generations on Terra. The story dramatizes adaptation to a new situation by making use of local resources and finding protection against unanticipated dangers. Biology and psychology fans will be interested in the use of "Imprinting" as the means by which human beings adopt their dragon companions of either size.

The books are exceptionally well written, especially as to literary style and well-developed characterization. They may be compared with other planet colonization novels, such as Engdahl's more realistic *This Star Shall Abide* and its sequel on the one hand, and Snyder's fantasylike trilogy (*Below the Root*, etc.) on the other.

A third book in the series, *Dragondrums*, focuses on the boy Premier, casting Menolly in a supporting role. No reference is made to existence on another world so that, taken by itself, the book is pure fantasy.

McGowen, Tom. **Odyssey from River Bend**. Boston: Little Brown, 1975. 166p.
Grades 5-7.

SUMMARY

The theme of this novel is the value of curiosity and, hence, scientific inquiry. Some time in the distant future, after the disappearance of the Long Ago Ones, the earth is inhabited by talking animals—some living in huts behind protective walls, others in the wild, each group scorning the other. A few of these animals can read, and dream of one day recovering the lost knowledge of the Long Ago Ones so as to overcome illness and seasonal hunger and cold. Among these is the now-aged badger, Kippatuk.

One day two of Kippatuk's pupils, young raccoons, find a relic of the Long Ago Ones, a container which turns out to hold a book. All during the particularly difficult winter which follows, Kippatuk studies the book, and in the spring he announces that he has decided to set out for the Haunted Land to find a storehouse in which the Long Ago Ones had kept all their knowledge.

After two harrowing experiences, one with a grizzly bear and the other with attacking eagles, Kippatuk and several companions reach the Haunted Land, a city partly buried under dirt and plant growths and now inhabited by chimpanzees. The latter describe the fate of the Long Ago Ones. Traditions tell that the animals who had called themselves "humans" had crowded and polluted their world until they realized something must be done. Some blamed their magic, called "science," and wanted to stop using it. Others argued that science could be used to solve the problems, but this viewpoint lost. So their old spells were forgotten and their magic was lost.

But the spirits of sickness, drought, hunger, and pain grew powerful. It was too late for the Long Ago Ones to recover their magic, so they died. Little by little plants, and then animals, spread over the earth.

Now, however, there is hope that the animals may be able to regain some of that same magic, for Kippatuk finds, and the chimpanzees are able to gain entrance to, a building inscribed with two words whose meaning he does not know, except that knowledge is kept there. The words are "Public Library."

NOTES

This story may be regarded as an extended fable on the Francis Bacon quotation which appears on the flyleaf: "Knowledge is power." The animals will move from wondering to science as humans had once done (Emerson quotation, also on the flyleaf). But they are determined to take care not to repeat the mistakes of the Long Ago Ones. A question to consider: Is there too much suspense connected with the two words that appear on the storehouse of knowledge, so that they come as an anti-climax? Note that in the final analysis it was abandonment, not misuse, of technology that led to the death of the Long Ago Ones.

Morressy, John. **The Drought on Ziax II**. Illus. by Stanley Skardinski. New York: Walker, 1978. 77p. Grades 3-6.

SUMMARY

The theme of this sequel to *The Humans of Ziax II* is strong and clear: Disturb the balance of nature to your peril. In this instance, the unanticipated by-product of the Earth Pioneers' wanton destruction of the monsters called sork is proliferation of an orange grass which absorbs moisture from everything it touches. The grass overruns the planet, causing a drought, crop failure, and withering of many food-bearing wild gampal trees.

Toren, a human boy, and Rilmat, his friend among the native Imbur, accompany a search party seeking water. The boys are attacked by the orange grass and saved by Toren's father, thus healing a rift between the two species. Rilmat recognizes the orange grass as sorkampal, food-of-the-sork, when he sees it growing on a small scale in the human scientists' laboratory. It is but one step from that to a realization that a natural balance can be restored only by nurturing the sork. Six specimens are found in a remote area, but they are already entwined by orange sorkampal. Humans cut down the grass, then Imbur use their chant to put the sork to sleep. Not only will the drought be alleviated, but also the humans have accepted the Imbur nonviolent method of dealing with the dangerous sork.

NOTES

A short, quickly read book, *The Drought on Ziax II* exemplifies the balance-of-nature theme clearly and simply. Therefore, it might be read first among the several titles listed under that heading in the index. Although one wonders why it took so long for the Imbur to recognize the sorkampal—Rilmat's explanation is a bit weak—the plot in general moves logically.

The novel's simplicity precludes complex characterization. Nevertheless, a secondary theme—human-alien relationships—may generate discussion. No need to belabor the symbolism, since the two groups are referred to as "races" (e.g., pp. 21, 54). Differences in language ("body of water," pp. 11-15), customs when sleeping outdoors (pp. 20-21, 62-64), and convictions regarding violence for self-protection (pp. 27-31, 75-77) are explored and at least partly resolved. *See* notes on Hoover's *The Lost Star* for other novels that deal with human-alien communication.

Morressy, John. **The Humans of Ziax II**. Illus. by Stanley Skardinski. New York: Walker, 1974. 62p. Grades 3-6.

SUMMARY

This brief story is a statement in favor of nonviolence on the ground that all creatures have a right to life. Toren, son of the commander of the human settlement on Ziax II, falls from an air-sled and is rescued and cared for by the Imbur. These beings resemble humans, but have six fingers and no nose. They are able to control the sork, dangerous animals during their breeding season, with a hypnotic chant. They rescue the humans from the sork and return Toren to his family with the charge of teaching them the Imbur way.

NOTES

The author's message is clearly stated, although the narrative suffers some from controlled vocabulary and sentence structure. *See* notes on Hoover's *The Lost Star* for other novels that deal with human-alien communication.

Morressy, John. **The Windows of Forever**. Illus. by Allen Atkinson. New York: Walker, 1975. 86p. Grades 4-7.

SUMMARY

Time travel stories inspire reflections on the nature of time. In this story, Thomas Gavin Bridger meets himself in various settings and in various ages. First he finds himself in the time of the mammoths, involved with a battle to defeat the teggloks. Then he journeys to the year 2860 A.D. where he helps to overcome the invading Kiv-Koorosh. In both cases he meets his older self, "Uncle Gavin," for whom these events have happened in reverse sequence. In between, he takes a brief trip to the year 3323, when everything has fallen to ruins. Finally, Gavin returns home and resolves to study to be a doctor so that he can return to the time of the mammoths with the ability to save his Uncle, or alter ego, who lies seriously wounded by a tegglok.

NOTES

At least three different Gavins are involved in this story—one a 70-year-old man, one about 20, and the narrator of the story, "Tommy," about 12. Young readers with a philosophical bent of mind will enjoy reflecting on the idea presented here, different from the assumption in many time travel stories that whatever happens in time travel to the past changes the time traveler in the present and future, rather than creating multiple "versions" of the same person. Some of the "science" in the story would bear checking as a student project.

Myers, Walter Dean. **Brainstorm**. Photos by Chuck Freedman. New York: Watts, 1977. 90p. Dell paperback, 1979. Grades 5-7.

SUMMARY

This adventure story pits man against computer. Human minds are being stolen by a ray from the distant planet Suffes, leaving the victims behaving like infants. A crew of 15-year-olds sets out toward the planet, expecting to go through time warp and therefore age to 30 by the time they reach their destination in three days' Earth time. But they are drawn in by the power of the computer which is emitting the mind-stealing ray, and so they must face the enemy as teenagers. Their task is made the more difficult by the fact that any strong emotion, such as anger or fear, makes them vulnerable to the ray. They find that the reason the computer is stealing human minds is to have material to present on screens for the entertainment of the Suffesians, whose lives are so regulated by the computer that they have lost all powers of creativity. After two failures, the teenagers find a way to disable the computer.

NOTES

The controlled vocabulary and sentence structure are very obvious in this story. Students may find it interesting to check out some of the science assumptions built into the story, and to study the photographs to see how the effects were created. They may wish to use some of the same techniques to create a story of their own. The photos, but not the text, indicate that the crew is ethnically mixed.

---

*Nelson, O. T. **The Girl Who Owned a City**. Minneapolis: Lerner, 1975. 179p. Dell paperback, 1977. Grades 6-9.

SUMMARY

"*Earning* the values for your life is more than just something, it is everything!" (p. 108). This libertarian motto becomes Lisa's guiding principle as she assumes the leadership role in planning for the survival of the children in her neighborhood when everyone over the age of 12 is struck dead by a plague. She thinks of visiting a farm, and then a grocery warehouse for supplies. She puts Craig in charge of the defense of their street. Although she loses her spirit for a week or so when her house is burned to the ground by a raiding gang, soon Lisa finds herself again able to "think of something."

She takes over the large high school building nearby and establishes a city which is open to children who will promise to contribute their share of the work and not to use force offensively. True to her beliefs, Lisa owns the city, and, although she has a council for advice, she makes all the final decisions. The city is briefly taken over by the Chidester gang, but Lisa regains her city with the help of the children who have come to look to her for encouragement and logical planning.

NOTES

A genuine utopia, this novel was written to demonstrate the values of libertarian philosophy in a situation young people might understand. This idea overshadows development of plot and characters, and may account for the underplaying of the immediate horrors of a world filled with dead bodies. Students interested in the theme of the novel will find it restated in the story of the king's advice for happiness which Lisa tells her younger brother, Todd (pp. 105-109). Apart from the libertarian idea, the novel reinforces the conviction that human beings, even at the age of 11 or 12, can survive in the face of disaster. The time setting is the immediate future.

---

*Norton, André. **Android at Arms.** New York: Harcourt, Brace Jovanovich, 1971. 253p. Grade 7 up.

SUMMARY

Adventure and intrigue are the mainstay of this novel, which comes to a close never having resolved the enigma which troubles its main character: is he human or android?

As the story opens, six prisoners, five men and a woman, are freed when an electric storm disables their robot-operated prison. Each a prince or other leader, they realize they may have been captive for periods ranging to nearly 80 years, yet they have not aged. And what has happened in their various realms? One of their number is a Veep, a Thieves' Guild boss, who reluctantly reveals that each of the others was probably replaced by an android programmed to obey the will of a group known as the Psychocrats, who want to control all the peoples of the galaxy.

The group commandeers an auto-guided supply ship, expecting to land on the planet Inyanga, home of Imperial Prince Andas Kastor. However, the Veep has switched tapes to take them to a guild port. When they land, he is astonished to find the port buildings long overgrown with vegetation. The Veep runs into the underbrush and that night is killed by a savage beast. The elderly Tsiwon, whose android double had apparently betrayed his nation, dies of a heart condition. The remaining four go to Inyanga, where they successfully penetrate the Triple Towers, Prince Andas' palace. Elys, the reptilian woman, attempts to betray Andas to the guards, but is killed along with the self-serving Grasty. Thus, only Andas and the feline Lord Yolyos remain alive to unravel the mystery of their imprisonment. Using secret passages known only to himself and his now-deceased father, Andas confronts the daughter of this impostor, and then the Emperor Andas himself. Androids, of course, cannot have children, but young Andas thinks the princess must have been passed off as the android's daughter. When he sees the emperor, however, and sees how he is aging despite a rejuvenation treatment, doubts assail him. Moreover, the emperor tells him that the Psychocrats' scheme had been uncovered and their headquarters taken, but no one had believed the tale of android doubles. So, the emperor surmises, young Andas is the android. Yet the young man has been able to take from its hiding place the key to a vault in the temple, a key which no one not of the royal house can touch with impunity. Who, then, is the android? Young Andas barely escapes capture and he and Yolyos hide again, while young Andas plans a way to get to the temple with the sacred key.

Suddenly, however, the pair is catapulted into a parallel world where he replaces another Andas, mortally wounded, and, after using that same key to unlock a similar vault in a similar temple, conquers the evil Old Woman who threatens this world as she threatens his own. If Andas is an android, no one, not even the doctors, can tell, so in this parallel world he remains as emperor.

NOTES

Whether Andas is human, or an android so nearly human that no one can tell the difference, is never fully resolved. If the six prisoners are androids whose creators had been conquered, then who sends the supply ships to their prison? And why does the real Tsiwon turn traitor while his android double remembers that he was to prevent the takeover by the Jauavum Empire? On the other hand, if the six are humans, then how can Andas's android double grow older or father three children?

The plot which occupies more than half of the novel is never concluded. Instead, the protagonist and his companion, together with two talismans—the key and a ring of evil power taken from the First Daughter of Emperor Andas—move into another plot, and another battle. Students might imagine a sequel in which young Andas eventually returns to or contacts the first galaxy and somehow resolves that conflict. They might discuss whether this joining of two plots is, or is not, an effective literary technique.

Some fantasy elements intertwine with futurism in this novel, most notably the possibility of creating a human android, and the witchlike powers of the Old Woman and her female devotees. André Norton has, of course, written many novels that are totally fantasy, rather than science fiction. As we shall see in the following discussions of her more futuristic books, she often combines fantasy and science fiction, sometimes to the degree that it is difficult to categorize a book as either one or the other.

Norton, André. **Breed to Come**. New York: Viking, 1972. 285p. Ace paperback, 1973. Grade 7 up.

SUMMARY

The interrelationship of environment and technology, and the problems and promises of interspecies cooperation are woven into this adventure story. Some 500 years after many humans had departed this polluted planet in spaceships, Earth is populated by four intelligent species: the feline "People," canine Barkers, rodent Rattons, and boarlike Tuskers. All four have developed from laboratory animals which mutated into larger, intelligent forms as a result of the same disease which had wiped out the remaining humans—a disease they created in their efforts to rehabilitate Earth.

Gammage, a particularly intelligent and long-lived feline, has dared to enter the lairs of the humans, or "Demons," and is gradually penetrating their secrets. Some of his finds are suitable for life in the caves, and these he sends back to the People from time to time. Gammage fears the Demons will return and urges an alliance with Tuskers and Barkers—though not including the treacherous Rattons. But an alliance with Barkers, who compete with the People for the same food supply, is a proposal so unthinkable that Gammage's own clan breaks off contact with him. His descendant Furtig, however, having lost his metal claws through defeat in the Trials of the unmated warriors, sets off to join Gammage in the Demon's lairs.

Furtig rescues two of the People from the Rattons, who lurk in the lower passageways of the city, before he finally reaches Gammage and joins forces with him. Furtig begins to learn along with the younglings, but soon after his arrival a spaceship lands, carrying a scouting crew of four Demons. These four have come to learn why their ancestors had left Earth—for the records had been deliberately destroyed—and to find, if possible, a means to counteract a lethal Cloud they had accidentally created and which was spreading inexorably across the surface of their new planet.

One of the humans goes mad and joins the Rattons, showing them how to activate powerful Demon weapons. The People, Barkers, and Tuskers combine forces with the three other humans and win the battle, though much of the city is destroyed. As the humans leave, promising never to return, they warn the People and their allies to develop their own technology in harmony with their way of life—else they will repeat the human errors.

NOTES

The notion of mutated cats, dogs, boars, and rats, if a bit far-fetched, nevertheless has the quality of reality rather than fantasy. The dangers of misunderstood and misused technology are clearly shown in Earth's history and in the new danger on the planet from which the scouts have come. The solution, however, is not proposed until Ayana's parting words, when she warns the People not to adopt technology they have not themselves developed.

A secondary theme is less obvious. Ayana speaks of Gammage saying, "He taught you that against a common enemy you can speak with Barkers under a truce flag, gather and unite tribes and clans. Remember that above all else, for if he had only done that much, Gammage would be the greatest of your race." (p. 287). Some modes of diplomacy had preceded Gammage's move, however, and readers might trace this development.

One could propose a number of sequels, following either the humans or the felines. Or one might reconstruct the state of science and society at the time disaster struck, for the "Demons'" technology had certainly advanced well beyond our own. Again, what might other species be like after similar mutations? The author's imagination stimulates our own speculation.

The People, Barkers, Tuskers and humans experience difficulty in understanding one another, but finally achieve some measure of trust and cooperation. Other novels which deal with such communications barriers are listed in the notes to Hoover's *The Lost Star*.

Norton, André. **Dark Piper**. New York: Harcourt, Brace & World, 1968. 249p. Grade 7 up.

SUMMARY

Survival is the predominant theme in this novel. The Four Sectors War is over; home to Beltane comes wounded Griss Lugard with rights to Butte Hold as his pension. Also roaming space are the ships of homeless refugees, some determined to take over a planet, rather than share it. Three such ships come to Beltane, trying to destroy it with bombs and germ warfare, but the latter backfires, killing those who unleashed it. Griss Lugard manages to save the lives of the half dozen young people of Kyvnet, though he himself dies in the attempt.

Thereafter Vere Collis becomes the leader. First the group escapes from the lava caves where Griss had taken them. They travel across the Reserves for animal mutants, some of whom are both intelligent and hostile. They gradually realize that they are the sole human survivors on the planet except for four of the refugees, who succumb to the virus even as they trail Vere and Thad. The group takes refuge in Butte Hold, venturing forth to raise crops and gain supplies, and to repair secretly the robots of the mutant animals in hopes of eventually making friendly contact. The book concludes three years after the disaster, as the group continues to struggle for survival.

NOTES

Something of a space age *Swiss Family Robinson*, this novel holds interest both because of the struggle to survive and because for some time the characters (and the reader) are unsure of the fate of their families and the other settlers. The first person narrative captures a bit of that Arthurian style which is appropriate in so many of Norton's novels, yet seems a trifle out of place here. By contrast with *Breed to Come*, which praises peacemakers, *Dark Piper* describes the awful consequences of trusting those whose only motivation is greed. It also demonstrates that many humans—though not all—can accept even the most dreadful experiences and move on to do whatever is required to carry on.

Norton, André and Michael Gilbert. **The Day of the Ness.** Illus. by Michael Gilbert. New York: Walker, 1975. 119p. Dell paperback, 1976. Grades 3-6.

SUMMARY

Cooperation is the theme of this story, which takes place ten years after the first alien landing on Earth. Until now, no one has seen the mysterious aliens who apparently live within a hill, making contact only to leave curious objects on the "trading rock" in exchange for such items as small tools. Even that contact broke off a year ago when two boys shot at the aliens just when they were about to reveal themselves to the personnel of the Project built to protect and learn about these visitors.

Now, however, the aliens call on Hal to help them defeat the evil Ness, also aliens, who plan to conquer the earth, making humans their slaves. The Ness have the upper hand because they have captured the Great Think-Think, without whose direction the Rav, the Clusters, and the Stalkers and Floaters—who act as the mouth, the eyes, and the hands of the alien group—cannot develop a plan. But working together to carry out Hal's plan, the aliens force the Ness to leave Earth with no means of return.

NOTES

Life in the U.S. has changed only minimally at the time of this story, which illustrates both suspicious and accepting attitudes toward aliens. The notion of several separate beings who function as parts of a disjointed body is the imaginative element bordering on fantasy in an otherwise simple adventure yarn.

Norton, André. **Forerunner Foray.** New York: Viking, 1973. 286p. Ace paperback, 1975. Grade 7 up.

SUMMARY

What would we learn if we could trace the history of an ancient, mysterious object? Ziantha, a psychic who serves a feline veep in the Thieves' Guild, begins to follow such an object, a gem encased in a rough stone, first to its planet of origin, then to the tomb in which it had been buried. Suddenly she is Vintra, warrior, chained within the tomb of Lord Turan. Another psychic has been catapulted through time into Turan's body. Together they try to find the mate to Ziantha's gem, which is a focus stone carrying residual power from centuries of use by psychics. To find it, Ziantha must enter still another body, that of D'Eyree, who controls the Lurla, the snails who build and repair her amphibian people's wall against the sea. Ziantha succeeds in carrying the second stone back to her own time, where she joins forces with the psychic she had known as Turan to pursue the history of the Forerunners.

NOTES

This mystery depends heavily upon psychic powers: telepathy, possession, and coercion. Hundreds of generations after the First Wave of settlers lift Terra, Earth's history is but a dim legend. Other peoples, too, have faded into oblivion; these are the Forerunners. The history of one of these groups is the mystery which Ziantha partially unravels, amid intrigues of Thieves' Guild and jack traders, law enforcement by the Patrol, and investigations of the reptilian Zacathans, whose passion is to be historians of the universe.

Norton, André. **Ice Crown.** New York: Viking, 1970. 256p. Grade 7 up.

SUMMARY

A tale of intrigue lightly touched with romance, *Ice Crown* also carries the theme that freedom means individual freedom to make choices. Roane Hume is the junior member of a team of three scientists who land on Clio, one of the now-defeated Psychocrats' experimental planets where humans with false implanted memories had been left to find a way to civilization—or to fail. Since no one knows how the truth would affect these involuntary colonists, they are sealed from outside contact. Roane's team lands on a secret mission to locate rumored evidence that the Forerunners—half-legendary space travelers whose history has been lost—had left artifacts on the planet.

The trio lands in the Kingdom of Reveny, where Roane, despite the prohibition against contacting the planet's inhabitants, almost immediately becomes involved with helping Princess Ludorica. Caught in a rainstorm, Roane takes shelter in a tower which also attracts the Princess and her captors, who have kidnapped her for Duke Reddick, rival for the throne. Roane helps the girl escape. The pair stumbles into an underground mind-control installation which, Roane realizes, must have been left by the Psychocrats to direct the inhabitants, or at least the rulers of Clio. Trapped by a mudslide, Roane signals her team for help. When opportunity comes, Roane again helps Ludorica leave the explorers' camp and reach her kinsman, Colonel Nelis Imfry, who in turn spirits the two girls across the border to a neighboring kingdom, where Ludorica hopes to find help in exchange for a suitable marriage alliance. Again captured, Ludorica comes under the influence of the ice crown and her ambitious cousin, Reddick. It is up to Nelis and Roane to alter the course of events. Eventually, Roane destroys the mind-control installation. Then, having violated the rules of her own people, she finds herself quite ready to adapt to life on Clio when her partners take to space without her. Nelis Imfry's encouragement certainly helps her accept her fate.

NOTES

Two choices reflect the theme of the novel. In one case, a choice is made to destroy the Psychocrats' installation despite the risk of driving all the citizens mad by its abrupt cessation. In the second instance, Roane decides to stay on Clio, thus asserting her right to abandon one way of life for another. The novel might be compared with Engdahl's *Enchantress from the Stars*, in which Elana, faced with a choice similar to Roane's, makes the opposite decision.

Norton, André. **Iron Cage.** New York: Viking, 1974. 288p. Ace paperback, 1976.
    Grade 7 up.

SUMMARY

The theme of *Iron Cage* is set forth in the quotation which serves as its preface: that man must "remove hate and fear from his heart" and acknowledge the "fundamental bond of affinity and affection" which unites all life forms, human and animal.

On a spaceship, humans had been handled as experimental laboratory animals by "the Big Ones." A human woman, her seven-year-old son Jony, and unborn twins, escape from the ship just before it takes off. Large bearlike aliens native to the planet adopt the defenseless humans and, when the mother dies several years later, assume the care of the three children. The aliens, who call themselves the People, communicate with the children by sign language. The People know, and eventually the children discover when they see paintings in underground tunnels, that humans had once landed and used the People as animals, controlling them with painful collars. Thinking Jony now intends to do the same, the People put one of those collars on his neck and leave him to fend for himself.

At this juncture a spaceship lands. Its human crew captures the twins and four of the People. They subject the latter to various tests after determining that they are of subhuman intelligence. Jony, too, is captured by the space crew and finds two of the People in the laboratory, held with metal bands and wires. Remembering his own experience as an animal, Jony becomes enraged and uses his powers of psychic control to help them escape along with Maba, the girl twin. Meanwhile Geogee, the boy, is taking some of the space crew to the tunnels which hold, besides paintings, boxes of ray-guns. Jony succeeds in preventing discovery of those weapons and in disabling the spaceship so its crew must remain stranded on this planet.

NOTES

The theme of the novel is underlined not only by the opening quotation, but also by a brief prologue set on Earth in our time in which a pregnant cat is thrown onto a dump, and an epilogue in which she and her newborn kittens are rescued by a boy who tells his friend, "I just have a feeling we've got to learn how to live so everything has a fair chance." Jony's experience as a mere animal of the Big Ones, and the Peoples' as former animals controlled by humans, are to be construed as parallel to the cat's plight. The unspoken moral is the Golden Rule: "Do unto others as you would have others do unto you."

The mysteries of the stone place left by the humans who had controlled the People are not unravelled. Finally, one wonders whether Jony will ever establish contact with the men now marooned. Students may wish to try tying these loose ends together through writing of their own. They might also critique the plot structure, including Jony's nearly incredible feat of disarming the spaceship.

The problems of alien-human communication are explored as the People and Jony interrelate. Other novels which treat this topic are listed in the notes to Hoover's *The Lost Star*.

___

Norton, André. **Moon of Three Rings**. New York: Viking, 1966. 316p. Grade 7 up.
Norton, André. **Exiles of the Stars**. New York: Viking, 1971. 255p. Grade 7 up.

SUMMARY

An adventure story on a distant, feudal planet, *Moon of Three Rings* makes heavy use of psychic powers. The Korburg Combine, a monopolistic trading entity, hopes to take control of the planet Yiktor as a base and supply depot by helping Osokun, a local lord, who will reign under its control. Krip Vorlund, Free Trader, is caught in this intrigue because Osokun's men hope to wring information about sophisticated weaponry from him, or failing that, to obtain such information in exchange for his release. Therefore, when Krip helps Maelen, a Thassa woman, rescue a mistreated animal, he is arrested. The arrest is but a ruse; in fact, he has been kidnapped. However, Krip is unable to reveal what he knows about the weapons because he is under mind lock, and he escapes before he can be ransomed.

Because she is obligated to Krip for his help, Maelen is summoned by Molastor, the spirit she serves, to help Krip reach the space port. First she exchanges his spirit with that of a barsk (animal), so that when Osokun's soldiers recapture Krip's body, he appears to have gone mad. Since Yiktor custom requires that a madman be delivered to a valley to be cared for by the priests of Umphra, Maelen intends to follow the soldiers and then, after they leave "Krip" with the priests, to exchange the two spirits again. Her plan is foiled when Osokun's father intervenes and, rejecting his son's intrigues, tries to avert the death penalty Osokun has incurred by returning Krip's insane shell to the Traders, along with an offer of money in recompense for the madness inflicted on him.

Krip, in the barsk's body, sets out in a frenzy toward the city, hoping only to find his body, though uncertain as to how to regain it. Meanwhile, war has broken out as the Combine tries to subjugate the planet by force. Krip encounters Maelen's co-worker, Malec, who convinces him that they must wait for Maelen, but soldiers of the now-outlawed Osokun set upon them, killing Malec.

Still, Maelen is obligated to help Krip. She travels with him to the valley of the insane and trades Krip's spirit into the body of a Thassa which has been inhabited by an animal spirit. In this form, Krip journeys to the port consul, even though his captain has lifted off to avoid being captured in the war. He hopes his ship will return long enough for him to change bodies, but learns that his body had died in the take-off. Krip, therefore, continues to live in the body of the Thassa. Meanwhile, Maelen has been taken captive. She is wounded and, to escape death, she, too, enters the body of an animal. In this form she accompanies Krip as he resumes his life as a Free Trader.

The sequel, *Exiles of the Stars*, finds Krip and Maelen, the latter still living in an animal body, traveling with the Free Traders. They land on Thoth, one of a five-planet system named for ancient Terran Egyptian gods, and enter into a contract to deliver certain treasures to the planet Ptah for safekeeping during civil war. However, the priest sent with them sabotages the ship, forcing it to land instead on uninhabited Sekhmet.

Here, as it turns out, are entombed the preserved bodies of four rulers of a long-gone civilization—perhaps forerunners of our ancient Egyptians. Still dwelling in each body is at least part of a living spirit seeking to inhabit another body so as to preserve its own. Three of the rulers exchange bodies with three crew members, then supervise a crew of "robos" and psychically controlled jack traders in loading the temple treasures of Sekhmet aboard a trade ship. After several psychic battles for control of the body or life force of Krip, herself, and others, Maelen finally regains human form by exchanging bodies with the queen. The crew members are restored to their original bodies and become wealthy with the planet's treasures.

NOTES

In these novels, Norton uses quasi-feudal style; students might identify examples of sentence structure and word order which create that impression. First person narration alternates between Krip and Maelen, the name of the narrator appearing at each change (*Moon*) or at the head of each chapter (*Exiles*). This shift of viewpoint increases the complexity of an already complex plot. Since the same incident is occasionally described by both characters, students may see some of the effects created by an author's choice of viewpoint character.

In *Moon of Three Rings* much of Krip's attention focuses on identity—what part of each mind-body combination he experiences is his essential self? Maelen, on the other hand, is largely preoccupied with unwinding her responsibilities as a wielder of psychic powers, a "Moon Singer." Since the planet is feudal, much of what occurs could have easily been placed in a fantasy world, but spaceships, interplanetary trade, and alien beings create a futuristic aura.

Exiles of the Stars is far closer to fantasy than its predecessor. The uninhabited planet Sekhmet could be a fantasy world, since spaceships, robots, and laser guns are but incidental to the central focus on psychic coercion and possession of alien bodies. Explanation such as we might expect in genuine science fiction is not provided. For example, the bit of guessing about the mechanism of the dead body housed in a freezing case which broadcasts psychic force through an amplifier does not begin to explain its operation or use. Neither are we told what interest the four rulers have in removing the temple treasures from Sekhmet. This second novel, then, is less useful than the first as a world-future image.

Norton, André. **Night of Masks.** New York: Harcourt, Brace & World, 1964. 191p.
    Grade 7 up.

SUMMARY

A scary adventure tale with a happy ending, *Night of Masks* is the story of Nik Kolheine, orphaned and disfigured when a spaceship had crashed in enemy territory on a barren moon. Now grown to young manhood, Nik has a chance to escape from the Dipple, something like a ghetto for lost souls like himself, and to acquire a new face by plastic surgery. This opportunity requires, however, that he kidnap a boy for the Thieves' Guild, meanwhile pretending to be the boy's fantasy companion, Hacon.

Nik kidnaps Vandy and they reach the dismal surface of Dis, a nightmare planet under an infrared sun, only to find that Guild members are quarreling among themselves. Why Nik was to spirit Vandy away never becomes clear, but Nik saves the boy's life more than once from the creatures, humanoids, and forces of Dis until both are finally rescued by Vandy's father.

NOTES

Imagination runs rampant to create alien life forms both repulsive and incredible. Norton handles her recurrent theme of the interplay of fantasy and reality somewhat differently here than in other novels. Most often she suggests that fantasy and reality overlap, but in this case she describes a boy's emerging recognition that they are separate.

Norton, André. **No Night Without Stars**. New York: Atheneum, 1975. 246p. Fawcett paperback, 1978. Grades 7 up.

SUMMARY

Sometimes the quest for technical knowledge turns out to be too dangerous to pursue, as Sander and Fanyi learn. Some 300 years after geological cataclysms (the Dark Time) have laid waste much of the earth, these two young people search for the knowledge of the Before Time.

Sander, a blacksmith, hopes to recover knowledge of alloys, then to return with an obvious claim to his rightful place in the clan group called Jak's Mob. Counter to Sander's belief in what he can see, Fanyi relies upon powers of telepathy learned through her Shaman training. She seeks a powerful weapon from the Before Time with which to avenge the raid which annihilated her village while she was away and unable to exercise her protective powers.

Accompanied by Sander's koyot, a mutated coyote large enough to ride, and Fanyi's two fishers, ferrets grown large, the two face hunger and thirst and several subhuman mutant attackers before reaching the ruins to which Fanyi's pendant guides them.

Here they find a storehouse of knowledge, but also power to control a human body. Guarded only by a mad old man, a computer installation has escaped destruction, presumably programmed with the knowledge from the Before Time. But whether by original intent, or through damage in the cataclysm, the machine is now bent upon controlling all living things. With the aid of that ancient protection against enchantment, cold iron, and of their animal companions, the two young people overcome the machine's evil power.

NOTES

No Night Without Stars may be regarded as a replay of the temptation in the Garden of Eden. However, the guiding principle is to refuse to surrender that which makes one human, rather than to observe a pledge to deity. Moreover, Sander and Fanyi already have a sense of good and evil, so scientific, rather than moral, knowledge is the forbidden fruit.

The element of adventure, however, lies in the pair's encounters with several mutant creatures, each of whose characteristics invites speculation as to the mechanisms of genetic change. These episodes of attack and escape occupy the bulk of the narrative. The author's attempt to borrow phrases from folk literature ("any such," "such a one") is sometimes cumbersome, but exemplifies a match of style to cultural level. Too, Sander's reluctance to trust anything he cannot see or touch continues a recurring motif in Norton's novels.

Norton, André. **Ordeal in Otherwhere**. New York: World, 1964. 221p. Grade 7 up.

SUMMARY

Ordeal in Otherwhere builds on the theme "divided we fall." When a plague kills the government officials and sympathizers on the colonial planet Demeter, Charis Nordholm faces suffering or death at the hands of fanatic survivors. She seizes the chance to be sold to a trader operating at marginal legality who in turn sells her contract to another fringer. Next Charis finds herself on the planet Warlock where her task is to negotiate trade with the reptilian females, Wyverns, who have the Power to control others through dreams.

Charis escapes from the trader's quarters and makes contact with both the female Wyverns and Shann Lantee, a Survey scout. Meanwhile, however, the male Wyverns, heretofore wholly dominated by the females' Power, have been provided with a machine which blocks the females' control. The latter then turn against all humans. Yet in their assembly, when the females consult Those Who Have Dreamed Before, a sign is given that Charis will reveal the answer to their problem. And eventually, having learned to link minds with Shann as well as a wolverine and a curl-cat, Charis does help the Wyverns see that as long as the females continue to hold the males in subservience, opportunity will remain for outsiders to exploit the males' resentment.

NOTES

Again, the author explores the boundary between fantasy and reality as well as the nature of psychic powers. For the most part, however, this novel is a combination of mystery and science fiction.

---

*Norton, André. **Outside**. Illus. by Bernard Colonna. New York: Walker, 1974, 126p. Avon paperback, 1976. Grades 4-7.

SUMMARY

"Believing is seeing"—but only those who have enough flexibility of mind to believe in what they cannot see can begin to build the new "London Bridge" to last a thousand years. Kristie belongs to one of the few Crowds still living in the vast, domed-over city—Inside. In some parts of the city, the breather machines have broken down; in others, rats have overrun the alleys. But Kristie wants to believe that Outside the poisons which forced the closing of the city gates have somehow disappeared.

Then the Rhyming Man comes, and some of the younger children, Littles, and older girls disappear. Lew, Kristie's older brother, stands by helpless and sees her, too, disappear before his very eyes. Kristie has gone Outside, whether by some magic or by means of a machine left by the adults. There she will join with others, who now have the power of telepathy, to build a new world, avoiding the mistakes of their elders. With Kristie's help, Lew is also able to muster belief in the unseen so that he can join her Outside.

NOTES

This story straddles the boundary between fantasy and science fiction, since we are never sure whether the Rhyming Man is an illusion, or some highly sophisticated machine. In either case the theme affirms the power of imagination.

Nursery rhymes are cleverly used; students may wish to trace their sources and original meanings. The Rhyming Man bears an obvious resemblance to the Pied Piper of Hamelin, although Kristie's sore leg does not prevent her from going Outside, as it held back the lame child in Browning's poem.

Norton, André. **Postmarked the Stars.** New York: Harcourt, Brace & World, 1969. 223p. Ace paperback, 1975. Grade 7 up.

SUMMARY

A space mystery, *Postmarked the Stars* is the story of a free traders' ship with a contract to deliver mail and freight to the colonial planet Trewsworld. Dane Thorson, assistant cargo master, barely survives death by poison, staggers to his spaceship, and finds that an impostor with a rubber mask has tried to take his place. When the impostor is discovered, just after lift-off, he is dead of a heart attack. But was he a spy, a smuggler, or an escapee? Eventually the crew finds a radiation box which has caused animals on board to retrogress—in one case to a primitive monster, and in the other to a far more intelligent, earlier form.

Dane and several other crew members land with the box and mutated animals in an uninhabited area while the main ship proceeds to the central port on Trewsworld. Soon, however, Dane's crew is involved in a deadly hide-and-seek with those who had hoped to drive off the colonists by creating primordial monsters, the ultimate intent being to take over and gain control of esperite, a rock which enhances psychic powers.

NOTES

This novel is pure adventure, and points up some potential risks of space colonization.

Norton, André. **Victory on Janus.** New York: Harcourt, Brace and World, 1966. 224p. Fawcett paperback, 1980. Grade 7 up.

SUMMARY

A mild statement on the dangers of technology and the virtue of living in harmony with the environment, *Victory on Janus* is primarily a contest of good against evil. Only a handful of Iftin survives in the forests of Janus and even these are changelings, or Ift spirits in human bodies. They carry dual sets of memories and have been modified by certain Ift characteristics, most notably green skin and hibernation through the winter.

The six Iftin of the forest Iftcan are wakened early with a warning of danger. The enemy is THAT WHICH ABIDES, the evil power thought to have been contained long since by the hero Kymon. THAT has created robot Iftin who have attacked the off-worlders at the port, setting the latter to destroying the forest in which they believe the enemy hides. Now that the Iftin are awake, THAT goes even farther and exerts mind control over port people, human colonists, and even machines, obviously gathering forces for the total destruction of the Iftin.

Aided by the power of Thanth, which is centered in the lake called the Mirror, Ayyar and Illylle lead the others to destroy THAT, which turns out to be an enormous computer trying to make the planet suitable for its long dead human cargo.

NOTES

The novel is a sequel to *Judgment on Janus* (pre-1964, and thus not within the scope of this bibliography), but can be read independently. The computer-run-wild may be regarded as symbolic of the potential dangers of artificial intelligence. Further, the notion that Iftin are native to and thus suited to Janus, while the computer's people—Larsh—regressed to a subhuman level in this alien environment, speaks to the flip side of that theme. However, this story is more of an adventure tale, with overtones of mysticism, than it is a strong environmental statement.

Norton, André. **The X Factor**. New York: Harcourt, Brace and World, 1965. 191p. Ace paperback. Grade 7 up.

SUMMARY

The X factor is that occurrence which the odds suggest will never occur. However, now and then the unpredictable does happen. In this novel, mere chance brings a mutant throwback whose body will not obey his mind to the one planet where that need no longer makes a difference.

Diskan Fentress is so desperate to escape from a world where he will never fit that he steals a spaceship tape to a world physically safe for humans, but questionable for colonization. There he finds himself in the middle of a conflict which involves the planet's furred natives, Zacathan archaeologists, and the outlawed Jack traders. Gradually he learns to cooperate with the intelligent animals to send all the others off the planet, while he stays to reunite the brothers-in-fur with the humanlike shapes of the brothers-in-flesh.

NOTES

As in several of Norton's novels, it is difficult to know whether the vision is real or illusory. Were spaceships and ray guns eliminated, the novel could be written as pure fantasy.

Norton, André. **The Zero Stone**. New York: Viking, 1968. 286p. Grade 7 up.
Norton, André. **Uncharted Stars**. New York: Viking, 1969. 253p. Grade 8 up.

SUMMARY

This pair of adventure novels centers around Murdoc Jern, gem trader, and an alien creature, Eet. Jern, an apprentice, and his master are selected as human sacrifices, but Jern escapes off the planet. The only purpose he can imagine for his attempted murder is to capture the zero stone, an alien artifact of unknown history which is the only remembrance Murdoc has taken from home after his stepfather's death.

It turns our that Murdoc has escaped the planet only to fall into the hands of the Thieves' Guild. En route to the Guild's mysterious space refuge, Waystar, Murdoc is aided in his escape by the strange creature Eet. Eet is a telepathic alien borne by the spaceship's cat after the latter swallows a mysterious, furry "stone."

Drawn through space by the zero stone, Murdoc and Eet reach a derelict spaceship, use its LB (emergency vehicle) to reach a strange planet, and then are recaptured by Guild members seeking more of the stones. They escape by surrendering the cache of zero stones to a Patrol officer, but Eet manages to spirit one of the stones away.

In *Uncharted Stars*, Murdoc begins a gem trading expedition, only to find himself "listed"—barred from legal trade. Certain that the Thieves' Guild is behind this blacklisting, Murdoc manages to find and penetrate Waystar, where he also rescues Forerunner artifacts just stolen from the alien, scholarly Zacathans. One of these artifacts is a map in the form of a bowl—a map which leads them to the source planet of the zero stones. Here Murdoc foolishly inserts a tray of stones into the machine which apparently turns them into zero stones. The machine blows up, but at the same time Eet (thought to be male) assumes *her* own beautiful "human" body.

NOTES

First person narration helps to reinforce credibility through some fairly incredible passages. The novel speculates on trade and piracy in the space age future. Alien beings and their customs, along with telepathy, are creative elements; however, the ending is anti-climactic. Eet's history is never fully explained, providing opportunity for students to gather the bits of information scattered through the two novels and then to develop a theory of their own.

---

*O'Brien, Robert C. **Z for Zachariah**. New York: Atheneum, 1975. 249p. Dell paperback, 1977. Grade 8 up.

SUMMARY

"I am hopeful," writes Ann Burden in the closing line of this novel, but to the reader there appears no reason to hope. Ann is nearly 16 and has been alone in her valley for nearly a year after the one-week nuclear war which seems to have wiped out all humankind. One day she sees a column of smoke, and each day the column comes closer until finally Mr. Loomis enters the valley. Meanwhile, Ann has hidden in a cave, not certain of what to expect. Loomis bathes in the one creek in the valley which carries radioactivity and when he falls sick, Ann comes to nurse him. In his delirium, Loomis speaks of a man named Edward; at last Ann realizes that Loomis had shot Edward to death in order to keep for himself the single safe suit which had permitted him later to walk across country until he happened upon her valley. As he recovers, Loomis becomes more possessive and more authoritarian, until finally he tries to cripple her leg with gunshot so that she cannot hide from him, as she has finally decided to do. Then Ann steals the safesuit and wagon and sets off across the dead landscape herself, certain that somewhere there is a roomful of children waiting for her to teach them.

NOTES

The novel is in the form of a journal, a device which effectively develops Ann's bewilderment at Loomis' actions and finally her decision to strike out on her own.

But the dream which inspires her is so unrealistic that the effect of the novel is depressing. This is a genuine dystopia in which materialism meets idealism to the detriment of the latter. Our pessimism is complete when we realize the meaning of the title, for Ann remarks that she had learned her letters from a Bible alphabet book which began with Adam and ended with Zachariah, so that for some time she had assumed that Zachariah was the last man, as Adam has been the first.

Ann skips writing in her journal for days at a time; students might chart these intervals and see how they permit the author to work in suspenseful bits of prediction from time to time. The poems, hymns, and stories to which Ann refers would be worth following up to enrich the meaning of the story. Hooker's *Kennaquhair* paints a more optimistic picture of a pocket of survivors after nuclear war.

Offutt, Andrew J. **The Galactic Rejects**. Illus. by Richard Cuffari. New York: Lothrop, Lee & Shepard, 1973. 191p. Dell paperback, 1974. Grades 6-10.

SUMMARY

The Galactic Rejects is a war adventure story involving alien species and telepathic powers. Three psychics commandeer a spaceboat on a damaged space transport and land on the previously unknown planet Bor. Here a humanlike species has evolved, but at a far more gradual pace than on Earth. Technology is developing slowly, although agriculture is well advanced. Crimes and acts of violence are nearly unknown in this pastoral utopia, where to cause embarrassment is to commit a major social error. The three psychics—one a poltergeist, one a teleporter, and one a telepathic receiver—make their living with a carnival and then with a magic act. A year passes, and their peaceful life is interrupted by news that the enemy aliens, the Azuli, have landed on the planet. Soon the Azuli are conscripting Borean young men and removing them from the planet to assist their war effort elsewhere. When one of their friends is taken by the Azuli, the three Earthsiders can remain neutral no longer. Invited to perform before the Azuli commander, they manage between them to blow up the base and release the latest group of Borean captives. Realizing that they can bring the 19-year-old war to an end by offering the Azuli immunization against a disease which they have contracted on the planet, two of the psychics take off in an Azuli spaceship for that purpose, although the third loses his life in the process.

NOTES

Although this pastoral utopia does not follow a cataclysmic disaster, it certainly questions the mad dash for technological advance. As a side benefit of their victory over the Azuli, the three psychics also preserve the utopian society of the planet Bor. Plot overpowers characterization in this novel, although the three "rejects," who prove very valuable after all, make an interesting team, especially as they combine their particular psychic gifts both to entertain the citizens of Bor and to destroy the Azuli base.

The author's use of isolated quotations and newspaper headlines in Chapter 11 demonstrates economical use of language to build toward a turning point in the story.

Packard, Edward. **The Third Planet from Altair**. Illus. by Barbara Carter. Philadelphia: Lippincott, 1979. 96p. Grades 3-6.

NOTES

One can hardly summarize a story which has over 70 plots! This story starts out with a mission to trace radio signals from the third planet in the Altair system. One of several "programmed novels" which this author has written, it asks "you," the reader, to select the next action from two or three at the bottom of the page. Because a number of the plots run into one another, there are 37 endings in the 96 pages of the book. Many of these endings involve the annihilation or marooning of the protagonist who is, in effect, the reader of the book. The various stories range in length from 8 to 22 pages each. More a novelty than a novel, the book might serve as a model for a creative writing project.

Parker, Richard. **A Time to Choose; A Story of Suspense.** New York: Harper & Row, 1974. 128p. Grade 7 up.

SUMMARY

This novel turns upon a theory that parallel worlds interpenetrate one another so that, at least for some individuals, it is possible to move between them and then to forsake one world and one identity for another. The choice, in this instance, is made for communal living and environment-conscious use of energy and machines in preference to familial indifference and auto-filled highways.

The setting is England. Stephen Conway first sees the other world through his automobile windshield as he comes to the top of a rural hill. Later both he and Mary Silver, a classmate, see and eventually move into and out of that world where the climate is warmer, life is communal, and moral sanction is given only "to operations that coincide with the workings of natural forces, using sun, wind, water, temperature changes, rainfall, but never destroying or interfering." Although the two worlds co-exist in present time, hints combine to suggest that the world consonant with nature is a century more advanced than the other.

At first Stephen, as Curwen, follows his friend Bitta to the Sike College, where she is embarking upon a five-year training program to become a sike healer. In a later visit, however, Stephen-Curwen, a fish hatchery worker, meets Mary, who is a member of the commune at the flour mill. Mary is, of course, Mary Silver. She walks through a doorway and is back in her familiar surroundings with no memory of her experience and no realization that she has been missing nearly two days. Stephen-Curwen is left behind, baffled, until he meets the "real" Curwen face to face. A few moments later he reenters his comatose body in this world and is once again just Stephen. Now Stephen and Mary decide that they must choose which world they want as their permanent home. The old warehouse at the wharf, one of the places where the two worlds intersect, is their place to cross through. They walk in, but a bystander looks for them inside and sees no one. A moment later, as the men who are there to judge a fishing contest decide the pair must have wandered elsewhere, the warehouse collapses.

NOTES

The author borrows the pastoral utopia model to create his parallel world, where advanced technologies are in accord with natural processes and gasoline engines have been eliminated. Little detail about that other world is provided, however, nor is the couple's decision to choose that world totally convincing. The several discussions of parallel worlds and the environmental concern will be useful for comparison with novels actually set in future time.

---

*Pesek, Ludek. **The Earth Is Near.** Trans. Anthea Bell. Scarsdale, NY: Bradbury Press, 1970, 1973. 206p. Dell paperback, 1975. Grade 6 up.

SUMMARY

"Perhaps the whole meaning of life really does consist in an eternal battle to prove that it is significant"; thus the narrator concludes the novel. If so, then this account shows the battle as costly, and with few rewards.

The Earth Is Near tells the story of the first manned space flight to Mars. The men reach their destination and all but three of them begin the return journey to Earth, but with many of their goals, especially the search for evidence of microorganismic life, frustrated. Human error is one contributing factor, but overarching that are the fine dust which hides deep pits and blows up into overpowering storms, and the strains, physical and mental, on human endurance.

As the months pass, the disagreements between the captain of the expedition and the second in command, who also has primary responsibility for the scientific purpose of the voyage, rupture into open conflict. O'Brien, the second, is determined to reach the site where evidence of life had been thought most likely, even though they have managed to land some kilometres from the area. Norton, the captain, is more concerned with the safety of the mission. Three attempts to reach the desired area, the Deucalionis Regio, fail at the cost of two lives. When at last the time comes to lift off from the planet, O'Brien cannot be found, having decided to stay and die on Mars.

NOTES

The strength of this novel lies not in its plot, but in the careful buildup of description and detail as the doctor on the expedition, the narrator, recounts his experiences, observations, and personal responses to the monotony, the dangers, and the psychological effects of the 258 days in space and 440 days on Mars. To have survived at all may be regarded as a human victory in the face of hostile nature. This story is useful as a corrective to some of the more glamorous accounts of space exploration, and as an introduction to the history of man's venture into space up to the present time.

---

*Phipson, Joan. **When the City Stopped.** New York: Atheneum, 1978. 181p. Grades 5-9.

SUMMARY

"I'll always know it's nothing but an eggshell we're living on." This statement by 13-year-old Nick Lorimer closes the book and captures its essence.

Various groups have been protesting the imminent construction of a nuclear reactor near Sydney, Australia. But one day, quite unintentionally, all major services are stopped by simultaneous protest strikes. The city is left without electricity, communications, garbage collection, deliveries of groceries and fuel—indeed, all the services necessary to the existence of its people.

Nick and his sister Binkie are left alone in this situation; their father away on a business trip and their mother unconscious after an automobile accident, her identification lost. Eventually the children find the home of Mrs. Piggott, their cleaning lady, and set off with her and her crippled husband, the latter pulled in a cart, hoping to hitch a ride from one of the huge trucks on the main highway. Jo Piggott, despite his handicaps, becomes the leader of the expedition, seeing them through rain, hungry dogs, looters and finally, the trip into the country, where a friendly truck driver puts them up in his own home.

For some time Jo has been pestering his wife to take him back to the country, for he has never become a city dweller in his heart. And the second night, he hobbles away toward the hills, until he dies peacefully beneath a tree, his eyes still turned toward the horizon. Nick and Binkie are reunited with their parents, and Mrs. Piggott takes in a motherless boy who has shared their adventures.

NOTES

The future of this book may be as close as tomorrow. Certainly the author succeeds in showing the dependence of city dwellers on the communication and transportation systems which provide the necessities of their daily life. Although something of a warning, the story conveys the notion that people can cope successfully with emergency situations, even if they make some mistakes along the way. Excellent characterization.

Reynolds, Pamela. **Earth Times Two.** New York: Lothrop, Lee & Shepard, 1970. 160p. Grades 6-8.

SUMMARY

In this variation on the theme of the power-mad scientist, Earth's twin planet Terra needs our technology to cope with its overpopulation. Dr. Hillis on Terra exchanges his daughter, Jessica, with Helene, niece of Dr. Hillis on Earth. Jeremy Hillis is also teleported to Terra and discovers how that planet's Dr. Hillis has forced people to obey him through psychic powers. Jeremy foils Dr. Hillis's attempt to control all Terra and returns himself, Helene, and his cat Charlie to Earth.

NOTES

Terra is a parallel, rather than a future, world. It may be compared with parallel worlds in Parker's *A Time to Choose* and other such novels listed in the index.

Dr. Hillis' fortress of mind control is a chilling dystopia for as long as it lasts, its direst feature being "Total Security Storage"—housing young teenagers asleep in cribs, their minds blank so that they can receive the technology information Jessica is to transmit from Earth. The ethics of psychic control are demonstrated in the confrontation between the Probers and Dr. Hillis on Terra, when the former move to stops Hillis' violation of their Sacred Law. This novel blends mystery, science fiction, and telepathy into an intriguing plot.

Richelson, Geraldine, adapt. **Star Wars Storybook.** 55p. New York: Random, 1978. Grades 4-8.

SUMMARY

A retelling of the motion picture *Star Wars*, illustrated with colored stills from the film. Luke Skywalker rescues the beautiful Senator Leia Organa from the Dark Lord Darth Vader with the help of a wise old man, Ben Kenobi, and the robots Artoo Deetoo and Threepio.

NOTES

This book offers no more than a plot outline as a text. However, it may serve as a resource for comparing portraits of the future in several media by helping students recall details of the film.

Simak, Clifford D. **The Goblin Reservation**. New York: Putnam, 1968. 192p. Berkley paperback, 1973. Grade 7 up.

SUMMARY

Simak weaves a tale of mystery and adventure, interlaced with speculations on the origin of the universe, varieties of nonhuman intelligent life, mythical beings such as goblins, and time travel. Some time in the twenty-sixth century, Associate Professor Peter Maxwell returns to the Wisconsin campus of University of Earth after a journey into space by means of an instant interplanetary transmitter. But there has been a mix-up—another Peter Maxwell has returned a month before, only to be killed in an "accident" within a few days. Maxwell himself had never reached his original destination, the Coonskin System, but had instead been snatched away to a crystal planet, which had survived the final shrinking together of its own universe before our universe was born. The ghostly inhabitants of this planet have asked Maxwell to serve as their agent in selling the knowledge accumulated in that previous existence. Maxwell's competitors in this transaction are the Wheelers, roly-poly hives of writhing insects on horn-rimmed wheels, former slaves of the trolls and goblins, now bent on becoming masters of the entire galaxy. On his side, however, Maxwell has a Neanderthal man brought forward by Time College, the Ghost of William Shakespeare, and a young woman who, with her bio-mech saber-toothed tiger, had rented Maxwell's supposedly vacant apartment. The people of the crystal planet will not tell Maxwell what it is they want in return for their "library," but eventually Maxwell discovers that they are interested in a particular Artifact which has been brought forward from the Jurassic period by Time College and housed in their museum. But too late—the deal has been closed with the Wheelers. Still, Maxwell decides to look at the Artifact through an interpreting apparatus given him on the crystal planet. He thereby releases a dragon, last of its kind and formerly a pet of the beings on the crystal planet. As a reward for freeing the dragon, which will now live on the Goblin Reservation, Maxwell's university will receive the crystal planet's data after all.

NOTES

The dominating features of this novel are its fast-moving plot and its astonishing array of creatures. No juvenile novel we have encountered suggests anything approaching the number and variety of alien beings encountered here—reptilians, hoppers, wrigglers, creatures who must stay in a tank of liquid, shrimp, spiders—and, of course, the Wheelers. Then there are the real ghosts, goblins, trolls, fairies, and banshees on Goblin Reservation. In all this panorama of intelligent life, Maxwell pontificates on the foolishness of intolerance, yet admits to revulsion at the voice and touch of a Wheeler.

University life in the twenty-sixth century involves a whole list of new disciplines, including time travel. However, alcoholic beverages remain a primary adjunct to recreation and problem avoidance.

Sleator, William. **House of Stairs.** New York: Dutton, 1974. 166p. Avon paperback, 1975. Grade 7 up.

SUMMARY

"This book is dedicated to all the rats and pigeons who have already been here." *House of Stairs* is the story of an experiment in psychological conditioning. Five orphaned 16-year-olds find themselves in a large area which consists of nothing but stairs and landings—they can find no entrance or exit. Eventually they meet at a food machine, but one which will operate only when its red or green light flashes, and then only sporadically. Gradually they find that they must behave in certain ways to obtain food, even then not always certain that the pellets of meat will roll from the chute. For a time they must dance; later the dance must become more complex in rhythm and movement. Then, they discover that they must make one another feel upset or hurt in order to keep the food machine working.

At this point, two of the young people decide that they will not respond to the machine—Lola, the girl who was forever getting into trouble at school, and Peter, who tends to withdraw into daydreams of his first state home and the boy who shared his room and bed there. After a bit, the machine begins to operate for the remaining three as long as they physically or psychologically abuse one another, even going so far as to urinate on the others from a high landing. Finally, the three turn to tormenting Lola and Peter on the distant landing to which they have withdrawn—dropping a shoe from above, physically assaulting them, and finally torturing them with food. The day comes when Lola knows she will soon die of starvation, so she begins weakly to descend to the food machine. Peter does not share her drive to live, but he decides to join her out of concern for her feeling of failure if he does not. Just at that moment, however, the experiment is brought to an end, the psychologist never realizing how close he had come to complete success. Lola and Peter are to be sent to an island for misfits. The other three are to be trained for intelligence work in the belief that they will do anything asked of them. In the final scene, however, the three see a flashing traffic signal and begin to dance just as they had in the experimental house of stairs.

NOTES

Not only this use of psychological conditioning, but also the glimpses of the overpopulated and polluted outside world class this novel as a dystopia. Swearing, homosexuality, and negative attitudes toward bathrooms and boy-girl relationships only accentuate the inhumanity these young people demonstrate toward one another. The reader does not know the purpose of the house of stairs until the final chapter, although Lola is the first to suspect what is happening. Lola and Peter and the island to which they will be exiled are the only bright spots in this well-written, but repelling, image of the future.

---

*Slote, Alfred. **My Robot Buddy**. Illus. Joel Schlick. Philadelphia: Lippincott, 1975.
92p. Avon paperback, 1978. Grades 3-5.

SUMMARY

Can a robot be a friend? In this lighthearted story of future technology, Jack
Jameson is given a robot playmate for his birthday—a very expensive robot, since it
is programmed to participate in sports, climb trees, and be happy. Of course, it cannot
eat, so the apple from the tree which they climb together, and Jack's chocolate birthday cake, are not experiences they can share. Still Danny One, the robot, will be able
to be reprogrammed to grow taller and smarter along with Jack.

Shortly after Danny comes to live with Jack, a robotnapper tries to capture
the robot. But Jack has become so good at imitating a robot's stiff-legged run that
the robotnapper becomes confused, not sure whether to take Danny or Jack. Meanwhile, Danny calls for police assistance using his "belly button," which activates his
two-way communication system with the factory. Afterwards, Jack's father realizes
he can use Danny's radio system instead of a mobile car radio to build up his business,
and soon he is able to buy a radio of his own, returning Danny to Jack as a full-time
playmate.

NOTES

A bit hard to believe, but nevertheless a well-written, easy-to-read bit of robot
whimsy. Careful study of the illustrations yields several notions about life in the future
which are not mentioned in the text, e.g., a Holiday Inn and a robot lawn mower.

Slote, Alfred. **My Trip to Alpha I**. Illus. by Harold Berson. Philadelphia: Lippincott,
1978. 94p. Grades 3-5.

SUMMARY

A bit of mystery and science fiction combine in this story. Jack Stevenson is
asked by his Aunt Katherine DeVanter to travel to Alpha I by Voya-Code to help
her pack for her move to Earth. With Voya-Code a person goes to sleep on Earth
and a dummy which looks like him or her is programmed by computer to be that
person's alter ego on the planet to be visited. When Jack's dummy wakes up on
Alpha I, he finds that Aunt Katherine behaves very strangely. Soon he realizes that
she is a dummy, illegally brought from Earth and programmed by Frank and Ruth
Arbo to deed over Aunt Katherine's property to them, with Jack as the legally
required family witness. The only way Jack can uncover the crime is to get his
aunt's dummy to the Voya-Code terminal, where her real body must be sleeping.
Pretending that he wants to return to Earth, Jack manages to accomplish his purpose,
and the criminals are apprehended.

NOTES

A lighthearted, easy to read adventure story, this story goes well beyond the
bounds of scientific probability, although provided with "scientific" explanations.
Unlike *My Robot Buddy*, which emphasizes the difference between human and
machine, *My Trip to Alpha I* assumes that a human being can be reduced to a computer program and moreover, that the dummy thus programmed seems to the human

to be himself, so that the reawakened person recalls his experiences in the dummy body. Students may wish to debate the viewpoints of Mr. Slote's two books.

Snyder, Zilpha Keatley. **Below the Root**. Illus. Alton Raible. New York: Atheneum, 1975. 231p. Grades 5-8.

Snyder, Zilpha Keatley. **And All Between**. Illus. Alton Raible. New York: Atheneum, 1976. 216p. Grades 5-8.

Snyder, Zilpha Keatley. **Until the Celebration**. Illus. Alton Raible. New York: Atheneum, 1977. 214p. Grades 6-10.

SUMMARY

In order that it may survive, must innocence be shielded from all contact with evil? *Below the Root* suggests, and its sequel *And All Between*, clearly declares, that the answer is "no." But *Until the Celebration* points out the difficulties of bringing them together.

On a moderate gravity planet, the people called Kindar live among the branches of an enormous vine. Wearing a filmy garment, or "shuba," they learn early in childhood to spread their arms and legs and float down from one branchway to another. Many aspects of Kindar life are controlled by the Ol-zhaan, or priests. Each year two 13-year-old Kindar are chosen to be trained for the priesthood. One of these, Raamo D'ok, is the central figure in *Below the Root*. Together with the other Chosen, the girl Genaa, and a slightly older novice, Neric, Raamo begins to question the teachings of the Ol-zhaan.

The one fear of the Kindar, who otherwise know only love and peace, is the Pash-shan, the terrible beasts who live imprisoned below the roots of the enormous Wissenvine. Sometimes infants fall to the forest floor and are snatched by the Pash-shan through the narrow openings between the roots. Rumor has it that even adults are seized by the Pash-shan, although no one knows how they could possibly be taken through such narrow spaces. When such worries bother the Kindar, however, they eat a Wissenberry or two and feel much too dreamy to worry about anything.

Because Raama and Neric suspect that some of the Ol-zhaan are in league with the Pash-shan, they descend to the forest floor in hopes of uncovering some clues to the conspiracy. There they find the child Teera, whom they believe is a Kindar child, captured as an infant, who now has managed to squeeze her way through one of the openings in the root. They hide her with Raamo's family and the three Ol-zhaan question her from time to time until one day Raamo's sister Pomma reveals that Teera is a Pash-shan (who call themselves Erdling). Finally Raamo, Genaa, and Neric learn from D'ol Falla, the revered priestess of the vine, that the Pash-shan are not monsters, but exiled Kindar, imprisoned below the root because they believed that Kindar, to avoid repeating their errors, had to know about the evil and destruction which had driven them all to Green-Sky from their original home planet.

Thus the Ol-zhaan became the guardians of the truth of their warlike history and the protectors of the Kindar's innocence. Over the years, however, the Spirit-skills (psychic powers) have been weakening, the wasting sickness spreading, and the roots of the Wissenvine shrinking. The only way to restore Green-Sky to its earlier state, D'ol Falla argues, is to release the Erdling and let the Kindar know the truth—but this must be accomplished gradually.

At this point the second novel picks up the narrative. Now told from Teera's viewpoint, *And All Between* begins with her escape between the roots and then traces the unfolding conflict between D'ol Falla and those who still insist that the Kindar must be kept innocent. The deciding factor is an all-unknowing demonstration of the psychic power "uniforce" by Teera and Pomma. During their weeks together in Pomma's home and their days in the Ol-zhaan temple, the two children, Kindar and Erdling, have rediscovered the Spirit-skills as they played their telepathic games, thus demonstrating the need of each group for the other.

Until the Celebration, however, shows that "Rejoyning" is not so easily accomplished. The Erdling are released from their prison; Kindar and Erdling leaders form a joint council; but the two peoples are accustomed to solving their problems in different ways, and innumerable disagreements arise. Their one symbol of unity is the two children, Pomma and Teera, who are regarded as holy now that the Ol-zhaan have revealed the secrets they had long withheld from the Kindar, and thus lost much of their status.

Further threats to unity arise from D'ol Regle, the Ol-zhaan who had opposed releasing the Erdling, and from Axon Befal, an Erdling who tries to rouse the people against the Ol-zhaan. Both have fled into the forest with a group of followers.

Tensions mount as the celebration of the first anniversary of the Rejoyning draws near. Finally, only days before the celebration, the two children are kidnapped and the dreaded tool-of-violence is stolen. The tool is returned and disposed of, though at the cost of Raamo's life, and on the anniversary day Pomma and Teera return. Not kidnapped, they had run away, afraid that they were losing their Spirit-skills and would be found out. But another pair of children they had been playing with while in hiding have learned to move objects with their minds. Thus the promise of the Spirit-force is renewed.

NOTES

One must ask first whether these novels are set in the future. The publisher describes them as fantasy; certainly the idea of humans living on an enormous vine created by psychic powers accords with that description. Nevertheless, escape from a war-torn planet is a common science fiction theme. When we had opportunity to ask Mrs. Snyder whether the books are set in future time, her answer was "yes and no." "Certainly," she went on to explain, "this is the future of a people who have escaped from an earthlike planet—a possibility I was exploring. But I am basically too much of an optimist to believe that the earth will really be destroyed."

Nevertheless, there are enough futuristic elements so that *Below the Root* may be compared effectively with other pastoral utopias. The use of religion to withhold truth from a people in the interests of survival occurs also in Engdahl's *This Star Shall Abide* and its sequel. Snyder suggests both the advantages and the dangers of such control of information, as well as of a tranquil—because tranquilized—society. Telepathy and other psychic powers are a crucial element in the narrative.

As already noted, the author uses Raamo as viewpoint character in the first book and Teera in the second. Since the novels overlap in time, a reader may observe the effects of this switch. The third novel is told in the omniscient third person.

Also of interest are the sources for the words created for the books; for example, Erdling is a German word (meaning earthling) and both Kindar (cf. Kinder, children) and Wissenvine (wissen meaning to know) appear to be Germanic in derivation. Note the relation of Wissenvine and Wissenberry to the "fruit of the tree of knowledge of good and evil" in the Biblical story of Adam and Eve.

Character development is skillfully handled, especially in the first two novels. The third volume does not focus on a particular character; its climax is less intense and its thematic message less clear. It probably appeals more to slightly older readers than do the first two volumes of the trilogy.

*Stone, Josephine Rector. **Praise All the Moons of Morning**. New York: Atheneum, 1979. 172p. Grades 7-10.

SUMMARY

This is a novel about the power of faith—the faith that with effort a better situation can be attained. Early in the twenty-fifth century, human colonists who landed on the planet Ix-Thlan were enslaved by the native Goldmen, a humanoid life form with chitinous skin. The means by which this is accomplished is an hallucinogenic fungus, later dubbed "loofah." Six hundred years later, we follow the story of Desta, a Strangeborn (human) girl who must take care of Barch, the simple-minded boy who will be burned on the altar as soon as his stone image is finished.

Desta's Uncle Gregorio has recently been banished in a purge of Old Believers, those who are convinced that the Mo-Pintural, lizards, will one day lead the Strangeborn to their beautiful Homeland. Desta goes into the desert, intending to hide the sacred relics her uncle had given her in the stone memorial set up to keep his spirit from seeking revenge. At the last moment, however, she fits the crystals together and hears the voice of Cass Williams. For a long time Desta does not realize—although the reader knows—that Cass was one of the original group of humans enslaved on Ix-Thlan, but Cass had escaped by projecting herself forward in time. A bit later in Desta's time, Cass emerges in the room where Desta is recovering from having had her foot cut off as punishment for nearly losing Barch in the desert.

Gradually, Desta comes to believe in the Homeland. Eventually she and Cass, who also has faith in the possibility of getting to a better world, rescue Barch, ride the Mo-Pintural across the treacherous desert, and finally use the crystals to travel through time to a future, and better, world.

NOTES

Cass Williams's taped messages open and are interspersed throughout the novel, clearly differentiated by typeface from Desta's story. These messages, diary-like, are in the first person, as contrasted with the third person narrative with Desta as viewpoint character.

Not all mystery is resolved; we never learn very much about the dreaded Tez and his Deadmen who frequent the desert, nor even about the Goldmen who hold the humans in slavery. Still, alien beings, lizards who are ridden like horses (compare McCaffrey's novels), telepathy, and time travel are among the interest-arousing motifs in this novel.

Stone, Josephine Rector. **Those Who Fall from the Sun**. New York: Atheneum, 1978. 153p. Grades 7-9.

SUMMARY

The force of willpower is the only genuine protection against evil, as Alanna learns in this novel. Earth has become overcrowded, its natural beauty destroyed. Techmen, thought to be aliens from another planet, have gradually taken over the machines and the food supply. Most humans have accepted the ypselite discs, implanted in their foreheads to put human creativity at the disposal of the Techmen. Independents like Alanna and her family have now been dragged away to a spaceship, to be set down on a distant planet where the Techmen hope they will accept the discs, since this must be done willingly.

Alanna finds herself alone, but she befriends a small rodentlike creature, which she names SymBo, and finally the seemingly fierce "dog-thing." She learns the power of dreams, then of telepathy and something like astral projection. With these gifts and the help of the dog-thing, Alanna finds some of the humans who had been aboard ship with her. Among them is the elderly man with his talisman from the pyramid-building DaHadood. He alone remembers the history of mankind, and the Techmen demand that Alanna give him up in exchange for her family, whom they say they are holding. At last, however, Alanna realizes that she cannot betray the old man. The Techmen, unable to overcome the power of her will, leave at least for the time being, as Alanna's family comes walking down a mountain trail.

NOTES

This story, a tale of good against evil, affirms the power of the human will and of history, which is described as the history of that will (p. 152). One might read the novel as an allegory of technology; however, the essential part played by psychic powers in overcoming the evil Techmen blurs what might otherwise be a clear confrontation between creativity and technology. Alanna suggests that SymBo is like the less mature self she had grown out of as a result of being wrenched from her family and familiar surroundings; if so, it is interesting that the rodent dies in the effort to defend her.

---

*Stoutenburg, Adrien. **Out There.** New York: Viking, 1971. 222p. Grade 7 up.

SUMMARY

Out There (same title as book by Mace) dramatizes the possibility that pollution, including nuclear and chemical contamination, might cause virtual extinction of wildlife. Early in the twenty-first century, Zebrina Morris Vanderbrook—white-haired, overweight, and regarded as "loony" by most adults—has gathered a "Squad" of five children who share her hope that somewhere in America's abandoned wastelands pockets of natural plant and animal life still survive.

At length, "Aunt Zeb" and her unlikely crew set off on a several days' jaunt across the Nevada desert and into the Sierra, searching for such survivors—just for the pleasure of seeing them. They drive along the potholed highway as far as it is still passable, then prepare to hike further.

Unfortunately, Lester breaks their compass and Aunt Zeb breaks her only pair of glasses. Although they succeed in finding game animals, they also encounter a young man who has taken to the wilderness, hunting to survive. In their confrontation the young man, Josh, is wounded in the leg. Immediately thereafter nearly all of the Squad's supplies are lost down a ravine in the destruction following upon the supersonic boom created by careless pilots.

The group takes refuge in an old resort lodge, waiting until Aunt Zeb's neighbor realizes they have been gone too long and searches for them. What seems a happy ending (even Josh will receive medical attention and then live with Aunt Zeb for an indefinite time) is marred by the clear intention of their rescuing pilot to consider reopening the resort for hunting and fishing—an action that will surely doom the precariously surviving wildlife.

NOTES

A dystopian novel, *Out There* bodes ill for people as well as wildlife. All five of these children are more or less unwanted; the most pathetic situation is that of little Knobs, whose parents left her clinging to a freeway fence with just a ball and jacks in her dress pocket, the same ball and jacks she plays with almost compulsively. The introspections of these unhappy youngsters slow plot movement and shift our attention from one to the other. The characters of Aunt Zeb, Patrick, Lester, and Knobs, and their development through these circumstances are well drawn, but somewhat difficult to identify with.

The main theme of pollution and its dangers to wildlife, however, is the most obvious basis for student discussion. Conflicting values are apparent in a world where the population crowds itself into domed cities, awaiting feasible means of space colonization—and where both Josh and Ed, the young pilot, do not hesitate to destroy an oasis of wild creatures to meet their needs for escape on the one hand, or wealth on the other.

Other books listed in Part IV under "Animal Extinction/Preservation" may be well compared with Stoutenburg's pessimistic approach. In addition, two books in picture book format will also be useful, although they are not set in future time. In the *Wump World* by Bill Peet (Boston: Houghton-Mifflin, 1970), alien Pollutians devastate the planet of the gentle Wumps. However, when the invaders leave in search of another new planet, the Wumps see signs that their world will eventually regain much of its natural beauty. *The Lorax* by Dr. Seuss (New York: Random House, 1971) tells how the Once-ler, who had destroyed all the Truffula Trees and the creatures who lived among them by his shortsighted expansion of a Thneed factory, entrusts the one remaining truffula seed to "you."

Sutton, Jean and Jeff Sutton. **The Beyond**. New York: Putnam, 1967. 223p. Grades 7-10.

SUMMARY

The Suttons tell an adventure story built around the idea that telepaths will eventually lead us to a better universe. The time is Galactic Year 3180—over three thousand years after the founding of the Federation which presently governs the galaxy. Near the outer reaches of that galaxy, on the forbidding planet Engo, a small colony of exiled telepaths struggles for survival. Despite their remote location, rumors continue that an underground conspiracy of telepaths, led by a mysterious Mr. Olaf, is plotting to take over the government. Especially feared are telepaths whose power is so strong that they can move objects without touching them. Thus the report that such a person, a "beyond," had been observed by a black market trader when he stopped at Engo soon reaches the ears of the Director of SocAd (Social Administration), whose responsibilities include identifying and controlling telepaths.

Two men are sent to Engo to investigate—Alek Selby, because the Director feels he will be objective, and Philip Wig, because the latter sees this as an opportunity to advance his own career. Selby soon accepts what he had long suspected: that he is himself a telepath. But his strongest power lies in sending rather than receiving messages. Thus he cannot at first discover the secret of the people on Engo, and they, fearing he might reveal the truth if Wig were to subject Selby to psychic probes, will not tell him.

Most confusing is Wig's insistence that young David Gant, the suspected
beyond, is dead, even after David's body is exhumed and identified. In fact, however,
when both Johnny and David were ill with fever, David had been caught in Johnny's
body as he tried to save Johnny's life by entering his mind. Wig does not understand
how this occurred, but that David has become Johnny he learns through illegal torture
of one of the Engo telepaths. Johnny now serves as the anchor for a psychic bridge
from Engo to a planet of telepaths in the neighboring galaxy, a bridge along which
the people of Engo are escaping. But how will Johnny himself escape?

The climactic scene finds Johnny, Selby, and Mr. Olaf (who turns out to be
the psychic prober from SocAd) the only telepaths remaining on Engo, confronting
Philip Wig and his sadistic cohorts. Selby finds he can enter Wig's mind to control
his body, a talent he uses to stop Wig's breathing. Meanwhile Johnny has been fatally
shot, but Selby prompts him to enter Wig's body. Consequently we find David-
turned-Johnny-turned-Wig and Mr. Olaf back at SocAd headquarters, given the
Director's go-ahead to work toward the day when telepaths will rule the world. The
Director believes that every man will then be equal for, unknown to anyone else,
he is himself a telepath.

NOTES

The mystery of David Gant's identity, fear for the fate of the telepaths on Engo,
and fascination with telepathic powers hold a reader's attention. The psychic abilities
incorporated in this novel, however, stretch credibility almost to the breaking point.
The means by which officials jockey for political power in this authoritarian federation offer another focus for discussion.

Sutton, Jean and Jeff Sutton. **The Boy Who Had the Power.** New York: Putnam,
   1971. 189p. Grades 6-9.

SUMMARY

What greater treasure exists than the secret of immortality? This is a story of
greed in seeking that secret. Psychic powers enhance the intrigue.

On the planet Doorn in Alpha Centauri, a boy named Jedro shepherds the flock
of gran belonging to his unkind master, Mr. Krant. Jedro cannot remember anything
about himself before the day four years earlier when he had awakened in Mr. Krant's
attic room. One day, however, a stranger named Mr. Clement appears, gives Jedro
an unusual stone, and tells the boy to hide because he (Mr. Clement) is about to be
murdered. Thus Jedro witnesses Clement's murder by a tattooed man, just as predicted.

Months pass while Jedro ponders Clement's brief words, especially his statement
that Jedro has "the power." Meanwhile, Jedro dreams of a man floating through space
in an oblong box.

Jedro runs away to town, where he joins a carnival from Earth—a carnival which
turns out to include The Tattooed Man, Clement's murderer. The latter is a henchman
of the carnival owner, Gerald Faust, who knows that a telepath named Holton Lee lies
somewhere in a cryogenic sleep, waiting to be awakened by the carrier of the memory
stone. The time has come for that awakening since Lee, who knows the secret of
immortality, has been waiting for the development of space technology so he can
lead his colony of telepaths to a home in the far reaches of the universe.

Faust is not the only one who covets Lee's secret; Old Granny, the fortune-teller,
is another. They will stop at nothing to obtain the stone from Jedro, who gradually

realizes his own telepathic skills. Driven by greed, Faust and Granny both fail, while Clement's daughter and Taber, a gentle lion who nevertheless kills three men to protect Jedro, assist the hero toward his destined task of awakening Holton Lee.

NOTES

A fast-paced mystery, this book holds a reader's interest by means of the gradual unfolding of Jedro's memory and mission. The interplay of several psychic abilities will fascinate many young people and may spark investigation of this field.

Sutton, Jean and Jeff Sutton. **Lord of the Stars**. New York: Putnam, 1969. 220p. Grades 6-10.

SUMMARY

A space adventure, *Lord of the Stars* recounts the adventures of Danny, marooned on the planet Wenda when his parents' colonial spaceship failed and he escaped in a lifeboat. On the planet, Danny is helped by Zandro, octopuslike leader of the Kroon, who wants to make use of Danny's telepathic powers in his scheme to take over the universe. Six androids like Danny are planted on the planet Makal to gather military intelligence about the human government there. Zandro can communicate with the androids only through Danny, but Danny's communications also put him in touch with Arla, an orphaned telepath living on Malak, who is horrified at Zandro's plan. In a final confrontation between Zandro and the telepaths, Arla links minds with Danny to overpower the Overlord, who is forced to withdraw.

NOTES

Alien creatures and artificial beings are combined with telepathy to create an exciting, if incredible, plot. As in some other Sutton novels, telepaths are feared by the government and are required to register.

---

*Sutton, Jean and Jeff Sutton. **The Programmed Man**. New York: Putnam, 1968. 192p. Grades 7-10.

SUMMARY

Spies and counterspies play with cunning and luck in this galaxy-wide tale of adventure. August Karsh is responsible for maintaining the power of a stagnating empire; his best agent, Daniel York, is charged with protecting the secret of the N-bomb. Dr. Golem Gregor directs intelligence operations for the outcast Zuman worlds, inhabited by telepathic mutants; his man is Myron Terle, a teleport, who hopes to obtain the secret which York is to protect. The first step toward capturing one of the bombs has, however, been taken by agents of Prince Li-Hu of the Alphan worlds; descended from emperors of Earth's ancient China, Li-Hu would like to be independent of the Empire.

An N-bomb cruiser is missing, has been sabotaged. York commandeers the destroyer *Draco* so as to locate the lost space vessel. Two attempts on York's life convince Captain Hull that traitors are on board the *Draco*. Meanwhile, Terle is skipping from one planet to another, leaving a disturbingly obvious trail. Terle himself is carrying out a program; each step emerges from his subconscious mind as needed. Terle recalls that he has submitted to this treatment so that, if captured, he can give no information either to Alphan or to Empire interrogators. Whatever Terle may be about, York's ship reaches the site of the lost cruiser's crash landing and picks up the few survivors. However, when York and Captain Hull enter the N-bomb chamber, they are astonished to find it empty. Nevertheless, York uncovers the identity of the saboteurs. Meanwhile, Terle has already been captured. Why, then, does York feel that his mission is not yet completed?

NOTES

Spies in outer space!—clearly, humankind have carried their ancient enmities along while spreading across the galaxy. There are no women in this novel; they are not even mentioned. Stereotypes associated with race and status are evident. Furthermore, the novel tells us little about circumstances in the world of the future. Nevertheless, its well-crafted plot and extremely clever ending will hold readers' attention to the very last sentence.

Only very careful readers will guess the identity of Prince Li-Hu's saboteurs before York names them (p. 175), the secret of the N-bomb before York reveals it to Captain Hull (p. 186), or the reason York still counts the minutes to Earth orbit after the saboteurs' imprisonment and Terle's capture (p. 191).

Tofte, Arthur. **Survival Planet; A Novel of the Future**. Indianapolis: Bobbs-Merrill, 1977. 187p. Grade 7 up.

SUMMARY

Sven Evenson pretends ruthlessness to drive the ruthless UnaTerran officials from his beautiful planet. Sven is one of five survivors living on the planet he knows as Iduna after a spaceship crash 13 years earlier. Other intelligent beings on the planet are the gentle Thrulls, seal-like aliens who sing to the sun each dawn and evening, and their more aggressive counterparts, the Maloons, who live some distance away.

The Evenson family has adjusted to life on Iduna, where the two youngest of the group, Sven and his sister Bretta, have grown nearly twice the height of their father and older brother and sister because they have been eating natural foods since childhood, rather than the artificial food packages which had been their fare on Earth.

The Evensons are astonished when a spaceship goes into orbit around Iduna. They learn that the food machines which have fed humans on Earth for 250 years are breaking down, and no one knows how to repair them. Consequently, Vice-Chairman Zurik and other officials have come in search of a new planet to settle. The UnaTerrans take over the Evensons' stone house, leaving the family to escape to their Thrull friends.

The two spaceship pilots are of a different sort from the officials, however, and join with the Evensons. In hopes of rescuing the pilots' loved ones, and perhaps showing survivors on Earth how to raise natural food, the two pilots as well as Sven and Bretta and their father set off for Earth, with a cargo of seeds and animals.

Having flown ten light years in six months, they reach Earth only to find famine and anarchy. Sven and one of the pilots venture into the city to find the latter's fianceé, but she is dead and the two men with the soldiers assigned to them barely make it back to headquarters, having injured and killed desperate, starving people to do so. The food machines are still working sporadically in the headquarters building, but the situation is hopeless. The Evensons, the two pilots, and the family of one of them, as well as another family, return to Iduna, soon to realize that they are being followed by Chairman Taggert and other officials. By claiming to have nuclear warheads trained on Taggert's ship, Sven forces the new arrivals to pick up the Zurik group and travel on to another planet.

NOTES

Iduna has the flavor of a pastoral utopia, although not as closely connected to previous human errors as is usually the case, and not following upon a catastrophic occurrence. Earth, on the other hand, is a dystopia, where man has let himself become so dependent upon machines that when they break down, no one can repair them; where every possible surface is covered with identical four-story apartment buildings whose roofs run one into the other; where famine has resulted in anarchy and brutality. The characters carry with them the attitudes which match the environments from which they come.

The typography of this book, designed by Terry McKee, is unusual and may spark student interest in typefaces and book design.

---

*Townsend, John Rowe. **Noah's Castle**. Philadelphia: Lippincott, 1975. 255p. Dell paperback, 1978. Grades 7-10.

SUMMARY

A man whose own alcoholic father often left the family hungry is determined that his wife and children will never suffer the same fate, even if that means hoarding food while others do not have enough. For Barry Mortimer, the situation creates a conflict between loyalty to his father and concern for those who are unable to obtain food.

Sensing that mounting inflation will lead to a crisis in England, Norman Mortimer buys a large, old home, well screened from neighbors' inquisitive eyes. There he installs shelves in the basement and begins to lay in supplies of canned and dried food, as well as a freezer full of meat and an electric generator. At first he keeps the secret from everyone but his son Geoff, but eventually Barry and Nessie, the two older children, are let in on the plan. It is Barry who first dubs the project "Noah's Castle," in allusion to Noah's Ark.

The father has always been something of a bully, but in his almost fanatic resolve to protect his family from hunger, he alienates them still further. The older daughter leaves home as soon as she turns 18. The wife and younger daughter move out temporarily as well. As prices rise—two million pounds for a loaf of bread—other nations no longer export to England the food it must have. Even those who are employed cannot use their ever-increasing wages to buy goods that are unavailable.

In order to save his father from prison, or from a beating when the hoard inevitably will be stolen, Barry decides to let the Share Alike group spirit the food away for free redistribution to the hungry. At the same time, however, both a profiteer's gang and an irresponsible group of raiders acting under the title Share Now also descend on the hoarded supply. The family manages to limp along thereafter, and the overall situation takes a slight upturn, but only his wife still offers comfort to the father who did his best to provide food, but not warmth.

NOTES

An author's note tells us that Townsend is "not predicting that the conditions [he] describes will actually come about." However, *Noah's Castle* explains the effects of inflation in language young people can understand. It also provides concrete examples of the lesser side of human nature which may emerge in the face of hunger, cold, and privation. There is Mr. Gerald, the father's former employer, who moves in for a visit, then threatens to report Mortimer if not permitted to stay, and finally tips off the violent Share Now group just as he moves out. There is the old man who is so busy eating his one meal in two days that he cannot look up, and the young man who steals a whole truckful of meals-on-wheels.

The most important issue in this novel, however, is not survival, but morality. Is Norman Mortimer wrong to place responsibility to his family above the public welfare? Is Jim Alsop right to lead undisciplined, violent raids on hoarders and profiteers? Is Barry right to betray his father by opening the door to the Share Alike group? Is Nessie right to move in with her boyfriend and his mother? Are the family members right to deceive one another for the various purposes described? Where does family loyalty fit on the scale of human values? The vivid characterization will facilitate discussion of these issues.

Townsend, John Rowe. **The Visitors.** Philadelphia: Lippincott, 1977. 221p. Grade 6 up.

SUMMARY

Katherine Wyatt and her parents travel back through time from the year 2149 to present-day Cambridge University. However, they give themselves away, their experiment consequently a failure. Meanwhile, Katherine and Ben Dunham have fallen in love. If Katherine stays, however, she must soon fall victim to a virus or bacterium to which she has not been immunized. So she and her family return to their time, and memory of them disappears from the minds of—almost—all persons they had encountered.

NOTES

This novel is essentially a present-time story. However, some direct information is provided about the Wyatts' future world, and additional bits may be inferred from their reactions to the twentieth century. The features of the apparently utopian twenty-second century contrast sharply with the faults of our own time.

Walters, Hugh. **First Contact?** Nashville: Thos. Nelson, 1973. 174p. Grades 5-8.

SUMMARY

Are advanced alien intelligences, far more advanced than humankind, watching our development? Two spaceships set out toward Uranus, hoping to discover the cause of radio signals whose regularity suggests they may be artificially, rather than naturally, created. As the eight astronauts approach Uranus, they discover that the mysterious radio signals, if heard for more than a few seconds, produce splitting headaches. More alarming, the signals suddenly jam the frequency used by the spaceships to communicate with one another and with Cape Kennedy Control. One of the astronauts travels across to the other ship and they establish a series of frequencies to be used as necessary, but the alien signals come in on each new frequency within ten minutes. In desperation, having noted that the signals follow voice communications only, not interrupting the telemetric frequencies transmitting data from the ships' instruments to Earth, the astronauts rig up Morse code keys. Soon garbled Morse signals come in. By repeating these back, and then switching to number series, which the unknown broadcaster carries forward, the astronauts become convinced that they have contacted an intelligent, nonhuman entity.

The ships land on Uranus. Contact is established when the alien, Vari, sets up an electrical field which aligns the atoms of the humans with those of his spaceship so that the astronauts can walk through its wall. Vari shows them his ship's gravity drive and other technological wonders, then begins to question them about humanity's spiritual development. His assignment, Vari tells them, is to decide whether Earth is far enough advanced to be ready for permanent, expanded contact with his own people. On the second contact, six of the eight men are inside Vari's ship so long that the remaining two become alarmed. When their laser guns fail even to scorch the alien spaceship, Morrey Kant decides he must persuade Serge to lift off in one ship and head for Earth while Morrey himself crushes the alien ship with his own. Convinced that his companions are already dead, Morrey sees this as the only way to protect Earth.

Vari is aware of Morrey's growing hostility and is holding the six hostages to learn what Morrey will do. When he understands Morrey's intended self-sacrifice, Vari intervenes; but, convinced that Earth is not yet ready to accept alien contact, he sends both ships and their crews back to Earth with no remaining memory of their encounter.

NOTES

This alien contact is handled with some originality. Students may be able to think of other ways to solve the problems of initial communication. When the astronauts exchange the number series with Vari (p. 60), one may conjecture as to how the number 81 is transmitted—does the author assume a base-ten number system, for instance?

From a literary standpoint, the novel offers little, since the characters (all of them male) are handled with condescension. But the plot takes a clever turn or two, and several interesting possibilities in space travel technology are explored.

Walters, Hugh. **Passage to Pluto**. Nashville: Thos. Nelson, 1973, 157p. Grades 5-7.

SUMMARY

A rescue mission in space, *Passage to Pluto* follows three astronauts on the first manned fly-by past that distant planet. They are to observe the surface and, if possible, investigate a body dubbed Planet X, whose presence has been hypothesized by mathematicians based on deviations in Pluto's orbit, but which has not been sighted by the most powerful telescopes.

When the astronauts wake from hypothermia in the vicinity of Pluto, they find that a million-to-one chance has occurred; the fuel tank for their return flight has been damaged by a meteorite and the fuel has escaped. Furthermore, Planet X, small but incredibly dense, is pulling them from their orbit around Pluto and into itself.

Planet X does not behave like a natural body, but almost like a space vehicle of some sort. The astronauts have two weeks to live; their commanding officer on Earth and former team member, Chris Godfrey, sets out in the backup ship, Pluto Two, and reaches them just in time. Pluto One almost immediately crashes into Planet X, causing a nuclear explosion which one of the astronauts had set into motion on the spaceship by way of paying back Planet X for the trouble it had caused. What seems to be a foolish and insubordinate act turns out to have saved the solar system, since Planet X would otherwise have pulled one planet after another within itself, with the destruction of Earth calculated at 100 years in the future.

NOTES

Essentially a suspense story like the two Ballou novels, *Passage to Pluto* unfortunately does not bring its characters to life. Scientifically oriented students may be interested in checking out the accuracy of the background information.

Watson, Simon. **No Man's Land**. New York: Morrow, 1975. 190p. Grades 6-9.

SUMMARY

Even in the wholly government-controlled England of about the year 2000, one may find a dragon and kill it. Life in the village of Hamerburgh was coming to an end. It was not only that Alan's family was moving to a giant-sized apartment complex in Easton, where row upon row of identical units housed 3,000 people. It was not only that the 65-year-old general who set up the boys' games in which they stormed the old stone keep was to be taken away to a rest home. Rather, the entire village was to be "rationalized"—razed to the ground and converted to uniformly smooth land for development.

Every Sunday, though, Alan returns to Hamerburgh on his motor bike. He finds that the general has not gone to the welfare home, but has escaped to abandoned Wood Hall, where he lives with an even more elderly, but equally independent, Mrs. Arbuthnot. After some months, Alan's parents and the authorities, believing that Alan's attachment to the past is unhealthy, send him to a boarding school. There Alan learns well from a teaching machine, but is confused between the advice of Carver, in a basement room, who encourages him to shoot at a moving picture with a sub-machine gun when he feels angry, and Mr. Christopher, on the top floor, who seems very kindly, yet not quite trustworthy. Disquieting, too, is the film about Kilda, an island where life is simple, even primitive. Fear of exile to Kilda, Alan's new friend Jay tells him, is intended to frighten the students into conforming, but Jay himself hopes to be sent there.

When Alan receives a letter from his sister mentioning the impending "rationalization" of Hamerburgh, Alan and Jay run away from the school to warn the general and Mrs. Arbuthnot. They find that the latter has given in to the security of a welfare home, but Alan and the general decide to make a heroic, though probably futile, gesture of protest on the battlements of the old keep. There they face the Giant, an enormous machine built originally for entertainment. A large audience has in fact gathered to watch the Giant at its new task of demolition. Giant had failed to locate Alan the day before, now fails to catch him in the keep, and becomes stuck in the masonry. In its anger, the machine shakes loose a section of the wall and is crushed. For his part in the escapade, Jay is exiled to Kilda, as he had hoped. The general is sent to the experimental geriatric center of his friend, Dr. Crabbe, who has managed to survive within the establishment without succumbing. As for Alan, he is apprenticed to Dr. Crabbe and so has the opportunity to fulfill his ambition of becoming a doctor. The village of Hamerburgh becomes an abandoned wilderness.

NOTES

The author notes on a flyleaf, "This story takes place in a possible future." A dystopia which projects a welfare state into the situation of over-control, *No Man's Land* is also a story of one boy's quest for a goal not yet clearly defined. As the general says (p. 189), Alan has "slain the dragon." Giant symbolizes both our ancient enemy, the dragon, and the new enemy, the giant of national planning. After Giant's defeat, the world does not change, nor have the characters learned much, but at least Alan, Jay, and the general reach the best niches available for them within that society.

In tone, although not in situation, the novel much resembles *Out There* by Mace, also a 1975 British publication with the Greenwillow imprint. Plot and motivation in *No Man's Land* are more clearly developed, but also more simplistic, than in Mace's story.

West, Carl and Katherine MacLean. **Dark Wing**. New York: Atheneum, 1979. 242p. Grade 8 up.

SUMMARY

The theme of this novel is freedom—social freedom vs. natural freedom, freedom to die vs. freedom to live. Gordon Travis approaches adulthood at a time when it is illegal to practice medicine or to sell medicines. Yet he has a natural bent for doctoring, an almost photographic memory—and he happens upon a decades-old paramedic kit, complete to computer tapes with diagnostic and treatment information. Fascinated, he absorbs and remembers that information, and finds ways to learn more. He helps a few people here and there, then finds himself virtually imprisoned by one of his patients, who sees in Gordon a means to illicit income.

Gordon provides treatments, prescribes medicines, often unsure as to whether he is doing the right thing. About to be arrested, Gordon escapes when his captor dies of a long-standing ailment. Meanwhile, he has lost track of his young friend, Iron Phedon, who is trying to return to his home planet of Centauri II, but is being prevented by those who have intrigued to "buy" the planet with an eye to vast corporate profits. Because Iron knows that his parents have not signed any contracts regarding Centauri II, there are those who would like to brainwash him, or kill him.

Gordon changes his ID for that of young Mark Talbot, enters the police academy, and becomes a cadet on Deathwatch. In what was once a hospital, the Ladies of the Watch bring a dying person to a moment of happiness, recalling past triumphs or thinking of loved ones, then quickly kill him, in the belief that the soul is thus released to eternal happiness. Eventually, Gordon realizes that he cannot carry forward this career because it is so diametrically opposed to his desires to heal the sick, a realization that comes to him when he finds himself unable to carry out his assignment to kill an elderly couple in their moment of happiness.

Gordon takes a vacation from the police force, finds Iron, again becomes involved in doctoring, and uses that skill to obtain his friend's passage to Centauri II. However, Iron's enemies catch up with him and poison him, upon which Travis again visits the ID-changer and arranges to take Iron's place on the spaceship to a planet of forests and sunlight.

NOTES

Gordon Travis flees the dystopian Earth for a new beginning elsewhere. Not only has medicine been outlawed on Earth, but sickness is considered evidence of immorality—one is sick because he chooses to be sick. In many other ways, however, individual choice has become the golden rule. The 47th amendment to the constitution has provided rights to juveniles, who may leave home and live in youth dens, where they receive a monthly stipend from the government as long as they refrain from having children. Should an individual want to become a parent, he must get a job, refuse the stipend, and thus avoid the sterility shots which are a condition of the stipend. The dens are self-governing; in one instance a den member is found not guilty of murder on the ground that the victim had been asking to be killed by his obvious behavior. Gordon is at odds with society because of his interest in medicine; it does not appear that there are many other actions, except perhaps advocacy against space exploration, that could get him into trouble with the law.

There is a quality of unreality about the novel, perhaps because Gordon's essentially negative attitude puts off the reader. He finally achieves his original goal—to become a space colonist—more by default than by design. Furthermore, it is nearly incredible that he can perform a tracheotomy, and even join tendons, and install pumps in the veins of an elderly man with a weak heart, just from studying instructions on a teaching machine. (Perhaps younger readers should be cautioned that such operations are much more difficult and dangerous than they sound. To the reader's knowledge, Gordon never makes a medical mistake!) The rather bizarre contrast between Tibetan and Egyptian rites for the dead and "feely" movies, holograms, and vidcubes contributes to the sense of unreality.

A comparable novel written for adults, although many older students will find it interesting reading, is *The Bladerunner* by Alan E. Nourse (David McKay, 1974), in which those persons over five years of age who have received medical care three times must be sterilized before any further medical care will be provided. In this situation, many doctors provide services through an underground, since people are understandably reluctant to seek their advice through legal channels. The title refers to the main character, Billy, who handles medical equipment and supplies for a doctor making illegal calls.

White, Ted. **Secret of the Marauder Satellite**. Philadelphia: Westminster Press, 1967.
　　171p. Berkley paperback, 1978. Grade 6 up.

SUMMARY

White blends mystery and science fiction, along with elements of boy-finds-himself and boy-finds-girl. The reader is led to speculate about nonhuman aliens who may have died out millennia ago.

The year is 1984. Paul Williams, first person narrator, has graduated from the NASA training academy and is assigned as a cadet on our orbiting space station. He leaves behind a United States troubled by unemployment, drought, pollution, and crime.

Gifted with an uncanny knack for handling himself at various gravities, Paul is assigned to salvaging material abandoned in space. His first find is a Russian spaceship launched in 1963, still containing its three, now mummified, cosmonauts. Their journal breaks off after noting they were on collision course with something they never had time to describe, yet the vessel obviously had not collided with anything. Paul goes out on another mission in his space tug and encounters the "black marauder satellite," which may have caused the Russian ship's failure. While Paul floats at the end of a mile-long cable, the marauder draws all power from the tug. Paul manages to get back to the space station using his air tanks as jets, with plenty of time to reflect on his personal problems along the way. Almost simultaneously comes word that a similar "black marauder" has been discovered in orbit around Mars, and also that the one nearby is on collision course with the space station itself. Three nuclear missiles are required to neutralize the marauder, which, scientists surmise, although now lacking some of its original capabilities, had been placed in orbit to intercept and destroy any spaceships that humans (or Martians) might attempt to place in orbit.

NOTES

Primarily an adventure story and already dated, this novel nevertheless touches briefly upon such concerns as pollution, crowding, bureaucracy, economic problems, and international tension. It should encourage questions about intelligent life in space, especially in eons past.

Careful readers will enjoy the word "¢o$tly" on page 75. They will notice that the first man on the moon is erroneously reported for 1972, and the first wheel of a space station for 1978. Unfortunately, the author takes a condescending attitude toward his characters.

---

*Wilder, Cherry. **The Luck of Brin's Five.** New York: Atheneum, 1977. 230p. Pocket Books paperback, 1979. Grade 7 up.

SUMMARY

The Luck of Brin's Five is a story of adaptation to change—both social change and the process of growing up. Dorn Brinroyan, a Moruian on the planet Torin, is 12 years old when his story begins. He is the child of a traditional family of five: the wife (Brin), two husbands, an "ancient" (elderly person, Brin's mother), and a "Luck." The latter is a mentally or physically deformed or abnormal person. In addition, there are three children, one still in the mother's pouch, for these aliens are marsupials.

The Luck of Brin's Five is elderly and dies just as the story opens. At the same time, however, a human who has come to the planet with a small scientific crew and taken off in their only reconnaissance plane, crashes near Brin's home. Scott Gale, the human, whom the family dubs "Diver," is quickly adopted as their new Luck, for by Moruian standards he has several physical abnormalities.

Afraid that the Great Elder, Tiath Gargan, will seek the pilot of the downed plane, Brin's Five sets off for the town of Cullin, there to consult a Diviner about protecting their Luck. She in turn sends the group further south, to inquire of an unnamed person in Rintoul as to how Diver might regain his ship and radio his companions. En route, however, the family comes upon the boat of three old women who have committed suicide in the belief that they had been dishonored when the passengers on their river boat were dragged away by Tiath Gargan's men. By discovering the three bodies, Dorn has become obligated to deliver their curse to Gargan.

Diver helps him with a tool which carries the message to the deck of Tiath Gargan's barge. By a secret agreement, seven men are obligated to Tiath Gargan and must now hunt Diver to his death. Meanwhile, Diver enters and wins a flying machine contest. The seven assailants are overcome, and Brin's Five journey on to Rintoul, only to have Diver and Dorn himself captured by men of Tiath Gargan. This time Scott and Dorn are brought before The Hundred, the governing council, where, despite the Great Elder's arguments, the right of Brin's Five to their Luck is upheld.

NOTES

This novel is of interest more because of the cultural contrasts and processes it depicts than for any future image, since Torin most closely resembles a feudal civilization which is not yet approaching space age technology. The Moruians come alive as real people. After a time, their family structure, their traditions, their feudal style of speech, even their marsupial pouches become familiar, and the blue-eyed human seems strange. The author creates this effect by using as narrator the young Moruian, Dorn Brinroyan, who views everything from his own cultural base, yet has enough empathy for the human Scott Gale to acquire a measure of detachment in considering his own people.

Also contributing to the reader's acceptance is Scott Gale's ready adaptation to his new home. He is apparently selected for, or conditioned to, such adaptation, for he says he is "under rule from my world to live out my life, if need be, in a new place" (p. 219). Certainly he rapidly learns the language, analyzes and accepts the customs, and commits himself to new family relationships in this setting.

Another topic for discussion is the novelist's portrayal of social change. The values of Brin's Five give way in part to the newer values of city dwellers as the novel closes. Social change, already under way before Scott Gale's arrival, is apparently to be hastened as a consequence of his mere presence, as well as of the technology he brings to Torin.

---

*Williams, Jay. **The People of the Ax**. New York: Walck, 1974. 145p. Dell paperback, 1975. Grades 7-10.

SUMMARY

It is necessary to recognize and reach out to the spark of humanity wherever it can be found. The boy Arne, the girl Frey, and others of the same age complete the initiation rites by which they receive their souls and change from Unfinished People to Human Beings. Now they can sense one another's emotions so fully that they can never hurt one another. The new initiates set out on an adventurous mock raid to steal the beaded blanket which is an important symbol to a neighboring village, knowing they will eventually be raided in turn. Arne achieves a coup by scratching his opponent's cheek with his ax, at which point the encounter is ended and a token exchanged. Just then both villagers and Arne's group join forces to fight off a band of the subhuman crom. The crom whom Arne engages in battle turns out to have an iron club, a matter of great importance, since if they have acquired iron weapons, the crom may be impossible to keep in check—and they do not share the Humans' aversion to violence. Unknown to himself, however, Arne has turned his enemy's club into iron by psychokinesis because his reluctance to kill is so strong that he cannot do so even to save his own life. Arne's village council suspects Arne's developing power and sends him on a journey, with Frey as his companion, to a wise old woman who will help him accept and train his "tendo."

Along the way, Arne is temporarily captured by the crom; he discovers that they express gratitude, laugh, and play—acts he had thought impossible except for Humans. In escaping these enemies, Arne and Frey find themselves inside the mountain on which lives the old woman they seek. They see tunnels which appear man-made, and even some inscriptions. When they reach Osan, the wise woman, she tells them that the mountain is really one of many collapsed buildings, the remains of a city built by the ancestors of the crom, who destroyed one another at some time in the distant past. Afterwards the Human Beings appeared, and they gradually awakened the soul in others. The crom, however, continued to be savage and uncivilized.

As Arne's training continues, he gradually becomes convinced that the crom are really Unfinished People, needing to have their souls awakened by someone with a power as strong as his own. After Osan communicates telepathically with other adepts, she grants Arne's desire to try out his belief, which the young man success-fully does.

NOTES

If it were not for the crom, *The People of the Ax* would fit the notion of a pas-toral utopia. Since those subhuman beings are going to be transformed as a result of Arne's empathy for them, perhaps it is accurate to class the novel in that genre. Whatever the catastrophe which caused the destruction of the cities, the Human Beings' incapacity for violence against their own kind, and their commitment to maintaining the balance in nature suggest that rejection of technology which is char-acteristic of the pastoral utopian form.

Students may wish to discuss why Arne's unusual gift also tends to isolate him from other people and at the same time to restrict his freedom to live as he chooses. It might be interesting to compare the civilization in which he lives with that of, say, the Vikings.

Williams, Jay. **The Time of the Kraken.** New York: Four Winds Press, 1977. 168p.
    Grade 7 up.

SUMMARY

Lack of understanding may divide people, yet truth may be too much to accept. In this novel, humans who fled centuries earlier from Iceland on the polluted earth have become divided over religious differences. Thorgeir Redhair's father has a blood brother among the enemy, and to him Thorgeir is sent in the hope of avoiding war. But Thorgeir's purpose is revealed and viewed as treason, his father is killed, and Thorgeir is exiled. On the journey back from the enemy village, however, Thorgeir has been told that the kraken is rising from its northern home and soon will descend upon the land, absorbing all the water it can and thus killing the crops. With his new wife, Ylga, and the nephew of his father's blood brother, who has sworn blood oath with Thorgeir, the young man sets off to the fabled Temple of Arveid, there hoping to obtain the weapons which had once before been granted to defeat the kraken.

The temple, however, is actually the spaceship in which the ancestors of all the people had come to this planet. The computer "Guardian" there provides Thorgeir with the weapons to slay the kraken. Thorgeir then tries to explain the truth in a way which will be understandable to the people, yet will reconcile the differences which have arisen from their misunderstanding of their origins. Finally, he returns to the temple, where he will live in exile with his companions.

NOTES

Forced back to an agrarian economy, the people have also revived much of their Nordic mythology, expanded by tales based on their forgotten journey to this planet and subsequent events. Students might identify the stylistic devices which create the folkloric style of the narrative. The typeface and book design are well suited to the story.

---

*Yep, Laurence. **Sweetwater**. Illus. by Julia Noonan. New York: Harper, 1973. 201p. Avon paperback, 1975. Grades 4-8.

SUMMARY

Things of beauty and relationships of value must sometimes be let go. Tyree Priest is a Silkie, one of a group left to themselves in Old Sion, a city half under water on the planet Harmony. More than anything else he wants to learn music, although his father objects. Tyree, therefore, slips away to Sheol, where the Argans live. An Argan is an intelligent being somewhat resembling a four-foot spider; among them Amadeus is an outstanding songsmith and he agrees to teach Tyree to play the flute until he "finds his song."

But Tyree inadvertently starts a tragic series of actions in motion when he takes a trumpet his father has salvaged to Amadeus as a gift of appreciation. According to his convictions, Amadeus now owes Tyree a gift such as no human has, so the Argans take away the Seadragon's treasure, while the Seadragon causes such disturbances in the sea that half the Silkies decide they can no longer live in Old Sion. They accept employment with Fuller Satin, the money-hungry businessman who wants to lay claim to Old Sion, perhaps keeping some of the Silkies as a tourist attraction. At the same time, Satin tries to buy the Seadragon treasure, a touchstone which gives Tyree's blind sister Caley such pleasure that she does not want to part with it at any price.

Concerned for the safety of the tourists, the Silkies who have gone over to Satin kill many of the hydras which infest the waters. By so doing, they interfere with the natural balance to the extent that the sunfish the Silkies need for food multiply far more than usual, attracting new populations of hydra from farther out in the sea. The hydra attack and eat the catch of sunfish and then attack the Silkies themselves. Now the last of the Silkies will be forced to leave their homes. Indeed, they are almost drowned by the Seadragon as she comes in search of her treasure— actually, her egg—so Caley must give up her touchstone. Shortly thereafter, Tyree must bid good-bye to Amadeus, but he still takes his music with him.

NOTES

This almost poetic novel talks about the essentially human qualities—music, stories, loyalty, independence. It also portrays the ways in which intelligent beings do, and do not, come to agreement; the relationship between Tyree and the Argan Amadeus is particularly worthy of study. *See* notes for Hoover's *The Lost Star* for other novels that describe efforts at human-alien communication.

Many names in this book are drawn from the Old Testament. Others are allusions to other sources, e.g., Amadeus the musician (Wolfgang Amadeus Mozart); Sebastian and Handel, two other Argan musicians; Fuller Satin, exploitative businessman (Satan, or a type of house paint?).

Tyree is the first person narrator of the story; occasionally he also reads from the log in old Anglic which had been kept by his Great-Great-Grandpa Lamech, first Captain of the Silkies after they had been stranded on Harmony.

PART IV

INDEX OF THEMES AND MOTIFS

This index provides access to the novels described in Part III by specific genres, themes, and topics. Subject headings have been chosen for their utility in developing classroom programs and activities in literature, social studies, and science, as well as for use in preparing book talks and providing reader guidance in libraries. Students may find it useful to locate titles on topics of special interest. Specific follow-up activities for novels which share common themes and motifs have been described in the closing pages of Part I.

Just reading through the subject headings on the following pages will suggest numerous topics for discussion and investigation. Listed below are several examples grouped to suggest the wide range of topics that might be pursued in connection with various units of study.

Literary Forms	DYSTOPIAS FABLES SURREALISM UTOPIAS UTOPIAS, PASTORAL etc.
Themes	CONFORMITY VS. INDIVIDUALITY INTER-GROUP CONFLICT MACHINE TAKE-OVER REALITY VS. FANTASY/FAITH etc.
Social Studies	ANTHROPOLOGY COMMUNAL LIVING EVOLUTION, CULTURAL FEUDAL LIFE GOVERNMENT headings INFORMATION CONTROL RACIAL CONFLICT RELIGION SEX EQUALITY SOCIAL CLASSES SYSTEM BREAKS WAR headings etc.
Settings	ALTAIR SYSTEM GREAT BRITAIN U.S.–SOUTHWEST TWENTIETH CENTURY FORTIETH CENTURY etc.

Biological Sciences	ANIMAL/PLANT EXTINCTION/ PRESERVATION
	BALANCE OF NATURE
	CLONING
	CONDITIONING, PSYCHOLOGICAL
	GENETIC ENGINEERING
	HYDROPONICS
	MUTATIONS
	POLLUTION headings

etc.

Technology	CITIES, ENCLOSED
	COMMUNICATIONS TECHNOLOGY
	COMPUTERS
	EDUCATIONAL TECHNOLOGY
	ENERGY headings
	ROBOTS
	SPACE headings
	TELEPHONES, PICTURE-SCREEN
	VEHICLES, SOLAR-POWERED
	WEATHER CONTROL

etc.

Special-Interest Topics	ALIEN BEINGS (INTELLIGENT)
	ASTROLOGY
	CIRCUSES
	MUSIC
	OLYMPIC GAMES
	PARALLEL WORLDS
	PSYCHIC headings
	TELEPATHY

etc.

As a further aid to locating books suited to various teaching purposes, the symbol † identifies a book which contains enough material on the topic under which it is listed so that the book could serve by itself to introduce the topic, and to provide basis for discussion, written composition, research into factual background, or other appropriate follow-up. Conversely, books which lack that symbol provide at least a few paragraphs of description or detail, but would best be combined with other novels under that same topic if follow-up activities are planned.

Under literary forms such as "dystopia" the symbol † indicates that the novel so identified is a good exemplar of that form. The symbol † has not been used under settings.

As compared with Part II of this manual, the "Index of Themes and Motifs" focuses for the most part on far more narrowly defined topics. Furthermore, whereas Part II discusses only selected novels, with the intent of describing the broad range of world-future images offered in children's literature within each topic, sometimes drawing appropriate comparisons, the "Index of Themes and Motifs," attempts to list every novel (by author's last name and first word of title) which contains useful information about, or is a useful example of, the topic. Therefore, when a number of books are under the same topic in this index, Parts II and III will provide assistance in selecting titles most suitable for the recreational or instructional purpose at hand. Furthermore, Part IV does not indicate literary quality of the various titles listed. For guidance in that area, the reader is referred to the asterisks which identify "first-purchase" titles in Part III.

INDEX OF THEMES AND MOTIFS

AIRPLANES, AUTO-GUIDED
see VEHICLES/AIRPLANES, AUTO-
GUIDED

ALIEN ANIMALS/PLANTS
  †Bova: Altair
  Bova: Flight
  †Bulychev: Alice
  Christopher: City
  Christopher: Lotus
  Dickson: Alien
  Dwiggins: Asteroid
  Earnshaw: Dragonfall 5
  Fisk: Escape
  Harrison: Men
  Hoover: Lost
  †Hoover: Rains
  Karl: Turning
  †Lightner: Space Ark
  †Lightner: Space Gypsies
  Lightner: Space Olympics
  Lightner: Star
  †Lightner: Thursday
  †McCaffrey: Dragonsinger
  †McCaffrey: Dragonsong
  Morressy: Humans
  Norton: Android
  †Norton: Dark
  Norton: Exiles
  Norton: Forerunner
  Norton: Ice
  Norton: Iron
  Norton: Moon
  †Norton: Night
  Norton: Ordeal
  †Norton: Postmarked
  Norton: Uncharted
  Norton: Victory
  †Norton: X
  Norton: Zero
  Packard: Third
  Synder: And
  Snyder: Below
  Snyder: Until
  †Stone: Praise
  †Stone: Those (cont'd)

  Sutton: Boy
  Tofte: Survival
  Wilder: Luck
  Williams: Time
  †Yep: Sweetwater

ALIEN ARTIFACTS
  †Bulychev: Alice
  Christopher: City
  †Dickson: Alien
  Engdahl: Beyond
  Hoover: Lost
  Key: Forgotten
  †Norton: Exiles
  †Norton: Forerunner
  Norton: Night
  †Norton: Uncharted
  Norton: Victory
  †Norton: Zero
  Simak: Goblin
  Walters: First
  Walters: Passage
  †White: Secret

ALIEN BEINGS (INTELLIGENT)
  Abels series
  †Anderson: Star
  †Asimov: Heavenly
  †Berry: Dar
  †Bulychev: Alice
  †Carlson: Human
  †Christopher: City
  †Christopher: Lotus
  †Christopher: Pool
  Corbett: Donkey
  Del Rey: Infinite
  †Del Rey: Prisoners
  †Dickson: Alien
  Earnshaw: Dragonfall 5
  Engdahl: Far
  †Fairman: Forgetful
  †Fisk: Grinny
  Goldberger: Looking
  Harrison: Men
  Hendrich: Girl
  †Hoover: Delikon (cont'd)

†Hoover: Lost
†Karl: Turning
†Key: Forgotten
†Kurland: Princes
 Larson: Battlestar
†Lightner: Space Ark
 Lightner: Space Olympics
 McGowen: Odyssey
†Morressy: Drought
†Morressy: Humans
 Morressy: Windows
 Myers: Brainstorm
†Norton: Android
†Norton: Breed
†Norton: Day
 Norton: Exiles
†Norton: Forerunner
†Norton: Iron
 Norton: Moon
†Norton: Night
†Norton: Ordeal
†Norton: Postmarked
†Norton: Victory
 Norton: X
†Offutt: Galactic
 Packard: Third
 Reynolds: Earth
 Richelson: Star
†Simak: Goblin
 Slote: My Trip
†Stone: Praise
†Stone: Those
†Sutton: Lord
†Tofte: Survival
†Walters: First
†Wilder: Luck
†Yep: Sweetwater

ALIEN INTERVENTION (SYSTEM
BREAK)
 †Carlson: Plant
 †Christopher: City
  Christopher: White
 †Hoover: Delikon
 †Karl: Turning

ALPHA CENTAURI (SETTING)
 Bova: Flight
 Sutton: Boy

ALTAIR SYSTEM (SETTING)
 Bova: Winds (cont'd)

Packard: Third

ANARCHY
 see also REVOLUTION
  Bova: City
  Christopher: Empty
  Dickinson: Devil's
  Hoover: Rains
 †Key: Incredible
  Norton: Outside
 †Phipson: When
 †Tofte: Survival

ANDROIDS
 see also ARTIFICIAL BEINGS
  Dwiggins: Asteroid
  Fisk: Grinny
  Harrison: Men
 †Norton: Android
  Norton: Victory
  Richelson: Star
  Slote: My Trip
  Sutton: Lord

ANIMAL/PLANT EXTINCTION/
PRESERVATION
 see also BALANCE OF NATURE
  Biemiller: Escape
  Biemiller: Hydronauts
 †Bova: Altair
  Bulychev: Alice
 †Carlson: Plant
  Christopher: Lotus
 †Hendrich: Girl
  Jakes: Time
 †Key: Golden
 †Lightner: Space Ark
 †Lightner: Thursday
 †Morressy: Drought
  Morressy: Humans
  Norton: Victory
 †Stoutenburg: Out

ANIMALS/PLANTS, ALIEN
 see ALIEN ANIMALS/PLANTS

ANTHROPOLOGY
 see also EVOLUTION, CULTURAL
  Carlson: Human
 †Engdahl: Enchantress
 †Engdahl: Far
  Karl: Turning (cont'd)

Offutt: Galactic
†Sutton: Boy

CITIES, ENCLOSED
Bonham: Forever
†Bova: City
Bova: Weathermakers
†Christopher: City
†Christopher: Pool
Engdahl: Beyond
Engdahl: Journey
Engdahl: This
Hendrich: Girl
†Jones: Moonbase
Kurland: Princes
†Malzberg: Conversations
McGowen: Odyssey
†Norton: Outside
Stoutenburg: Out
Tofte: Survival

CITIES, MULTILEVEL
Bova: Dueling
Fairman: Forgetful
Snyder: And
Snyder: Below
Snyder: Until
West: Dark

CITIES, UNDERGROUND
Biemiller: Escape
Biemiller: Follow
Biemiller: Hydronauts
Campbell: Legend
†Eldridge: Shadow
†Hoover: Children
Hoover: Treasures
Lightner: Space Olympics
†Martel: City
Norton: Day
†Snyder: And
Snyder: Below

CLAIRVOYANCE (perception of object or event not within view)
see also PRECOGNITION
PSYCHIC headings
Biemiller: Hydronauts
Carlson: Mountain
Engdahl: Far
Key: Forgotten
†Key: Golden (cont'd)

McCaffrey: Dragonsinger
McCaffrey: Dragonsong
Norton: Breed
Norton: Exiles
Norton: Forerunner
Norton: Ice
Norton: No
Norton: Outside
Norton: Postmarked
Norton: X
Reynolds: Earth
†Stone: Those
Sutton: Beyond
†Sutton: Boy
Wilder: Luck

CLONING
Bonham: Forever
Hendrich: Girl

COLLEGES
see SCHOOLS AND COLLEGES

COMMUNAL LIVING
Carlson: Human
†Carlson: Mountain
Christopher: Sword
Grohskopf: Notes
Hooker: Kennaquhair
Hoover: Children
Hoover: Treasures
Jones: Cast
†Kestavan: Pale
Kesteven: Awakening
Mace: Out
†Malzberg: Conversations
McCaffrey: Dragonsinger
McCaffrey: Dragonsong
Parker: Time
Snyder: Until
†West: Dark
†Wilder: Luck

COMMUNAL NURSERIES
Biemiller: Follow
Hoover: Children
Hoover: Treasures
Lightner: Day
Norton: X

ENERGY DEPLETION (SYSTEM
BREAK)
   Christopher: Wild

ENERGY, EARTH-CORE
   Martel: City

ENERGY, GRAVITATIONAL
  see also VEHICLES, ANTI-GRAVITY
   Dwiggins: Asteroid
   Key: Magic
   Walters: First

ENERGY, LASER
  see also GUNS, RAY/LASER
   Biemiller: Escape
   Bova: Weathermakers

ENERGY, MECHANICAL (REVER-
SION TO)
  see also FUEL headings
   Christopher: Beyond
   Christopher: Empty
   Christopher: Pool
   Christopher: Prince
   Christopher: White
   †Dickinson: Devil's
   †Dickinson: Heartsease
   †Dickinson: Weathermonger
   Hooker: Kennaquhair
   Hoover: Children
   Hoover: Treasures
   Jones: Cast
   †Kestavan: Pale
   Kesteven: Awakening
   Key: Incredible
   Mace: Out
   McGowen: Odyssey
   Norton: No
   O'Brien: Z
   Williams: People
   Williams: Time

ENERGY, NUCLEAR
  see also SPACE TRAVEL
     TECHNOLOGY
     WAR, NUCLEAR
   Ballou: Bound
   Ballou: Marooned
   Biemiller: Follow
   Christopher: Wild
   Jones: Moonbase (cont'd)

   †Phipson: When
   Sutton: Lord
   Walters: Passage

ENERGY, SOLAR
  see also VEHICLES, SOLAR-
     POWERED
   Biemiller: Follow
   Bova: City
   Hendrich: Girl
   Hoover: Children
   Hoover: Lost
   Hoover: Treasures
   Key: Golden
   Key: Incredible
   Key: Magic
   Kurland: Princes
   Lightner: Day
   Lightner: Space Gypsies

ENGLAND (SETTING)
  see GREAT BRITAIN

ENVIRONMENT
  see BALANCE OF NATURE
     CITIES headings
     POLLUTION headings
     POPULATION headings

ESP (EXTRA-SENSORY PERCEP-
TION)
  see PSYCHIC headings
     TELEPATHY

ETHNIC GROUPS
  see GYPSIES
     RACE headings
     RELIGION

EVOLUTION, BIOLOGICAL
  see GENETIC ENGINEERING
     MUTATIONS

EVOLUTION, CULTURAL
  see also ANTHROPOLOGY
   †Anderson: Star
   †Carlson: Human
   Del Rey: Infinite
   †Engdahl: Beyond
   †Engdahl: Enchantress
   †Engdahl: Far (cont'd)

FUEL SHORTAGE
see also ENERGY headings
   Benford: Jupiter
   Bonham: Missing
   Bova: City
   Kestavan: Pale
   Nelson: Girl
   Phipson: When
   Townsend: Noah's
   Walters: Passage

GALACTIC WAR
see WAR, GALACTIC

GAMBLING
   Christopher: Prince
   Larson: Battlestar
   †Lightner: Space Olympics
   Sutton: Programmed

GANG WARFARE
   †Bova: City
   †Bova: Exiled
   Nelson: Girl
   Norton: Outside

GENETIC ENGINEERING
see also MEDICAL TECHNOLOGY
       MUTATIONS
   †Biemiller: Escape
   †Biemiller: Follow
   †Biemiller: Hydronauts
   †Bova: End
   †Bova: Exiled
   †Bova: Flight
   †Carlson: Human
   Goldberger: Looking
   Harrison: Men
   Hendrich: Girl
   Hoover: Children
   Hoover: Treasures
   Jakes: Time
   Martel: City
   Norton: Dark

GEOLOGIC DISASTER (SYSTEM
BREAK)
   Christopher: Beyond
   Christopher: Prince
   Christopher: Sword
   Norton: No

GERM WARFARE
see WAR, GERM

GERMANY (SETTING)
   Christopher: City

GOD
see RELIGION

GOVERNMENT
see also ANARCHY
       COMMUNAL LIVING
       ELITISM
       FEUDAL LIFE
       INFORMATION CONTROL
       LIBERTARIANISM
       REVOLUTION
       STRIKES
       WAR headings

GOVERNMENT, AUTHORITARIAN
   Anderson: Star
   Bonham: Forever
   Bonham: Missing
   Bova: Dueling
   Campbell: Legend
   Christopher: City
   †Christopher: Guardians
   Christopher: Pool
   Christopher: White
   Corbett: Donkey
   Eldridge: Shadow
   Engdahl: Beyond
   Engdahl: Far
   Engdahl: This
   Hoover: Delikon
   Jackson: Endless
   Kesteven: Awakening
   Mace: Out
   Malzberg: Conversations
   Mark: Ennead
   Martel: City
   †Reynolds: Earth
   Snyder: And
   Snyder: Below
   Stone: Praise
   Stone: Those
   Sutton: Beyond
   Sutton: Lord
   Tofte: Survival

VEHICLES, SOLAR-POWERED
(continued)
    Hoover: Treasures
    Key: Golden
    Lightner: Day
    Slote: My Robot

VEHICLES/SUBMARINES, ANTI-
GRAVITY
    Biemiller: Escape
    Biemiller: Follow
    Earnshaw: Dragonfall 5
    Key: Golden
    Key: Magic

VIRGO (SETTING)
    Yep: Sweetwater

WAR
see also DEFENSE TECHNOLOGY
           GANG WARFARE
           WEAPONS TECHNOLOGY

WAR (SYSTEM BREAK)
    Eldridge: Shadow
    Hendrich: Girl
    Hoskins: Jack
    Kesteven: Awakening
    Key: Golden
    Norton: Android
    Snyder: Below

WAR AND PEACE
    Anderson: Star
    †Bova: Dueling
    Bova: Winds
    †Carlson: Human
    Christopher: Guardians
    Christopher: Pool
    Christopher: Prince
    Christopher: Sword
    Hooker: Kennaquhair
    Hoover: Treasures
    †Kurland: Princes
    Morressy: Windows
    Myers: Brainstorm
    †Norton: Breed
    Norton: Moon
    †Snyder: And
    †Snyder: Below
    Williams: Time

WAR, GALACTIC (SYSTEM BREAK)
    Hoover: Delikon
    Karl: Turning

WAR, GALACTIC
    Dwiggins: Asteroid
    Larson: Battlestar
    †Offutt: Galactic
    Richelson: Star
    Sutton: Lord

WAR, GERM (SYSTEM BREAK)
    Engdahl: This
    Norton: Dark

WAR, MAGNETIC (SYSTEM BREAK)
    Key: Incredible

WAR, NUCLEAR (SYSTEM BREAK)
    Biemiller: Escape
    Biemiller: Follow
    Biemiller: Hydronauts
    Engdahl: Far
    †Hooker: Kennaquhair
    Jakes: Time
    †Lightner: Day
    Martel: City
    †O'Brien: Z

WATER SHORTAGE
see also FOOD SHORTAGE
    Bova: Weathermakers
    Campbell: Legend
    Dickinson: Devil's
    Engdahl: Beyond
    Engdahl: Journey
    Engdahl: This
    †Harrison: California
    Hughes: Crisis
    †Jones: Moonbase
    †Morressy: Drought
    Norton: No
    Stoutenburg: Out

WEAPONS TECHNOLOGY
see also DEFENSE TECHNOLOGY
           GUNS, RAY/LASER
           WAR headings
    Biemiller: Follow
    †Bova: Dueling
    Bova: Exiled (cont'd)

APPENDIX: NOVELS ANNOTATED IN PART III

Listed below by primary author are all of the books annotated in Part III of this volume.

GENERAL INDEX

This general index provides access to Parts I and II by subject, futurist, and title of novel and to each entry in Part III by author, coauthor, illustrator, title, and publisher. To find comments about a novel in Parts I and II, look under the title of the novel in this index. To locate novels related to particular futuristic topics, genres, etc., turn back to Part IV, "Index of Themes and Motifs."